6/07

IN THE SHADOW OF
Wounded Knee

In the Shadow of

Wounded Knee

>>>————————————→

The Untold Final Chapter of the Indian Wars

ROGER L. DI SILVESTRO

WALKER & COMPANY

NEW YORK

Map on pages 36–37 is from *Red Cloud: Warrior-Statesman of the Lakota Sioux*, by Robert W. Larson. Copyright © 1997 by the University of Oklahoma Press, Norman. Reprinted by permission of the publisher. All rights reserved.

Map on page 63 is from *The Last Days of the Sioux Nation* by Robert M. Utley. Copyright © 1963 by Yale University Press. The map may not be reproduced, in whole or in part, in any form (beyond that copying permitted by Sections 107 and 108 of the U.S. Copyright Law and except by reviewers for the public press) without written permission of Yale University Press.

First published in the United States of America in 2005
by Walker Publishing Company, Inc.
Distributed to the trade by Holtzbrinck Publishers

For information about permission to reproduce selections from this book, write to Permissions, Walker & Company, 104 Fifth Avenue, New York, New York 10011.

Library of Congress Cataloging-in-Publication Data

DiSilvestro, Roger L.
In the shadow of Wounded Knee : the untold story of the Indian Wars / Roger L. DiSilvestro.
p. cm.
ISBN-10 0-8027-1461-7 (alk. paper)
ISBN-13 978-0-8027-1461-9
1. Wounded Knee Massacre, S.D., 1890. 2. Dakota Indians—Wars, 1890–1891. I. Title.

E83.89.D57 2005
973.8'6—dc22
2005044264

Book design by Maura Fadden Rosenthal/Mspace
Book composition by Westchester Book Group
Printed in the United States of America by Quebecor World Fairfield

Visit Walker & Company's Web site at www.walkerbooks.com

2   4   6   8   10   9   7   5   3   1

For Jeanne

With appreciation for your confidence in my writing and for your uncomplaining toleration of my absences, moods, and obsessions, including the buffalo skull under my desk.

CONTENTS

Acknowledgments   ix

Prologue   1

1   An Officer's Life   7

2   Conflict on the Plains   21

3   Freedom's Final Days   41

4   The Coming of the Ghosts   53

5   Death Comes for Sitting Bull   77

6   Gunfire at Wounded Knee   87

7   Casey's Last Ride   93

8   Ambush or Self-defense?   103

9   The Last Battle   117

10   A Fractured Life   135

11   On Trial   159

12   Justice Deferred   179

Epilogue   201

Notes   205

Bibliography   241

Index   245

ACKNOWLEDGMENTS

THESE ACKNOWLEDGMENTS REPRESENT SLIM THANKS to only a handful of the people to whom I am indebted for their help and support.

The staff of the archives of Historic New England, which was called the Society for the Preservation of New England Antiquities when I visited its Boston headquarters, won my deep appreciation and respect when they let me extend my time there beyond the restricted visiting hours. Their collection of material from Edward Casey's family, and their kindness in providing it to me, was invaluable.

Also helpful in giving me access to the Casey family home near Newport, Rhode Island, was the staff of the Casey-farm historic site. It's such a beautiful place that it is hard to believe that Edward Casey did not want to spend his life there.

I owe special thanks to Theresa Norman, registrar of the Siouxland Heritage Museums, who let me examine the rifle Plenty Horses used to kill Lieutenant Casey, now stored at the Courthouse Museum in Sioux Falls, South Dakota. Ms. Norman also was patient in dealing with my many queries and provided important research materials to me over the course of the final two years of research and writing.

I also thank John McCabe of the Springfield Armory National Historic Site in Springfield, Massachusetts, who offered information on the type of rifle Plenty Horses used to kill Lieutenant Casey.

My appreciation is deeply felt for the staffs of the various public libraries that helped me with great patience as I rummaged through their archival material. These include the libraries at the Pine Ridge Lakota Reservation; Miles City, Montana; and Sturgis, Sioux Falls, and Rapid City, South Dakota, as well as the archival staff at the Philadelphia Historic Society, which houses the records of the Indian Rights Association.

I would be remiss in not expressing my gratitude to my agent, Gail Ross, in seeing this project through and in helping to shape it by providing the expert and well-reasoned input of her editorial advisers, Jenna Land and Howard Lee. They made the early stages a pleasure. Along similar lines, I offer my appreciation for my editor at Walker & Company, Jackie Johnson, who gave me the key to clarifying the structure of the book and provided exquisite editing and enhancement.

I thank Birgil Kills Straight and Sophie Lone Hill, a descendant of Few Tails, for the time they gave me in interviews that helped add dimension to the story of Wounded Knee and its aftermath. I also thank Casey Barthelmess for his help in obtaining photos of Lt. Casey and providing information on the subject of Casey and Wounded Knee.

Personal thanks go to friends and colleagues who read various drafts of the book and who, through their comments and attention, encouraged my commitment to the project. These include Vince Cosentino, whose reading of practically every long work I have written, both published and unpublished, serves as a reinforcement to my commitment to writing; Kathy Shay, who has remained a friend despite our scarcely seeing each other since my army days more than thirty years ago; Mike "Smoke" Pfeiffer, an archaeologist with the U.S. Forest Service and old college friend; Linda Gallagher, who long ago urged me to write more nonfiction; and Dan Smith and Laura Gemery, former colleagues at the National Wildlife Federation.

Finally, I cannot acknowledge sufficiently my very old friend Don Nelsen, who after forty-some years, mostly with little personal contact, has managed to remain part of my professional and personal life. With his extensive knowledge of genealogical research, he turned up vital information I might otherwise have missed. His skill and efficiency often gave me the feeling that I had my own personal researcher on whom I could rely without question. Thank you very much.

This man wears a war bonnet because he has killed enemies. Therefore he is a good man. And men make him a leader because of his many deeds in battle. He has killed many men from all tribes of Indians and white men, too. Therefore he won leadership. It is so.

—Thunder Bear

IN THE SHADOW OF
Wounded Knee

Prologue

A FRIGID DECEMBER WIND WHIPPED across the South Dakota plains, rushing down from some distant arctic wasteland. In the southwestern part of the state, near the Nebraska border, snow dusted the trees and lay a foot deep over the hills and flats surrounding the creek the Lakota Indians call Cankpe Opi and maps call Wounded Knee.

But the treacherous cold did not stop Birgil Kills Straight and the 115 Lakota with him that day in 2003, when they came on horseback to Cankpe Opi at the end of a 350-mile ride that had taken nearly two weeks.[1] Kills Straight and the others had gathered at this place, in the heart of the Pine Ridge Lakota Reservation, to honor the youths who rode among them, to teach them courage, self-discipline, and respect, to put them in touch with their history and culture, and to remember the Lakota who had died there more than a century before, cut down by the rapid fire of automatic weapons.*

Perhaps it was the ghosts of those dead that, in the late 1980s, had troubled Kill Straight's dreams, urging him to make these annual spirit rides, to start far north where the great chief Sitting Bull had been killed by Indian police and to follow southward the path of Lakota refugees seeking escape from U.S. Army troops. It had all happened so long ago, but it was fresh in Kills Straight's memory and in the memories of his people—that terrible December in 1890.

THE LAKOTA IN 1890 COULD not leave their six reservations without permission from a politically appointed white agent. They were not allowed to practice traditional religion. A far-roaming hunting people, they were forced to adopt an agrarian lifestyle in an arid land from which even experienced

*Pine Ridge Lakota Reservation was called Pine Ridge Sioux Reservation during the late 1800s.

farmers could not eke out a living. Railroad tracks, telegraph wires, and the crude roadways of a new and growing society crisscrossed the plains that the Lakota recently had claimed as theirs. Aspiring commercial farmers busted prairie sod for crops. The wild grasses that for millennia had nourished vast numbers of bison now fed domestic livestock. South Dakota had attracted the business of six rail companies, promoting the development of some three hundred new towns. The U.S. Census Bureau in 1890 announced that the American frontier was closed, based on the number of people settled in the West and the amount of land in agriculture, rendering the Indians more or less officially a landless people, confined on reservations at the mercy of the latest immigrants.[2]

And yet the Lakota did not give up. Ground down by poverty and defeat, they and other Indians in the West turned in 1889 to the deep spiritual beliefs that permeated their cultures, finding hope in a religious revival that featured endless dancing to induce visions of long-dead relatives. A Paiute holy man who had learned the dance in a vision preached that if the Indians danced and kept peace with the whites, God would banish the whites from the continent, resurrect all dead Indians and restore them to their families, and bring back the wildlife that had fed, housed, and clothed the Indians.[3]

The religious revival threw fear into settlers who lived near the Lakota reservations and thought they were witnessing a war dance. Newspaper editors, backed by politicians who wanted to grab Lakota lands, added oil to the fire by writing stories and editorials that predicted an Indian uprising. This incendiary combination led in autumn 1890 to the largest military buildup since the Civil War as U.S. soldiers poured into the Lakota reservations. Eventually, the ghost dancers would yield to the army and give up the new religion, but not without paying a price in human lives.

In mid-December the U.S. Army was tracking down a wandering band of some four hundred Lakota led by a sick, elderly chief named Sitanka, or Big Foot. After several days of pursuit, the army caught up with the Indians and made them encamp along Wounded Knee Creek. There, on the sunny but cold morning of December 29, the Seventh Cavalry had Sitanka's band surrounded, heavy guns staring down at the Indians from a hill that overlooked the camp. The soldiers assembled the warriors and demanded their weapons. During the disarmament, a warrior named Black Coyote held his rifle over his head and said he would not give it up unless he was paid for it. U.S. soldiers tried to wrestle the rifle away from him, and it went off. As the shot reverberated, a volley of gunfire ripped through the camp. Whether the gunfire came from U.S. troops or Lakota Indians is unclear, as eyewitness accounts disagree.[4] In any event, a lieutenant ordered the soldiers to fire. Within moments, frenzied killing began. For four hours, long after most of the Lakota men were killed in the opening volleys, troops on horseback tracked fleeing women and children and cut them down. When the killing stopped, the soldiers gathered up their dead and wounded along with wounded Indians and headed for the Pine Ridge Sioux Reservation headquarters for medical help, leaving scores of slain Lakota where they had fallen.

As word of the slaughter spread like a bloodstain across the reservations, young warriors took up weapons, mounted horses, and rode off in pursuit of U.S. troops, determined to protect their families and elderly from another attack. Among the warriors rode a twenty-one-year-old Brulé Lakota who had lost a cousin in the gunfire along Wounded Knee Creek. The rider was called Tasunka Ota—Many Horses—although the whites translated it as Plenty Horses and sometimes as Young Man with Plenty Horses. Right after the shooting at Wounded Knee, he had joined other warriors to fight the U.S. soldiers.

The warriors wanted revenge. Plenty Horses did too, but he also wanted something far more important to him and his troubled life than mere vengeance. By the time Plenty Horses was ten years old, he had seen his people defeated and bereft of their lands. His adolescence had begun on a government-controlled reservation, where he was often hungry and, like all his people, powerless to do anything about it. At fourteen, Plenty Horses was spirited away by the government to a boarding school in Carlisle, Pennsylvania, and enrolled for five years in a program designed to make Indians look and act like conventional whites. When the government finally permitted him to return to the reservation, many Lakota no longer accepted him, perceiving him as tainted by white contact. "I was an outcast," Plenty Horses would say. "I was no longer an Indian."[5]

And then, two years after his return, came Wounded Knee and a chance to ride the warpath with the others, to prove that he was a true warrior, facing the enemy with bravery and fortitude in the Lakota tradition. Plenty Horses and the other warriors roamed the plains and skirmished with U.S. soldiers in the weeks following the massacre. The fights inflicted little damage to either side until a chance encounter on January 7, 1891.

While Plenty Horses rode with the warriors, another relatively young man was riding with the U.S. Army. Lieutenant Edward Wanton Casey was a West Point graduate who had served in the army for almost twenty years. He had participated after Wounded Knee in some of the skirmishes with the Lakota. By the end of the first week of January 1891, the fighting had wound down, and the last of the hostile Lakota, some four thousand men, women, and children, including eight hundred to one thousand warriors, were encamped along the White River in the western end of the Pine Ridge Sioux Reservation. Reaching that camp was Casey's objective when, on January 7, 1891, he mounted his black horse at nine in the morning and rode out of his base camp with two Cheyenne Indians who had enlisted in the U.S. Army.

Later, officers who knew of Casey's activities would say that he went to try to make peace with the last of the fighting Lakota. Others would say he was seeking information on the hostiles' activities, dispersal, and intentions. His motives may remain forever unknown, but what is certain is that within sight of the camp he met warriors who had just come from there. They approached him amicably, and Casey sent a messenger into the camp to ask for a meeting with the principal chiefs. While waiting for the answer, Casey spoke for perhaps an hour with one of the warriors, Plenty Horses. Among other things, Plenty Horses told Casey he could come no closer to the camp because women and children were sheltered there.

The messenger finally returned and told Casey to leave immediately, that his life was in peril. The warning came from an old and respected chief, Red Cloud, who in the 1860s had forced the U.S. Army to withdraw from Lakota territory. The young warriors were crazed with anger and with lust for the glory of battle, Red Cloud said. They would kill any military officer who came near.

Accounts differ on Casey's reaction to the message. Plenty Horses would insist that Casey threatened to return with more soldiers and capture the chief. Other witnesses reported that Casey simply said he would come back later. In any event, Casey turned his horse to head home, and Plenty Horses shouldered his Springfield rifle, aimed down the heavy muzzle, and fired a bullet that crashed through the back of Casey's skull and exited below his right eye. Casey's horse reared, and Casey fell to the ground, instantly dead.[6]

Within days after the shooting, the last hostile Lakota surrendered to the military. Shortly after that, the army arrested Plenty Horses for Casey's murder. The following spring, the young Lakota stood trial in a federal court in Sioux Falls, South Dakota. Newspapers carried his story nationwide. The *New York World* even assigned a reporter to the trial full-time. During courtroom breaks, women flocked around the erstwhile warrior to ask for his autograph.

Accounts of Wounded Knee generally close with the end of hostilities in late January 1891, but in fact Wounded Knee continued to echo for months afterward in the trial of Plenty Horses, which for a brief moment threatened to raise the specter of whether the soldiers who killed scores of Lakota at Wounded Knee were not every bit as guilty of murder as Plenty Horses appeared to be.

The trial of Plenty Horses is now largely forgotten, a piece of America's past that constitutes something of a dark secret from a time when the hammer of history was forging the modern era. *In the Shadow of Wounded Knee* shows America at the instant it was shifting from a wild frontier country into a modern nation and how the cost of building America was paid not just in human lives but with the sacrifice of human hopes and dreams and the future of entire cultures. The Indian wars did not end at Wounded Knee, nor even with Casey's death, but rather in that Sioux Falls federal courthouse, where a lone warrior awaited his fate at the hands of a society that had killed countless numbers of his people and seemed determined to kill at least one more.

CHAPTER 1

An Officer's Life

LIEUTENANT EDWARD WANTON CASEY WAS born into a long line of military officers. His great-great-grandfather had fought as an officer in the French and Indian War, and his grandfather, Wanton Casey, was an officer in the Revolutionary War. His father, Silas, was a West Point graduate and hero of the Mexican War who won honors for gallantry in the Civil War. Silas also rewrote the army training manual on tactics, which became known as *Casey's Tactics*.[1]

Edward Casey's brother Thomas Lincoln had been first in his West Point graduating class in 1852 and, as head of the U.S. Army Corps of Engineers' District of Columbia Office of Public Buildings and Grounds, finished the Washington Monument after twenty-five years of desultory construction under the command of other officers.[2] Brother Silas III, a naval academy graduate in 1860, had built a distinguished Civil War record and in 1907 would be promoted to commander of the Pacific Squadron. Edward's sisters married officers.

Edward Casey was born on an army post—the Bernicia Barracks near Berkeley, California—where his father was a captain in the Second Infantry. He grew up to the cadence of marching men, to the clank of sword and clink of spur, to the rumble of cannon on national holidays. He saw his father march off at the head of a military unit to fight Indians, and he collected the Indian artifacts his father sent him.[3]

Edward in 1873 graduated thirty-fourth in a West Point class of forty-one. By the end of the year he was on frontier duty at Fort Sully in Dakota Territory. He volunteered in 1874 to go with George Armstrong Custer and the Seventh Cavalry on an exploration of the little-known Dakota Black Hills, land that by treaty belonged to the Lakota. Instead, the army sent him to New Orleans to help quash civil disturbances.

In 1875 Casey was reassigned to the West. The following year the

Second Lieutenant Edward Wanton Casey at the time of his West Point commencement, June 1873. (*Montana Historical Society, Helena*)

Cheyenne and Lakota killed Custer and a large portion of the Seventh Cavalry in a battle on Montana's Little Bighorn River. After the battle, several thousand Indians who had camped together fragmented into smaller groups to wander across traditional hunting grounds in Montana and the Dakotas. The battle-scarred army determined to round up the Indians and put them on reservations.

During this 1876–77 campaign Casey was stationed at a temporary army supply depot in Montana where Glendive Creek flowed into the Yellowstone River, marking the point beyond which riverboats on the Yellowstone could not pass. Building materials for a fort farther upstream, near the mouth of the Tongue River, were being left at the Glendive depot. Casey's commander and the builder of the fort was Colonel Nelson Miles.

For months after the Battle of the Little Bighorn, Miles pushed his men hard and the Indians harder, attacking Cheyenne and Lakota all through the winter, when they were most vulnerable. He destroyed whole villages— tepees, meat, supplies, everything—during a season of scarce game and brutal weather. Hundreds of Lakota and Cheyenne surrendered to him, including Crazy Horse, the top Lakota warrior.

Late in April 1877 Miles heard from scouts that Indians were hunting bison at the mouth of Rosebud Creek, about one hundred miles from where Miles was busily turning his smattering of primitive huts into a respectable fort. He immediately rounded up the troops for a foray against these Indians. The soldiers left on May 1, with Casey in command of white and Indian scouts.[4]

When scouts on May 6 located a camp on Muddy Creek made up mostly of Miniconjou Lakota led by Lame Deer—Tacha Ushte in his own language—Miles prepared to attack the next morning, while the Lakota were still asleep. His strategy called for twenty-six-year-old Edward Casey to lead thirteen scouts and six soldiers in the opening charge. At the first light of dawn Miles gave the order, and Lieutenant Casey and his men spurred their horses, hooves thundering as they swept in among the tepees like a cyclone.

Killing Indians was not Casey's priority. His job was to capture the ponies without which the Indians could neither fight effectively nor flee swiftly. In one rush, Casey stampeded the entire herd of some 450 ponies out of the village. Another wave of cavalry entered after Casey, and then another, and the shooting started. The soldiers chased the Lakota into the wooded hills, but the Indians got away. In all, three soldiers and six Indians were killed. Miles destroyed all the tepees and reportedly also tons of dried meat and hundreds of bison hides—everything the Indians had. He also brought back to his cantonment all of the Lakota ponies, letting his infantry use them as mounts. Miles brevetted Casey for gallantry.

AFTER MUDDY CREEK, CASEY SERVED another year in the West before the army sent him to control striking workers in Chicago and Wilkes-Barre, Pennsylvania. Next, he spent about two years on Indian campaigns in Texas, Indian Territory (now Oklahoma), and Colorado. From 1880 to 1884 the army gave him a breather from war, making him an assistant instructor on tactics at West Point.[5] At the end of 1884 he rejoined the Twenty-second Infantry, stationed at Fort Lewis in southwestern Colorado.[6]

In September 1887 he volunteered to lead a reconnaissance expedition from Fort Lewis into a little-known region—the area surrounding the Grand Canyon, which cut across Arizona Territory about 450 miles away.[7] The government had begun sending topographers and scientists into the canyon as early as the 1850s, and by the 1880s enough was known of the place that it was attracting adventurous tourists and gold-seeking speculators. On September 2, 1887, Casey sent a letter through the proper military channels to the assistant adjutant general of the Department of the Missouri at Leavenworth, Kansas, asking permission to lead an expedition to the canyon. "According to my information," he wrote, "no military itinerary has been made for the route I propose and the details of the country are not laid down upon any map I have ever seen. The country mentioned is in proximity to the reservations of the Navajo, Moqui and Pueblo Indians and for that reason some knowledge of the details might be of military interest."[8]

Casey received approval on November 1 and set out at 4 p.m. the next day. With him went three other officers—one of them an assistant army surgeon— eight enlisted men, two civilian packers, fifteen pack mules, a wagon, and seventy-five days' rations. Among the group was a German immigrant, Christian Barthelmess, who was the Twenty-second Infantry's chief musician and semiofficial photographer.[9]

The men had traveled only three miles south of the fort when they stopped to make camp, a short jaunt that allowed them to check their equipment while still close enough to have to go back for forgotten items. That evening, the regimental band and a number of officers came out to serenade the explorers. At eight o'clock the next morning they set out in earnest.

But the going was slow. For a while they wrestled fruitlessly with an odometer mounted on a wagon wheel, but it was not designed for the type of equipment with which the expedition was outfitted. The expedition also stopped every hour for five minutes to take weather readings. "This was done with as exacting care as if the specific security of the United States and general welfare of the rest of the universe depended on it," wrote Barthelmess in a private account that he planned to publish in a German-language newspaper.[10]

As the expedition continued, accidents befell the group. A mule kicked Private Charles Reid, fracturing a kneecap. Casey left Reid at Fort Defiance in the care of a doctor. Another private made it across the desert country to the Grand Canyon and then back to Colorado, within about forty miles of Fort Lewis, before suffering a bizarre accident as the expedition rested in Cortez, a young community where Casey bought grain for the hoofed stock and arranged for his

Casey's 1887 Grand Canyon expedition stops for water at Baker's Peak, Arizona. Lieutenant Casey, in striped trousers, looks down at the water barrels. *(Christian Barthelmess, Montana Historical Society, Helena)*

men to sleep in an empty store near a stable. He gave his men the night off in a town that was still very much in the making. The dirt streets were unlighted, and a well five feet wide and sixty feet deep was being sunk at one intersection. The well was unmarked and unfenced, and the private stepped into it while returning to his quarters after dark, falling straight to the bottom.

A crowd gathered, and Casey and the other officers arrived. With a rope they lowered Lieutenant F. B. Jones of K Company into the dark hole. He tied the rope around the private, and both men were hauled out. The expedition's surgeon, Lieutenant Nathan S. Jarvis, and a local doctor agreed that the soldier was too badly injured for further travel. Casey left the private in the care of the civilian physician, agreeing to cover all costs himself.

Next day, the rest of the men and animals headed down the trail toward Fort Lewis. Unfortunately, the trail led through the La Plata Mountains and a pass three feet deep in snow. The expedition had used up its food—seventy-five days of rations in sixty-four days of travel—and had almost worn out the horses and mules. The men made only eighteen miles that day. By the time they got to the fort, on January 5, 1888, three of the men had frozen feet.

Despite the effort and strife, Casey had not accomplished all he had set out to do. In a brief report he filed the day after his return to Fort Lewis, he wrote:

"I made the Grand Canyon of the Colorado at a point ten miles below the mouth of the Little Colorado River. I was unable to make the north side of the Canyon owing to the snow on the Buckskin Mountains."

CASEY WAS, BY CONTEMPORARY ACCOUNTS, a good soldier, bright, promising, and well liked. But his career had stalled. By 1890 he had not risen above the rank of first lieutenant, and he had not been promoted in ten years. Unfortunately for him, Congress had repeatedly downsized the army after the Civil War. By the 1880s the U.S. Army numbered fewer than twenty-five thousand soldiers and two thousand officers. Promotions came slowly.

If Casey's career needed a boost at the time of Wounded Knee, his personal life needed resuscitating. Approaching middle age—he had turned forty on December 1, 1890—he was an unhappy bachelor whose finances were a debacle. In the late 1880s he had invested his own money and his sister's children's money in a cattle ranch that not only swamped him with debt but left him struggling to pay back his relatives. He also was involved in a seemingly hopeless love affair with Nettie Atchison, a divorcée or widow who lived at least part-time in Paris, France, with her two daughters.[11] She and Casey wanted to marry but felt that her daughters and his financial woes made a wedding impossible.[12]

Casey had no clear way out of his troubles. The Wild West was growing tame, the Indian wars were largely over, and Casey was stationed in eastern Montana at Fort Keogh, the military installation Colonel Miles had built upriver from the Glendive supply depot where Casey had been stationed in 1877. By 1888 the fort had been transformed from a collection of crude cabins, constructed of cottonwood poles stuck upright into the ground and roofed with logs and dirt, into the sort of post that soldiers call a country club.[13] As early as 1879 officers could communicate with several Montana and Dakota Territory military installations by telegraph and could enjoy the service of the first telephone in Montana, although the line ran only from Miles's house to the post telegraph office. By 1880 the troops had put in 650 miles of telegraph wires, which the public also could use, and by 1884 Miles could phone all the way to a cow town and stockyards depot on the other side of the Tongue River, founded at about the time the fort was built and named Miles City after the commanding officer. The soldiers also built roads throughout the area, eight hundred miles of them within a few years after the fort was founded, a boon to public transportation.

Casey lived in a spacious, two story, brown clapboard duplex with a yard, dormers, porch, and a red shingle roof. He shared it with another officer and a pair of large wolfhounds. Casey's personal effects included curtains and drapes, a meerschaum pipe, doilies, theatrical costumes, watercolors, and oil paints in addition to such typically western equipment as pistols, swords, a buffalo robe, and fly-fishing gear.[14]

The fort itself, named for an officer who had died with Custer at the last stand, did not even have a stockade. The only fortifications were strategically placed stacks of firewood.[15] Home to perhaps 1,400 people, including not only 600 to 800 troops but also the civilians who helped keep the caissons rolling along, the fort offered its soldiers a wide range of entertainment. It boasted a good library and a canteen—like a clubhouse for the soldiers—that provided food, games, and entertainment designed to keep the men from spending their paychecks in Miles City saloons.

Dances were as frequent as marches, beginning in 1882 with grand balls every Wednesday evening. The Fort Keogh Dramatic Company, led by various officers down through the years, staged plays popular throughout the area. The officers also threw parties at the slightest excuse, celebrating promotions, returning troops, birthdays—they even held a party in honor of Martha Washington, who had been dead for most of a century. The regimental band put on regular entertainments, and traveling shows also stopped in, including the European Female Brass Band and Minstrel Company.

In warm weather, the main form of combat for Keogh soldiers was baseball, the troops taking on teams from nearby towns and other army posts. The games made headlines in the Miles City newspaper. Tennis and bowling were popular, as was boxing. Sleigh rides were a favorite winter recreation.

However dissatisfied Casey may have been with his position and his place, he grew skillful at mixing business with pleasure. A fellow officer, in a letter to Casey's brother Thomas, remarked that the lieutenant was always in the midst of any plan for a good time.[16] He was well liked by other soldiers, who used him as an example of what a good officer should be.

But Fort Keogh provided Casey with little chance of fulfilling his potential, and his responsibilities often were menial. Once he led a contingent in banking

Officers' quarters at Fort Keogh at about the time Lieutenant Casey lived there. One of two surviving houses is open to the public at the Range Rider Museum outside Miles City, Montana. *(Christian Barthelmess, Montana Historical Society, Helena)*

the Fort Keogh parade ground so it could be flooded for ice-skating. In a three-page letter to the post adjutant, dated January 6, 1889, Casey reported on his slop barrel inspection.[17] He wrote that ice and snow were polluted with slops and "from spittoon cleaning." He concluded: "I request that sufficient slop barrels be furnished the entire post and will direct that they be asked for where needed and also that the barrels and stands be properly secured. They are sometimes upset by the cattle. Very Respectfully, Your Obedient Servant, EW [*sic*] Casey, 1st 22 Infty." The following day, Colonel Peter Swaine, then commander at Fort Keogh, referred the letter to all post officers and ordered that they "comply with its requirements and recommendations."

Yearning for unmapped lands and far horizons, Casey must have rankled at inspecting slop barrels and setting policies for their care, but he soon found a more amenable assignment. Late in 1889 he read a paper on training Indians as soldiers, the first in a series of three written by army major William Powell, who suggested that the U.S. government should stop pushing agriculture on these natural warriors and instead "make soldiers of them." The idea had been in the air since at least 1878, when Ezra Hayt, commissioner of Indian affairs, urged the formation of an Indian cavalry force of up to three thousand men.[18]

In 1880 an army captain published an article in a military journal, *The United Service: A Monthly Review of Military and Naval Affairs,* suggesting that the Indians, given their skills on horseback, be enlisted as cavalry.[19]

Casey caught the fever and promptly recommended to Colonel Swaine that they enlist reservation Indians to form a regular troop.[20] Swaine liked the idea and told Casey to recruit local northern Cheyennes. From the commissioner of Indian affairs, Thomas Morgan, Casey got permission to enlist up to one hundred of them.

Casey became so thoroughly identified with the idea of enlisting Indians that the plan was credited to him by another officer, Lieutenant S. C. Robertson of the First Cavalry, who commanded a contingent of Crow Indians:

> Last year Lieutenant Casey, of the Twenty-second Infantry, a dashing and able young officer, stationed then at Fort Keogh, Montana, conceived the idea of employing this Indian material on a more substantial and permanent basis. His idea was to enlist the Indians of the different tribes in separate troops or companies, and for definite periods of say a year or six months. They were to be thoroughly drilled and disciplined, required to keep two pony mounts of serviceable quality, for which the government was to allow forage and extra pay, and to be allowed to continue in the service, by re-enlistment, during good behavior. This was intended to serve the double purpose of giving a leaven of civilization and military training to each of the tribes represented, and at the same time furnishing the army with a number of bodies of light irregular cavalry scattered among its Western stations. These levies were to be known as "scouts," but in arms, equipments, uniform, and drill they were to be assimilated as rapidly as possible to the condition of regulars.[21]

Robertson reported that Casey went to Washington, D.C., to win Secretary of War Redfield Proctor's support for raising a troop of Cheyennes.

Indians had served in the military since the nation's beginnings. In 1637 Narragansett and Mahican fought beside New England colonists against the Pequot. Indians allied with both the British and the French in the aptly named French and Indian War, and the British rallied Indians against American patriots during the Revolutionary War.[22] The first army mustered by the thirteen original colonies to fight the British included a company of Stockbridge Indians from Massachusetts. Indians fought on both sides of the Civil War, and in

1866 Congress authorized enlistment of one thousand Indian scouts in the West. On behalf of the U.S. Army, Apache fought Apache, while the Pawnee, Arapaho, Cheyenne, Crow, and Shoshone signed up to fight the Lakota, who in turn helped the army fight the Nez Percé.[23]

Eventually, the secretary of war authorized twenty-six regiments stationed west of the Mississippi River to enlist a company of Indians each. These Indians generally signed up as civilian scouts and did not receive military training and other benefits. Casey instead would enlist his men as army regulars. They would sign up for six months at a time, receive standard uniforms and equipment, right down to the white gloves, and twenty-five dollars monthly, comparable to soldiers' pay.

Enlisted Indians offered many advantages to the army.[24] On a practical level, as scouts they neutralized the only significant advantage the Indians had over the U.S. military, their superior knowledge of the land. Signing up the Indians was also a good safety valve for warrior aggression. Officers in the 1870s often enlisted former hostile Indians virtually on the day they surrendered, hoping to keep restless and potentially dangerous young men from starting trouble. For example, when some three hundred Cheyenne surrendered to Nelson Miles in late April 1877, he immediately signed on several of the warriors as scouts. Only a few days later, they helped lead him to Lame Deer on Muddy Creek.

Enlisted warriors also were good propaganda. By making scouts out of men who surrendered, the army showed hostile Indians that giving up was not all bad. And if that example did not tempt hostiles to surrender, the army was hoping that warriors would be demoralized into submission when they saw their own compatriots leading U.S. soldiers into their hidden camps.

Indian recruits in turn had their own good reasons for signing up to fight other Indians. Among the plains tribes, warriors achieved status by fighting enemies and taking their horses. Allying with the U.S. Army allowed defeated warriors, who might otherwise be left idle on reservations, to pursue these traditional activities. Alliances among plains tribes were fluid—allies one season might be enemies the next—so in most cases, no loyalties were strained when Indians enlisted.[25]

The Cheyenne at Tongue River fit the mold for eager recruits. On their enlistment papers, many who signed on with Casey put down their occupation as "hunter."[26] But little wildlife remained to hunt. The bison were gone, as were the pronghorn and deer. Even the Cheyenne who had been to the federal schools had no work. And here was the army offering them a chance to recapture their pride.

Casey presented his plan to tribal elders at the Tongue River Cheyenne reservation. He needed their approval to approach younger men about enlisting, but at first the elders opposed him. After all, white men in blue uniforms had never brought good news to the Indians. Moreover, in a letter to his brother Thomas, Casey wrote that the Cheyenne were "much exercised over the report of the coming of a Christ and had been having religious dances before my arrival."[27] He was referring to the ghost dance. "The Indians are perfectly peaceful," he added, "as their new faith teaches good will to all—the punishment to be left to the Christ."

The elders were vexed about Casey's proposal for scouts because they had heard that he would make Cheyenne troopers leave their families and cut their hair. But when he explained that neither would hair fall nor families break up, "their fears vanished," he wrote Thomas.[28]

During a two-day visit at Tongue River, Casey enlisted twenty-seven Indians and turned away about half that number as unsuitable. Another sixteen soon volunteered. Within weeks Casey had more recruits than he could handle.

Casey's challenge was to get the scouts to think as a unit, instead of functioning in battle as independent individuals, and to teach them fundamental skills that they tended to find repugnant, such as building cabins and gardening. At first the Indian troops lived with their families in tepees and tents on the bank of the Yellowstone River about a mile and a half from the fort. Casey led them into nearby mountains to cut trees so they could build their own cantonment. Other soldiers helped them float nearly three thousand logs downriver. Frederic Remington, an artist, magazine correspondent, novelist, and denizen of various troubled parts of the West who wrote for such popular magazines as *Century* and *Harper's Weekly*, described the results of their work in a magazine article.

> I saw a long line of well-constructed log buildings, corrals, and stables, also a large garden fenced and cultivated. I entered the houses and saw comfort and cleanliness. I saw smiling faces and laughing children. I saw perfectly kept cavalry arms and accoutrements, and fine Indian soldiers, who stood like

bronze statues, and saluted in the best possible form, while never a muscle of their stern faces twitched, and they looked a soldier, and felt a soldier, and were in fact the finest I had ever seen. I saw them mount and fall in and drill in admirable shape, all by a sign of Lieutenant Casey's right hand, because they do not understand English well enough. I admired the indomitable zeal of Lieutenant Casey, and hoped his work would lead to greater things. Indeed, if he were properly supported, why could not Fort Keogh be abandoned at some future day, and why could not Casey and his company of the First Irregular Cavalry do the work of the garrison, and let the Eighth Cavalry and the Twenty-second Infantry go to Fort Snelling, and there perfect themselves, so that when we call for the skeleton of our army organization in time of war, we will find it worthy to be built on to.[29]

In a May 1890 letter to his brother Thomas, Casey wrote with pride of his troops: "Some of them have never handled an axe in their lives. Yet the first forenoon I put them to work they cut 275 logs. I had 18 axes when I made them stop as I had more than I could haul with my few teams."[30] The following July, he wrote again: "My Indians have done splendidly. They have worked harder by far more than [sic] white recruits would have done under the same circumstances."[31]

Casey soon found that the Cheyenne were more diligent in meeting their responsibilities than was the U.S. Army. He persistently complained to Thomas that the army had not sent promised equipment. Once he asked Thomas to use his influence to get uniforms that were two months overdue. "Pardon this letter Tom," he wrote. "It is one string of 'wants'—but what can a miserable Lieutenant do single handed especially when he is in the wilderness."[32]

One thing he did was pay for his troop's general expenses from his own beleaguered pocket. But Casey offered his scouts more than financial support. When Colonel Swaine commandeered the wagons Casey was using to move logs and supplies at the Indian camp, the lieutenant persuaded Swaine's superiors to order the colonel to give back the wagons. Casey also sided with the Indians in disputes with civilians. In one case he filed a complaint with the post commander on behalf of an Indian boy who was assaulted by the son of the fort's hospital matron. And when three of Casey's scouts were accused of killing a rancher, Casey scraped the bottom of his pocketbook to help pay for their legal defense. He also determined to investigate the scene of the shooting

Lieutenant Casey (seated on a tree branch) with his new Indian scouts, camped in 1889 on the Yellowstone River west of Fort Keogh. *(Christian Barthelmess, Montana Historical Society, Helena)*

personally, even though it was three hundred miles from the fort. To his brother Thomas he wrote:

> The Cheyennes have been charged with the murder of a white man. Three of my scouts have been arrested. I believe it is a put up plan on the part of rich cattlemen to oust the Cheyennes from their Reservation. I see by the papers they have sent their representative to the Secretary of War for more troops to protect the settlers. On my honor as an officer there is no more need of protection for those miserable rascals than there is for your family now. The cattlemen are working this for all it's worth. . . . A number of the officers came to me and told me they would subscribe towards the expense of council [*sic*] for the Indians now in jail. I have employed council & we will see the Cheyenne have a fair play as long as our money lasts but we can never stand against the cattlemen. Could not the Indian Dept. lend a hand in some way—if only for the sake of fair play and simple justice. These people are bound to hang some body [*sic*] and they do not care whether it is a guilty or innocent party. As soon as I get my camp established I will leave [Lieutenant Robert] Getty in charge and go to the scene of the murder to collect evidence for the defense. It is a 300 mile trip & I dread it but there is no body [*sic*] else to go or that will go.[33]

Casey's concern for his scouts paid off in their response to his training. Remington described Casey's men, whom he first saw on a cool Montana morning at Fort Keogh: "Patter, patter, patter—clank, clank, clank; up comes the company of Cheyenne scouts who are to escort the general—fine-looking, tall young men, with long hair, and mounted on small Indian ponies. They were dressed and accoutered as United States soldiers, and they fill the eye of a military man until nothing is lacking."[34]

In December 1890 Fort Keogh shrugged off the tranquil regularity of peacetime life. The Lakota, scattered across six reservations in South Dakota and into North Dakota, were engaged in the frenzied religious dancing that newspaper editors, nervous settlers, and skittish reservation administrators interpreted as a prelude to "a Sioux outbreak." Nelson Miles, now a general headquartered in Chicago as commander of the army district that included the Dakotas, began pouring troops into the Lakota reservations as winter began. When the shooting started at Wounded Knee, Miles had 3,500 men ready to fight and 2,000 more in reserve. Add to that number a few hundred Indian troops, and he had more than a fifth of the entire U.S. Army concentrated primarily on the Pine Ridge Sioux Reservation. Nothing like this buildup had been seen in the United States since the Civil War.[35]

Casey received orders on December 12, 1890, to lead his men to the Pine Ridge Sioux Reservation, where the most zealous of the Lakota dancers were concentrated. He wrote his brother Thomas, "Our orders are to capture the Sioux, which of course means fight should we meet them. . . . I hope and pray my Scouts will acquit themselves well as so much will depend upon their example."[36] The "much" that made him fretful was a bill Congress had just passed authorizing the enlistment of one thousand Indian recruits.

Casey and his men rode out of Fort Keogh on Sunday morning, December 14.[37] He was eager to test the mettle of his troops in the field. A week later he wrote from Pine Ridge to Nettie Atchison: "My scouts have behaved splendidly. . . . They are full of fight and I think I can make a good showing when the time comes. If I don't, I don't care to come back."[38]

CHAPTER 2

Conflict on the Plains

PLENTY HORSES IN 1891 GAVE his age as twenty-two, suggesting that he may have been born in 1868 or 1869, because the Lakota measured their lives by winters rather than calendar years. They gave each year the name of an event important to them or their tribe, although different individuals kept differently named winter counts. The Miniconjou Iron Shell called 1868 the Year Fish's Wife Died. Eighteen sixty-nine was the Year the Sun Died.[1] A count kept by another Miniconjou, based on his people's history, covered the years 1781 to 1932.[2] He called 1868 the Year Fifteen People—meaning Lakota—Were Killed (in a battle with the Crow Indians). He called 1869 the Year Thirty Crows Were Killed.

If Plenty Horses was born in the Year the Sun Died, the name was fitting, because in 1869 the world of the Brulé Lakota—his people—had began to spin out of orbit. The Brulé would soon give up their life of freedom and of the hunt, of wandering across wild lands and of warfare, and begin life on the reservation. For them, as for all Lakota, the reservation would be a twilight world where the old ways were well remembered but impossible to follow.

LONG BEFORE THE LAKOTA BECAME the masters of the northern plains they had lived much farther to the east, perhaps in the Ohio Valley or even in the Southeast. They were pushed out of there late in the fifteenth century by the well-organized and powerful Iroquois. By the 1600s they were living in what is now northern Minnesota, hunting in the forest and gathering wild rice in marshes.[3] Colonial Europeans found them there and came to know them as the Sioux, a name derived from the Ojibwa word *nadoweisiw,* for snake—and meaning, in this context, enemy.

The Sioux had become a powerful force in their region. They were divided into seven tribes: the Mdewakanton, Sisseton, Wahpekute, and Wahpeton, collectively known as the Santee; the Yankton and Yanktonais; and the Teton. They called themselves "the allies," although tribal dialects varied the name. Among the Santee it was "Dakota." The Yankton and Yanktonais rendered it "Nakota," and the Teton, "Lakota."[4] They warred successfully on neighboring Cree and Ojibwa until the arrival of the French and English in the Great Lakes region abruptly changed the balance of power.[5] By the 1650s the Ojibwa and Cree, in regular contact with the Europeans, were trading furs for firearms. The more distant and isolated Sioux, lacking access to guns, soon found themselves fighting with arrows against rifles.

Staggering under the effects of European weaponry, Sioux tribes one by one began leaving the Mississippi headwaters, eventually crossing the Minnesota River and going first south and then west toward more open country, where they found vast herds of buffalo, creatures that offered huge amounts of meat as well as hides for clothing and shelter.[6] Around 1700 the Tetons, who became known as the Lakota, joined this westward movement, which continued for roughly a century as they spread across the plains and even beyond the Missouri River, pushing out other Indian peoples, such as the Omaha and Iowa, and evolving into wandering hunters ever in search of game, particularly buffalo. As the eighteenth century progressed, fur companies began sponsoring annual trade fairs on the plains, giving the Lakota access to firearms.[7] Then, late in that century, the Lakota encountered another of the benefits of European contact: the horse.

Horses had originated in the New World and had emigrated into Siberia and across Asia millions of years before humans arrived in North America. When the ancestors of the American Indians arrived in the New World, at least fifteen thousand years ago, horses were extinct in North and South America. But they survived in Eurasia, where they were widely hunted for food until agricultural peoples started to domesticate them about six thousand years ago. They soon became draft animals, pulling wagons, and also were used for riding. The Spanish first brought the horse back to North America early in the 1500s. Ponce de Leon took horses with him to Florida, and the conquistadores who invaded the Southwest brought in herds of horses and began breeding them. Some horses escaped, and some were traded to the Indians.[8]

One turning point for the horse in North America, and therefore for the Indians, was the Pueblo Revolt of 1680, in which sedentary, agricultural tribes in what is now New Mexico drove out the Spanish, who had virtually enslaved them. The Spanish left horses in their wake, and the Indians quickly took advantage of these animals. The more nomadic tribes of the Southwest, such as the Apache, became master horsemen. Through trade and theft, horses passed from tribe to tribe, arriving in the northern plains, where they fell into the hands of the Lakota.[9]

And so the Lakota emerged from the eighteenth century as mounted warriors armed with rifles. After decades of retreat, pushed hither and yon by other tribes, the Lakota were now fierce and demanding warriors who roamed the Great Plains from the Missouri River to the Bighorn Mountains, from the Canadian prairies to the Platte River and down into the Kansas plains. The Lakota split into seven tribes: the Oglala (Scatters Their Own), Miniconjou (Planters by Water), Two Kettle, Sans Arc (Without Bows), Hunkpapa (Campers at the Opening of the Circle, so named because when they camped with other tribes, the Hunkpapa always took an outermost position, the one most exposed to danger), the Siha Sapa (Blackfeet, not to be confused with the Blackfeet people found farther west), and the Brulé.[10] The Brulé, with the Oglala, almost always had been in the vanguard of the movement west, blazing a path that the other tribes had followed.[11] Taken together, the Lakota were not just a force to be reckoned with in the northern plains; they were *the* force.

ON SEPTEMBER 24, 1804, A band of about nine hundred Brulé Lakota under Chief Tatanka Sapa, or Black Buffalo, was encamped in what is now central South Dakota near the mouth of the Bad River, which empties into the Missouri. Black Buffalo and his people were in a celebratory mood—only two weeks earlier they had battled and beaten the neighboring Omaha, killing seventy-five warriors and capturing forty-eight women and children—when they heard that a party of white men in boats and pirogues was coming up the Missouri. Just the day before, three teenage Lakota boys had made contact with the white men, who gave the boys two or three pounds of tobacco and asked them to tell their chiefs that the white men wanted to meet the next day.[12]

By and large, the arrival of the boats was good news to Black Buffalo, because the Lakota supplemented the rewards of hunting and tribal warfare with tribute demanded from riparian passersby. Usually the property of white trappers and fur companies, these boats were often loaded with trade goods when heading north and with furs when returning south. Jean Baptiste Truteau, a Canadian-born representative of the fur-trading Missouri Company who was waylaid and robbed by the Lakota during a 1794 expedition, wrote in his journal that "all *voyageurs* ought to avoid meeting this tribe, as much for the safety of their goods as for their lives even."[13]

The Lakota had no reason to think that this latest arrival of white immigrants would differ from the traders they had encountered in the past. They did not know that these men composed the U.S. Corps of Discovery, sent upriver under the military leadership of Captain Meriwether Lewis and Lieutenant William Clark. President Thomas Jefferson had tasked these men with traveling across the virtually unknown northern West, starting at the junction of the Missouri and Mississippi and ending at the Pacific coast. The United States had just purchased that vast region from France, and officials wanted to learn more about what they had bought. Among other assignments, Lewis and Clark had been ordered by Jefferson to make a good impression on the lordly Lakota so that the Indians would become friends with America and trade with the young nation, exchanging furs for items such as guns.[14] The Lewis and Clark expedition thus amounted to the first official contact between Plenty Horses' people—he was himself a Brulé—and the United States.

The result of that contact was not what Jefferson had sought. The time that the Corps of Discovery spent with the Lakota was punctuated with the baring of swords, stringing of bows, cocking of rifles, and, very nearly, the firing of cannons. Much of the tension grew from Brulé dissatisfaction with the gifts that Lewis and Clark offered them. Suspicions about one another's motives festered on both sides, and tension between the whites and the Lakota nearly exploded on September 27, as the expedition prepared to proceed up the Missouri. About two hundred Lakota gathered on shore, some with firearms, others with spears, cutlasses, and bows and arrows. Warriors laid hold of the ropes to the expedition boats and demanded tobacco. When Lewis and Clark finally tossed a few pounds ashore, the Lakota let them go, although by then Clark was preparing to light the fuse of a cannon.

By and large, the first encounter of Lakota and Americans, while it did not go well, nevertheless accurately presaged the decades ahead.

*   *   *

LAKOTA LIFE WAS SHAKEN TO its foundations in the years following Lewis and Clark. By 1825 the Lakota, like so many other tribes, had come to depend on certain goods supplied by whites: guns, cloth, tools, pots, and pans. That year, the United States and the Lakota, as well as other related tribes who lived farther east, signed a treaty recognizing one another's sovereignty, although whether this had any real meaning to the Indians is open to debate.[15] For the United States, the treaty was a means for normalizing relations with the intimidating Lakota. From the Lakota perspective, the treaty was an agreement with a weaker nation—the United States—that recognized Lakota dominance in the upper Missouri. In return, the Lakota agreed to a U.S. demand for a monopoly on their trade.

That the United States might not be as weak as it seemed, and that the Lakota might not be as much in command as they had believed, started to become apparent in the 1830s as white settlers infiltrated Lakota territory, and the United States dotted the northern plains with forts. By then Plenty Horses' Brulé ancestors were living in what today is southwestern South Dakota, largely in the watershed of a river they called Makazita Wakpa, which literally means "Earth Smoke River" but is more accurately rendered as "Dust River."[16] They gave it this name because the white clay beds through which the upper portions of the river ran made the water look milky. Today it is called the White River. Other streams in the area, such as White Clay Creek and the Milk River, were given their names for the same reason. The White River country was rich in grass, water, and game such as bison, deer, and pronghorn—a perfect paradise for mounted hunters. The Lakota could even find wild horses roaming the Sandhills to the south, in what today is Nebraska.

Once the Brulé in the late 1700s took control of this area from the crop-growing and more sedentary Arikara, other Lakota tribes and even more distant relatives from as far away as Minnesota moved in. The area began to suffer. The newcomers cut cottonwood groves along streams for firewood and stripped off bark to feed horses. Game grew scarce. The degradation was compounded when the fur trade boomed after the War of 1812.[17] The Lakota switched from killing animals for food to killing them to provide hides for trade. A hunter knew when he had killed enough to feed his family or his band, but what was the limit in commercial hunting?[18] In the winter of 1829–30, at least 6,000 bison hides from the Black Hills alone—the heart of Lakota country—were shipped to St. Louis.[19] Those hides were a drop in the bucket.

That same year, 26,000 bison hides from north of the Big Sioux River reached St. Louis, along with 25,000 pounds of beaver pelts, 37,500 muskrat skins, 4,000 otter, and 150,000 deer.[20] The Lakota, enamored of a trade that brought them firearms, ammunition, blankets, kettles, fabrics, beads, needles, and such exotic foods as coffee, flocked to trading posts set up along the Missouri.[21]

By the 1820s White River wildlife was ebbing away, and rival fur companies were plying the Indians with bad liquor in an effort to win their trade. The fur dealers sold the booze at a loss or even gave it away.[22] Drunken Lakota often would quarrel and fight. People were killed.[23]

Soon, much more powerful impacts hit the Lakota. In 1835 Brulé wandering along the Platte witnessed something they had never seen before—caravans of wagons enclosed under white canvas, like tents on wheels. At first the Indians were not alarmed and even approached wagon trains for trade and guided the settlers to fords in streams.[24] But the Lakota became increasingly hostile after they recognized in the 1840s that these whites were coming in endless numbers, using up grass and firewood and killing off game. Marauding Lakota attacked small parties of mounted white hunters and sometimes robbed them of everything, literally stripping them naked and setting them on foot to walk back to the wagon trains.

The federal government in 1845 responded by sending out Colonel Stephen W. Kearny, who rode at the head of a force of dragoons and met with Brulé and other Lakota he found in June at a fur-trading outpost just south of the Platte River in what today is eastern Wyoming. He gave the Brulé an intimidating demonstration of five companies of sword-wielding soldiers parading about on horses that towered over the Indian ponies—the Indians dubbed the Americans *milahanska,* "long knives," and called these big animals *sunkawakan milahanska,* "American horses." Having exhibited his might, Kearny reinforced his message with cajolery, giving the Lakota presents and telling them to leave the wagon trains alone.[25]

The army in 1848 reinforced Kearny's warning by building a fort named after him on the Platte River in what is today south-central Nebraska. Fort Kearny stood in the heart of hunting grounds used by the Lakota and the Pawnee, who frequently fought one another over access to the region. The army also purchased the trading post where Kearny had met with the Lakota, reincarnating it as Fort Laramie. Many wagons moved through the area. In

1849 some 4,400, carrying twenty thousand settlers, had passed Fort Kearny by May, still early in the travel season.[26]

The superintendent of Indian affairs, D. D. Mitchell, visited Fort Laramie in 1851 and found himself "much surprised to witness the sad change which a few years and unlooked-for circumstances had produced. The buffalo, upon which [the Indians] rely for food, clothing, shelter, and traffic, are rapidly diminishing. The hordes of emigrants passing through the country seem to have scattered death and disease in all directions. The tribes have suffered much from the small-pox and cholera, and perhaps still more from venereal diseases."[27]

To reduce tensions, in 1851 the U.S. Congress appropriated one hundred thousand dollars for negotiating another Lakota treaty. Promises of gifts for participants brought ten thousand Indians to Fort Laramie to talk things over. The treaty signed at Fort Laramie on September 17 assigned boundaries to territories controlled by the Lakota and other tribes. Lakota territory covered what today is North Dakota south of the Heart River, South Dakota west of the Missouri, northwestern Nebraska, and eastern Wyoming between the North Platte and the western slope of the Black Hills. The Lakota agreed to let white travelers cross the Platte River valley in Nebraska and Wyoming and to allow the United States to build roads and outposts—including forts—in Indian territory. For these benefits, the government promised for the next fifty years to pay the Indians fifty thousand dollars yearly in various types of goods and equipment and to protect the Indians from settlers. The U.S. Senate reduced the term of the contract to ten years and gave the president the option to renew the terms every five years.

In the early 1850s none of the Lakota knew what they were up against in their dealings with the U.S. government. They thought of the *milahanska* as merely another enemy tribe that could be beaten into submission when needed. The Indians reached the conclusion that such measures were necessary in August 1854, when a young lieutenant, John L. Grattan, rode with thirty other soldiers, a twelve-pound fieldpiece, and a mountain howitzer into a Lakota camp near Fort Laramie and tried to arrest a Miniconjou Lakota for shooting and killing an ox that had passed by with a Morman wagon train. The camp included some two hundred lodges, almost all of them Brulé.

Fresh out of West Point, Grattan—like many another brash officer—was convinced he could beat the entire Lakota nation with a handful of soldiers and some artillery. When he reached the camp, he set up his men in battle order, palavered with the Indians for a while, lost his patience, and ordered his men into action.

The Brulé went into action, too, annihilating Grattan and all his men. Flushed with victory, the warriors instantly went off to raid nearby trading posts. The next day, cooler and somewhat older heads prevailed as the Lakota recognized the vulnerability of their position, camped as they were with women and children along a main immigrant thoroughfare with the U.S. military nearby. The Indians broke camp and melted into the wilder parts of the prairie to begin their annual autumn bison hunt.[28]

The Grattan affair marked the first battle between the Lakota and the U.S. Army. After it, the Lakota returned to such conventional activities as attacking the Crow and the Pawnee, hunting buffalo, and holding a sun dance, a key religious ritual that preserved tribal unity through individual sacrifice on behalf of all Lakota. Then, in spring and summer 1855, they again attacked trading posts, primarily to steal horses and other goods. The traders warned friendly Lakota that the army would soon retaliate for the Grattan affair and these other affronts.

In fact, earlier in the year, Brigadier General William S. Harney had begun putting together an attack force at his base in Fort Leavenworth, Kansas. In August the Indian agent at Fort Laramie told the Lakota that friendly bands should move their camps from the north to the south side of the North Platte River and keep close to the fort. Any bands north of the river would be deemed hostiles. The bulk of the tribe crossed over.[29]

The alacrity with which the Lakota complied was a measure of how wary they had become of the whites. Only a few years earlier they would have ignored such an order. But not all the Lakota submitted, including most of the Brulé. About 250 of the latter were camped on a Platte tributary called Bluewater. Among them was a young warrior of growing fame who would not only shape but also personify the changes that the Lakota, particularly the Brulé, made in dealing with the United States. Born in 1823, Sinte Galeska, or Spotted Tail—so named because in battle he always wore a raccoon tail attached to his headdress—was tall and aristocratic in bearing, with a round face, narrow nose, and wide mouth.[30] He had by the age of sixteen won so sterling a reputation as a warrior that he had already served as an advance scout for at least one war party.[31] At seventeen or eighteen, in a knife fight over a woman, he killed a Brulé chief named Running Bear. Badly wounded, Spotted Tail survived to marry the woman, his first of several wives.[32] By 1855 he was becoming a Brulé leader, had taken more than one hundred enemy scalps, and with two other warriors was wanted by the military for his role in a November 1854 mail-wagon attack that resulted in the death of three whites. He was ardently anti-white and pro-war.[33]

Although, as would happen nearly forty years later with Plenty Horses, the army demanded the surrender of Spotted Tail and the other two warriors, in this case the Brulé shrugged off the order. They would soon learn, however, that the army meant to impose its authority. On the morning of September 3, 1855, Harney and six hundred soldiers, backed with artillery, attacked the Bluewater village.

Accustomed to dishing out harsh punishment to enemies, the Lakota for

Spotted Tail, an important Brulé chief. He advocated peace after a visit to Fort Leavenworth, Kansas, persuaded him that his people could not win a war against the United States. *(Library of Congress)*

the first time in living memory lost one of their big camps to foe. When the attack ended, eighty-six Lakota had died, and the army had captured seventy women and children. Spotted Tail was among the wounded who fled. His wife and child stood among the captives.

Harney went on to Fort Laramie, where he cut off the goods that the government had promised to provide yearly for friendly Lakota. He also ended all trade with them and vowed that his ban on trade and annuities would not be lifted until the warriors involved in the mail-wagon slaughter were turned over to the military. He then headed off with his troops on a raid through the heart of Brulé country.

Harney's scouring of the countryside ended when cold weather blew in, closing the war season. But Harney, whom the Lakota called the Hornet, vowed to buzz back in the spring. During the ensuing weeks, Lakota chiefs begged Spotted Tail and the two other warriors to turn themselves in.[34] The tribe could withstand the loss of three warriors, but it could not survive without trade. And so, decked out in elaborate war costumes and mounted on their best horses, the trio rode into Fort Laramie on October 18, 1855, singing their death songs and fully expecting that they would be hanged.[35]

The surrender marked a turning point for the Brulé, if not for the Lakota as a nation, in at least two ways. First, the Brulé had chosen not to rebuff the U.S. military over the issue of the surrender of the three warriors, a sure sign that some of the fight had been taken out of them. Second, when Spotted Tail and the others arrived at Fort Leavenworth on December 12, 1855—having crossed what was, for Lakota people, a vast chunk of ground, taking them into alien territory—they discovered for the first time the magnitude of the force against which they had been fighting. The Kansas plains were swarming with whites— white men, white women, white children—scattered in homesteads, clustered in towns, passing through in countless streams of wagons. Among the whites, surrounded by them, were the Kaw Indians, the native people of this land, boxed up on a reservation. In Kansas, too, lived Indians the U.S. government had transported from distant reaches beyond the Mississippi—Delaware and Shawnee Indians who wore Euro-American clothing, lived in houses, and farmed the land. In them Spotted Tail saw the bleak future of his own people.[36]

The army did not hang Spotted Tail and the others. Their agent, working through the superintendent of Indian affairs, won a pardon for them from President Franklin Pierce. Spotted Tail then lived at Fort Leavenworth until the following spring, learning the ways of U.S. society while charming and be-friending army officers and their wives.[37]

However socially buoyant he was, something within Spotted Tail died at Fort Leavenworth. A year earlier, he had been a Brulé firebrand, a strong advo-cate for war with the whites. But now, seeing the vast numbers of settlers, of their soldiers, of their houses, of their weapons, he knew that fighting these newcomers would destroy the Lakota nation. Fort Leavenworth alone held more soldiers than there were Brulé warriors in all the world.[38] And more im-migrants were coming west all the time—Spotted Tail saw them passing by on the crowded steamboats that plied the Missouri, within sight of the fort. The question on his mind concerned how his people would adapt to the challenges the new settlers posed and how he would convey to them a sense of what he had seen and learned. In the process of answering those questions, he would create the new Brulé world in which Plenty Horses would grow up. But between his realization that the Lakota could not survive a fight with the United States, and actually giving up that fight, lay a few more years of hostility and aggression.

BY 1857 THE BRULÉ OF the Platte country were mired in trouble. U.S. settle-ment was pressing upon them from the south and east, and the federal govern-ment was planning to put a railroad right in their midst. They had no choice but to find ways to get along with the whites. Although they sometimes joined Lakota who lived in more distant hunting grounds around the Powder River, in what today is Montana and northern Wyoming, that region could feed only so many Indians, and the bison were ebbing. Anyway, the lands in Nebraska Territory and in southern Dakota Territory were the Brulé home. They did not want to leave, and the only way to survive there was through accommoda-tion with the whites.

The settlers continued to come. Bison and other Lakota prey dwindled fur-ther. During the 1860s fighting between Lakota and the newcomers intensified, and forts went up in Montana along the Bozeman Trail, blazed as a thorough-fare to Oregon by an explorer who would later be killed by Indians. In January and February 1865 Spotted Tail joined in two raids on Julesburg, Colorado, killing soldiers and citizens and raiding stagecoach stations and trading posts. As many as 1,500 Lakota took part in these raids. Spotted Tail would later declare that he had participated in what he saw as futile battle only because of tribal pressure.[39]

In summer 1865 the army invaded the Brulé hunting grounds. With soldiers lurking about, the Lakota could not leave their families to hunt. Desperate, they retreated north to the old White River country, but they had already hunted out the game there. Spotted Tail and other leaders decided that seeking peace was the best avenue for returning safely to the Platte River. The following spring they went to Fort Laramie with these hopes in mind.

By then the Lakota people were fractured by white contact. Among the Brulé were bands that had learned to plant corn, although traditional Brulé considered planting crops demeaning and would threaten the corn bands when they tried to farm. Year round at Fort Laramie lived bands of Lakota who counted among their number many who had intermarried with white traders, soldiers, and others. In the early days of white contact, these marriages, usually between white men and the daughters of chiefs, were seen by the Lakota as creating useful ties with the newcomers. But by the 1850s the independent Lakota of the Powder River area looked down on these stay-around-the-fort Indians because they had given up traditional ways. The wilder Lakota called them Waglukhe, or Loafers. The Waglukhe, in turn, looked down on traditional Lakota as the equivalent of country bumpkins who had not grasped the new reality.[40]

One of the key leaders of the independent Lakota was Red Cloud, an Oglala whose people, ironically, had lived and hunted for years in the country just north of Fort Laramie. Red Cloud had known Fort Laramie since its trading-post days during his childhood and, like others of his people, had gone there often to sell furs and hides.

Red Cloud was not a hereditary chief. In fact, his father had besmirched the family by dying of alcoholism when Red Cloud was only about five years old, forcing his mother and siblings to live with relatives.[41] But Red Cloud won status through success in battle. Born around 1820, he had already taken a scalp by age sixteen, while on his first war party.[42] A few months later, he joined a war party that trapped fourteen Crow warriors who gave up in despair, sitting down and covering their heads with their blankets to await death. Red Cloud rode up and struck three of them with his bow, leaving himself open to retaliation, but rode away unscathed.[43] To these coups he would later add seventy-seven more. Once, he and a friend rode ahead of a war party and swooped down on an unsuspecting Crow guarding a herd of fifty horses. Red Cloud killed the guard, and he and his friend made off with the horses.

In 1866 Red Cloud was leading a war meant to drive the new enemies out of Lakota territory. This war hit a high note on December 21, when Captain William Fetterman led a contingent of soldiers out of Fort Phil Kearny in northern Wyoming to pursue half a dozen Lakota warriors who had attacked a detail of men cutting wood near the fort.[44] The warriors were led by Tasunka Witko, or Crazy Horse, a man in his midtwenties who was idolized by the Lakota as one of their top warriors.

The fort commander had ordered Fetterman not to chase the Indians beyond a nearby highland called Lodge Trail Ridge. However, the thirty-one-year-old captain—eerily echoing the Grattan affair—was an overconfident hothead who had bragged that he could beat the entire Lakota tribe with eighty soldiers, exactly the number with which he left the fort.[45]

Once the soldiers rode out on the plains, the Lakota with Crazy Horse taunted Fetterman, who promptly veered away from the woodcutters and chased after the Indians, rushing without pause over the top of Lodge Trail Ridge and straight into several hundred warriors waiting in ambush. The attack on the woodcutters and the taunts by Crazy Horse and his men were a mere ruse to lead soldiers to doom. For Fetterman, that doom came in the form of an Oglala Lakota named American Horse, who clubbed Fetterman to the ground and cut his throat so deeply that the knife slashed all the way to the bone. The rest of Fetterman's troops suffered a similar fate in a battle that U.S. historians came to call the Fetterman Massacre. The Lakota called it the Fight of One Hundred, as they thought one hundred soldiers were fighting under the feckless captain. When it was over, the Indians dispersed to hunting grounds around the Powder River in what today is southern Montana.

The Fight of One Hundred caused considerable grief in Washington, D.C.[46] The army, particularly Civil War hero General William Tecumseh Sherman, wanted to punish the Indians severely.

Sherman was expert at punishing enemies, having laid waste to much of Georgia during his march from Atlanta to the sea toward the end of the Civil War. He was perfectly willing to use the army, which he saw as "the picket line at the front of the great wave of civilization," to scour away the Indians.[47] He declared to General Philip Sheridan, commanding troops on the southern plains, that war in the West would lead to the "extermination—the utter annihilation of these Indians." He told Sheridan not to restrain his troops in battle, promising to fend off in Washington anyone who tried to chastise the military for any excesses. "I will say nothing and do nothing to restrain our troops from doing what they deem proper on the spot, and will allow no mere vague general charge of cruelty or inhumanity to tie their hands, but will use all the power confided in me to the end that these Indians, the enemies of our race and of our civilization, shall not . . . carry on their barbarous warfare."[48] Shortly after the Fetterman battle, he wrote President Ulysses S. Grant specifically about the Lakota: "We must act with vindictive earnestness against the Sioux, even to their extermination, men, women and children."[49]

But he was at least partly thwarted by the civilian Department of the Interior, which was responsible for Indian affairs. Interior officials contended that hostile actions by the military had incited the Lakota to attack at Fort Phil Kearny. Congress reacted to the conflicting views by appointing a commission to go west and investigate.

The Lakota leader with whom the commission most wanted to speak was Red Cloud, widely credited with planning the Fetterman battle. He was also well known to the government because of his long association with Fort Laramie. Nevertheless, the commissioners failed to get him to attend the 1866 council. They traveled to various parts of Lakota territory, but only lesser chiefs would meet with them. One exception was Spotted Tail.

Spotted Tail was regarded around this time both by his people and by the U.S. military as the head Brulé chief. On June 27, 1866, he and other peace-seeking chiefs signed a treaty with the whites. The Powder River Lakota, particularly Red Cloud, refused to sign and continued fighting in the north, but Spotted Tail had to make peace if he and his people were going to live in their homeland. Unlike the Powder River region, the Brulé hunting grounds were studded with forts and lay along one of the main U.S. wagon-train thoroughfares. His choice was to sign or to starve, so he signed, and then, with his people, he went home.[50]

Despite the treaty, Brulé warriors continued to join Red Cloud in fighting the whites, causing Spotted Tail to worry that the army would ride in and punish even his peaceful people. But he was in for a surprise. When the commissioners returned to Washington, they urged the government to stop the war against the Indians and to send yet another panel to talk with the Lakota. In response, Congress in July 1867 created the Indian Peace Commission, authorized to seek peace not just with the Lakota but with Indians throughout the plains.[51] This commission, which gathered in St. Louis, Missouri, on August 7 for its organizational meeting, was composed of three civilians who wanted peace with the Indians and three soldiers who leaned more toward extermination.[52]

The most prominent of the soldiers was General Sherman himself, who had troops out in the field trying to find Lakota with whom to fight even as the commission was being assembled. His hope was that, by marching large units of soldiers into the heart of Lakota hunting grounds, he would entice equally large numbers of warriors into battle. In this way he planned to wipe out the Lakota in sizable gulps, rather than piecemeal in skirmishes with individual war parties.[53] Even while serving on the commission and meeting with the Lakota, he wrote to his wife, "I don't care about interesting myself too far in the fate of the poor . . . Indians, who are doomed from the causes inherent in their natures, or from the natural & persistent hostility of the White Race."[54]

Sherman notwithstanding, the panel's desire to negotiate an end to hostilities was a harbinger of a revolution about to sweep down on the plains and the Lakota. Protecting settlers was not the government's only goal in terminating hostilities. Perhaps even more important, the government did not want an Indian war to derail one of America's most-ambitious nineteenth-century undertakings: construction of the transcontinental railroad. Everyone well knew that the Union Pacific railroad would cross Lakota lands in the Nebraska area and that further construction would bring steel track to the northern parts of Lakota territory as well.

This development would introduce change on a scale the Lakota could scarcely imagine. Wagon trains carrying settlers to California and Oregon had alarmed the Indians, but those settlers were just passing through. The railroad would create new towns from which goods could be shipped to market.[55] The *milahanska* would follow the iron trail more swiftly and in greater numbers than ever before, and they would make their homes on Lakota lands. The last of the game herds would vanish as sport and commercial hunters took advantage of the railroads. Under these circumstances the 1868 treaty would be not so much a permanent solution to Lakota hostilities as a delaying tactic abating Indian aggression until the United States was poised to take over in the West.

But completing the railroad was not the only challenge for the government. The Civil War had just ended, and rebuilding the South required funds and

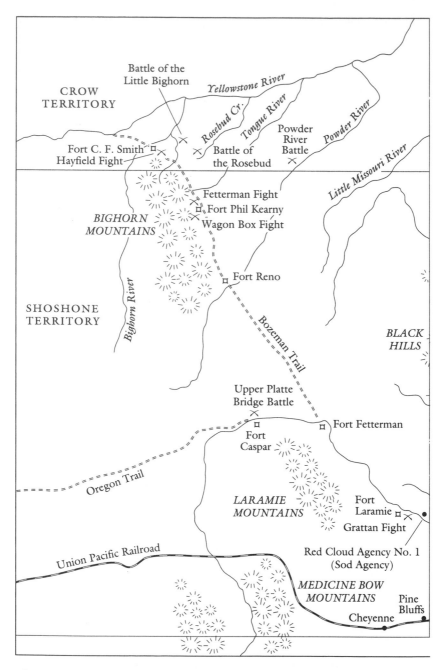

Lakota reservations and important sites of the Lakota Wars of the 1860s and 1870s.
(Copyright © 1997 by the Oklahoma University Press)

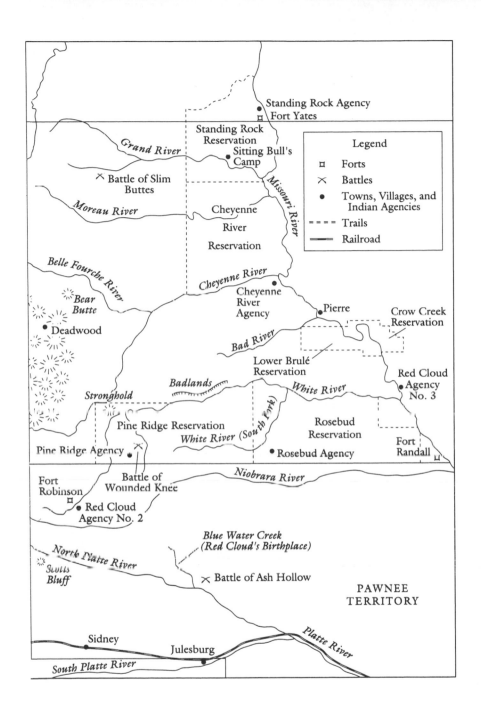

Standing Rock Agency
Fort Yates

Standing Rock
Reservation
Sitting Bull's
Camp

Grand River

Battle of Slim
Buttes

Moreau River

Cheyenne
River
Reservation

Missouri River

Legend

◻ Forts
✕ Battles
● Towns, Villages, and
  Indian Agencies
- - - - Trails
——— Railroad

Belle Fourche River

Bear
Butte

Deadwood

Cheyenne River

Cheyenne
River
Agency

Pierre

Crow Creek
Reservation

Bad River

Stronghold

Badlands

Lower Brulé
Reservation

White River

Red Cloud
Agency
No. 3

Pine Ridge Reservation

White River (South Fork)

Rosebud
Reservation

Fort
Randall

Pine Ridge Agency

Rosebud Agency

Niobrara River

Fort
Robinson

Battle of
Wounded Knee

Red Cloud
Agency No. 2

Blue Water Creek
(Red Cloud's Birthplace)

North Platte River

Scotts
Bluff

Battle of Ash Hollow

PAWNEE
TERRITORY

Platte River

Sidney

Julesburg

South Platte River

troops. Consequently, the government lacked the personnel and the money needed to protect both the Union Pacific and the Bozeman Trail.[56] Compared to the need to put America on rails and the South on its feet, fighting the Lakota over the Bozeman paled in significance.

To settle these issues, the Indian Peace Commission intended to move the Lakota to reservations and to teach them to farm, blithely ignoring the fact that reservations and farming were anathema to nomadic plains hunters. Using steel plows to tear the flesh of Mother Earth also carried dark religious overtones for the Lakota. For such evil, traditional Lakota presumed, the spirits would punish them.[57] Even among the few Brulé who had learned to farm, growing crops was considered women's work and was performed on the scale of a home vegetable garden. And those who planted crops risked being policed by other Lakota, who might destroy the would-be farmers' homes, horses, and other possessions.

Although some army officers and most western settlers still favored killing off the Indians, or at least subduing them, the federal government was in no mood for protracted battle and sided with the more peaceful of the peace commissioners.[58] Red Cloud, however, continued to take a hard line in negotiations, refusing to meet or to sign a treaty unless the United States first closed not only a chain of forts along the Bozeman Trail but also the trail itself.

The government was so eager to bargain that on March 2, 1868, President Grant ordered General Sherman to close the three forts that offended Red Cloud. The new treaty also promised that the government would close the Bozeman Trail, which after all would be less important once the railroad was built. These concessions to Red Cloud did not please Spotted Tail, even though he had helped to negotiate them.[59] Spotted Tail sensed that the government was rewarding the warring Lakota while his own peace-seeking people were beleaguered by settlers and soldiers along the Platte. He and other peace chiefs knew that if this ironic state of affairs persisted, they would lose authority among their own people, including their ability to restrain eager young warriors.

In the fall, after months out west, the Indian Peace Commission gathered in Chicago without ever getting Red Cloud to sign the treaty. Sherman, as commander of the army's Division of the Missouri, which included the plains region of the Lakota, pushed through his own policies.[60] He not only took the lead in dissolving the commission itself but also succeeded in getting the Bureau of Indian Affairs transferred from the Interior Department to the War Department, where the military could take more direct control of the Indians. Although civilians would remain in charge of Indian reservation agencies—the administrative offices for specific Lakota groups—military commanders were to monitor the activities of the civilian agents and to serve as agents for Indians who did not live on reservations.[61] Sherman also initiated a policy in which Indian tribes would no longer be treated as separate nations, ensuring that in the future Indians would be held individually responsible for obeying U.S. laws.

By this time the U.S. government had largely met Red Cloud's demands. The forts were closed around the end of July 1868, and Red Cloud and his warriors burned two of them to the ground almost as soon as the army left.[62] Nevertheless, Red Cloud did not come to Fort Laramie to sign the treaty until November, a month after the Indian Peace Commission had ceased to exist. Despite his intransigence, the commissioners had hammered out a treaty that met his wishes, surrendering to the Lakota their Powder River hunting grounds and other sites above the North Platte River. The treaty labeled these regions "unceded territory," where the Lakota could hunt but not settle and where the United States could build roads and railroads.

The treaty also established the Great Sioux Reservation, composed largely of South Dakota west of the Missouri and off-limits to white settlement. Reservation agencies would be built to supply the Indians with rations and annuities and to teach them to farm. Another provision allowed each Indian family to lay claim to 320 acres within the reservation, along with other considerations designed to encourage them to grow crops. Even after signing the treaty, Red Cloud refused to go to the reservation. He and his people headed back to Powder River, where they continued to engage in occasional shootouts with white interlopers.

Spotted Tail had signed the new treaty on April 29, 1868. In the absence of Red Cloud, he had played a leading role in treaty negotiations. He had stressed the need for firearms and ammunition for hunting but generally had acceded to white demands in the belief that he and his people would then be allowed to return safely to their Platte River homeland.[63] He had failed to notice that the treaty required his people to move to the new reservation in southern Dakota Territory.

CHAPTER 3

Freedom's Final Days

NONE OF THE LAKOTA TRIBES understood that the 1868 treaty required them to move to a reservation. The first to learn of this plan were the Waglukhe, the Loafers who had lived around Fort Laramie for a quarter of a century. Shortly after the signing, army officers ordered the Waglukhe to move to a reservation on the Missouri River in southern Dakota Territory. The Loafers had abandoned the old ways so long ago that many of them did not even own horses for travel. The U.S. government had to supply wagons for transport, and the Waglukhe went along docilely if unhappily.[1]

The military then turned its attention to the Brulé hunting along the Republican River in southern Nebraska. When the army told Spotted Tail's people they must move northeastward to the Missouri, the Indians could scarcely believe what they were hearing. They had acquiesced in everything the U.S. government had asked of them, while their wilder northern counterparts had fought back. Now the Brulé were to be rewarded by being put on a reservation in a land exhausted of game, while the warring northern Lakota remained on their hunting grounds leading the old life.

But the chiefs knew that they were not in the northern Lakota's enviable position on the pristine Powder River. Brulé hunting lands were pressed on all sides and divided within by white encroachment. Some Brulé warriors might slip off to join northern brethren in fighting, or might raid settlements along the Platte, but the chiefs knew, and persuaded most of the Brulé to believe, that warfare against the whites could not be won. And so the Brulé packed up and headed for the Missouri River, the boundary they had crossed one hundred years earlier when they had swept as conquerors onto the high plains. They were back in the lowlands, and they despised it.

The Brulés' assigned home lay along Whetstone Creek, which flowed into the Missouri from the west about twenty-five miles above the Nebraska border. The agent was General William Harney, who in 1855 had fought the Lakota on

the Bluewater, capturing Spotted Tail's wife and child. In 1868 he had served
on the Indian Peace Commission and had endorsed informal promises to provide the Lakota with food and other goods in addition to what the treaty offered. But when he prepared to take charge as the Brulé agent, he told a
newspaper reporter in Sioux City that he would avoid spending any time with
the Lakota, because he did not want them to ask him where all the horses,
cows, chickens, and other promised gifts were to be found.[2] Instead, he ordered thousands of acres along Whetstone plowed, so the land would be waiting for the Lakota to sow it. He also ordered all manner of agricultural
equipment: rakes, plows, corn planters, threshing machines, harrows, even a
mill for making flour.

And then reality struck. Harney could order all the farming equipment he
wanted, but he could not make the Brulé farm. The Lakota were divided into
two fundamental groups: the conservative "traditionalists," who resisted U.S.
efforts to change Lakota culture, and the "progressives," who were willing to
go along with federal plans and adapt to the new system. The traditionalists
could take a very hard and effective approach to stifling government plans. For
example, when farming instructors came to the reservation, the conservative
faction kept them from teaching by letting them know they would be killed if
they strayed from agency headquarters.[3]

The life of a reservation agent in many ways was no better than that of
their defeated charges. As political appointees, the agents often lacked mana-
gerial skills and knew nothing about Indians. For an annual salary of $1,500,
they worked on isolated prairies surrounded by seasoned warriors who re-
sented them. Some $2 million in government funds went yearly to the Lakota,
and graft occurred often enough to damage the reputation of almost any man
who became an agent, honest or otherwise. Chiefs used this situation to keep
agents in line, sending letters to Washington officials accusing agents of theft
when the chiefs wanted to get rid of them.[4]

Nevertheless, the reservation administrators were the men in charge, and
they were largely convinced that Indians were best dealt with by destroying
their tribal system and turning them into farmers and ranchers.[5] The agents
devised plans for achieving this goal. One of the first was to undermine the
conservative chiefs, the most visible artifact of the old ways. These hard-
liners helped maintain tribal independence and served as authority figures
through whom the Indians could demand concessions from the federal gov-

ernment. Initially, the government backed the chiefs, who offered some chance of keeping order among the warriors and the rest of the people. Agents turned over rations to these leaders, who would distribute the food to the people. This practice meshed with Lakota traditions of generosity and gift giving and helped preserve the tribal line of authority.[6]

But when the agents finally realized that the chiefs were not always amenable to government plans, they set out to replace them with handpicked, malleable progressives who would do as told. The agents also changed the rules for distribution of rations, ordering that the head of each family come to the agency to receive goods personally. This arrangement posed a problem for Lakota who lived far from agency headquarters. They would have to ride in every two weeks, even if the trip took several days one way. While they traveled, they neglected the little farms that the agents had insisted they set up. For the Lakota, here was one more maddening aspect of life under U.S. government rule. Moreover, the agents succeeded in heightening the opposition between traditionalists and progressives, and the Lakota turned to fighting one another for influence on the reservation.[7]

In 1883 the secretary of the Interior, Henry Teller, ordered the agents to ban ceremonial feasts and dances, including the sun dance, that brought the Lakota together for social as well as ceremonial purposes. The agents also established Indian police forces that reported to the agents rather than to the chiefs, diminishing the chiefs' authority and driving another wedge between progressives and traditionalists. Young Lakota were eager to sign up, because serving on an agency police force was a plum job that could ingratiate a politically astute warrior with his agent. The assignment not only paid hard cash but also echoed the role of the warrior in *akicita* societies, the Lakota men's clubs that often were assigned by the chiefs to keep order on hunts or when traveling.

The government also sought to destroy Lakota culture by eroding the relationship between parents and children. Educating the offspring in reservation schools helped remove children from parental influence. An even better tool was the boarding school, where children could be kept for years, sometimes hundreds of miles from family and friends.

The chiefs did not stand by idly and accept these changes, but some were more adept than others at evading the authorities. Spotted Tail's skills at running his agents was legendary. As late as 1879 he persuaded an agent not only to permit a sun-dance ceremony—the dance reservation administrators most wanted to forbid—but also to send out invitations to Lakota at other agencies.[8] He curtailed open rebellion among his people, too, even as he himself worked to preserve traditional ways. Crafty enough to ensure that the agency police were loyal to him, he strengthened his political base.

The Brulé adjusted slowly to the new order. In early 1869 some Brulé wanted to travel south to the Republican River to hunt. Spotted Tail warned them not to go, fearing they would be shot. They went anyway, and several were killed in fights with Pawnee army scouts. Also, Oglala Lakota who in 1868 had stayed on the southern hunting grounds, refusing to go north to the reservation, arrived in spring 1869 destitute after encounters with army troops who had shot them up and destroyed their tepees and other property. These developments supported Spotted Tail's contention that resistance could only fail.[9] During the early 1870s, when Spotted Tail attempted to have his agency moved onto the high plains around the White River, he pressed his plan diplomatically on his agent and on various federal bureaucrats during a trip to Washington, D.C.

Meanwhile, life on the reservation established its own rhythm. Each year the Brulé received their annuities. A shipment for 1871 included 2,450 of the dark blue, dark green, or dark red blankets favored by Lakota men; cases of blue, red, and print cloth; forty-eight cases of camp kettles; 576 axes; cases of shirts, socks, pants; and boxes of tobacco.[10] Lakota who had no interest in these items would swap them with local traders for rifles, ammunition, and other goods. When annuities were handed out, the Indians would come in from their scattered prairie camps and gather at the agency, setting up tepees, staking out horses, and socializing much as they had at the old tribal gatherings they had held at various times of year.[11]

On the reservation the Lakota also received rations at regular intervals—every ten days, or two weeks, or month. Rations included staples such as beans, coffee, and flour, even though the Lakota had little use for flour. The main attraction was the dispersal of beef on the hoof. The animals would be released from corrals, and Lakota men would chase them on horseback and shoot them down like bison.[12]

The Brulé in the early 1870s continued to live in some strange twilight world in which old traditions and new ways shaded into one another. Spotted Tail even finagled permission for occasional buffalo hunts to the south.[13] But

Lakota women gather at the Pine Ridge Reservation agency for rations in 1891.
(www.PictureHistory.com, Photo #1890.0134)

by 1875 the bison were nearly gone from the Republican and Platte, and the Brulé were sinking into the unmitigated despair of reservation life.

By the mid-1870s, however, Spotted Tail had succeeded in getting his people moved away from the Missouri and up to the high plains around the White River. He had even won support for this relocation from white settlers in southern Dakota Territory, who thought they would make good money hauling supplies by wagon to the distant Brulé. The move was appealing to Spotted Tail and his people because it gave them a chance to uproot and wander, as they had all their lives, plus the land around White River was not suitable for farming—the earth itself would become an ally in the battle against agriculture.

Meanwhile, the northern Lakota fought a defensive war against the military. These battles did not disturb the uneasy peace of the Brulé, although Spotted Tail did play an active part in the northern war as a peacemaker. In 1877 he tracked down one of the most inveterate of the Lakota war leaders, Crazy Horse, and persuaded him to give up the fight. The army rewarded Spotted Tail by turning over to him the 1,200 ponies that the surrendering Lakota had yielded to the military. Spotted Tail responded in generous chiefly fashion, returning many of the horses to the Indians he had talked into surrendering.[14]

Once Crazy Horse surrendered, the U.S. government told Spotted Tail that he had to move back east to Ponca Creek, a tributary of the Missouri River, where the government had already established a new agency. Reluctantly, the Lakota set out.[15] While traveling near Wounded Knee Creek on the way east, some Sans Arc and Miniconjou who had recently surrendered and were traveling with the Brulé broke away to join Sitting Bull in Canada. At the same time, the Brulé balked, refusing to go farther east than Rosebud Creek, which fed into the south fork of the White River. Spotted Tail could not budge them, and so they wintered there, with supplies brought from the Missouri River one hundred miles away.[16]

This move revealed deep political schisms within the Brulé people. Some wanted to move on to Ponca Creek. These were primarily Waglukhe and Corn Brulé, willing to try farming if the traditional Brulé would let them. In spring, after a grueling winter in which diphtheria and measles killed many Brulé children and elders, including, it seems, one of Spotted Tail's sons, some progressives headed for the Ponca.[17] Other Brulé wanted to join Sitting Bull, and another segment wanted to go on the warpath in Nebraska to punish cowboys who had stolen hundreds of Lakota ponies during the winter. Spotted Tail was consumed with keeping these various factions in one piece.

Good news came in March 1878, when federal officials in Washington, D.C., told Spotted Tail that his people themselves could choose a new agency site. The Brulé promptly picked a place along Rosebud Creek, near the Nebraska border, and wanted to move immediately. However, Spotted Tail's remaining progressives preferred Ponca Creek and abandoned the traditionals to go there. Spotted Tail countered by moving his full-bloods down to the Ponca, too—some six thousand Lakota living in seven hundred lodges that extended for fifteen miles along Ponca Creek.[18] These traditionalists strong-armed the progressives into agreeing to move back to Rosebud.[19] But officials in the Department of the Interior delayed the departure until July. By then the Brulé had had enough. On July 22 a portion of them headed for Rosebud. A week later, all were gone.

While the Brulé traveled, more dissension arose. Having thrown off the federal yoke, if only temporarily, some warriors did not want to reinstall it. They headed north and joined Sitting Bull. The government by then had given implicit approval to the Rosebud plan: The Brulé agent, a seasoned westerner named W. J. Pollock, hired wagons, at the cost of $1.25 for each one hundred pounds hauled one hundred miles, to transport old or poor Brulé who lacked horses.[20] He also sent rations and beef to the camps and asked the Brulé to let two cavalry troops shadow them. He tried to visit the camps but initially was rebuffed. The Brulé believed they had to settle this move on their own.[21]

Pollock finally got into the camp on August 28. After giving Spotted Tail and another chief, Hollow Horn Bear, silver medals from President Rutherford B. Hayes, Pollock went to work trying to set up the new agency at the site Spotted Tail and his people had chosen: a bowl of land along Rosebud Creek, surrounded by pine-speckled hills. The Corn Brulé and Loafers settled close to the agency, and Spotted Tail encamped several miles to the north.

The new agency was about two hundred miles from the Missouri, where annuity and other goods for the Lakota were shipped by steamboat to a site the whites called Rosebud Landing and the Lakota called Black Pole. Getting the goods from Rosebud Landing to the new agency proved a boon to the Brulé, who discovered a task that, unlike farming, they enjoyed: They became teamsters, hauling freight in wagons. While traveling they camped, setting up tepees along streams as in the old days. At the end of the trip they were paid in dollars. Such work required strong horses, and so the Brulé began to cut hay for their ponies, keeping them well fed even in winter, rather then letting the animals fend for themselves on snowy prairies. The hauling business combined cash commerce with the Lakota yen for travel and horses.[22]

And so the free-ranging days as plains nomads were over, the wars were over, and the hunting of the buffalo was over. Nevertheless, the Great Sioux Reservation was a huge patch of land. Covering all of what is now South Dakota west of the Missouri River, its forty-three thousand square miles of prairie seemed big enough to insulate the Lakota from the schemes and plans of the United States.[23]

BY THE LATE 1880S SOME four hundred thousand immigrants had settled in the parts of Dakota Territory that were not designated as Indian reservations. They came from surrounding states in search of new land and new hope, and they came from across the sea, primarily from Scandinavian countries and from Germany as well as Russia. Most came to farm, but many to ranch or to mine for gold.[24]

They were a new breed of pioneer. They arrived at their destinations more quickly than did their predecessors in the 1840s, traveling "in the cars," which is to say by railroad, or churning along rivers in steamboats. One Iowan wrote: "I bought a ticket for Aberdeen, and entered the train crammed with movers who had found the 'prairie schooner' all too slow. The epoch of the canvas-covered wagon had passed. The era of the locomotive, the day of the chartered car, had arrived. Free land was receding at railroad speed. The borderline could be overtaken only by steam, and every man was in haste to arrive."[25]

They were in a hurry because they saw the promise of fortune ahead of them, because they felt the thrust of progress all around them. Their century had arrived on horseback and under sail, but now they crossed the country by rail and sailed by steam. They felt inside them the power they had created around them, and their power seemed boundless. Within a generation or two, they had industrialized their world, and miracles were happening everywhere. They had grown accustomed to the way photography, an invention of the 1830s, had almost humbled the passage of time, preserving the image of the distant and the dead. And then, in the 1870s, along came Thomas Edison with his recording machine, which preserved voice, song, and music. These Americans were a people whose images would be remembered long after they were gone, as if fate itself were marking their passage on Earth for all eternity, and they knew it, just as they knew they were giving birth to a new era for humankind. Even the boundaries of night and day were being blurred. In 1879 Thomas Edison lit up his laboratory in Menlo Park, New Jersey, with the world's first incandescent electric lightbulb. Despite early fears about electricity in the home—that it caused freckles,[26] for example—no-soot, no-fumes, no-wicks electricity in the 1880s began to outcompete gas fixtures and kerosene lamps for lighting.

Nothing better signified the changes that were engulfing their lives than did the imminent decline of the horse as a universal source of power for such things as transportation and agriculture.[27] In the 1880s the horse was still an important beast of burden, but it was edging toward obsolescence—a major development in human history, in which the horse had played a critical role for thousands of years. In 1887 in Richmond, Virginia, an electrical engineer named Frank Sprague, who had worked previously for Thomas Edison on such projects as the lightbulb, opened the first urban electric streetcar system, the Union Passenger Railway. By the time of the Wounded Knee shoot-out, more than forty U.S. cities hosted electric streetcar lines. That number would increase more than twentyfold in the following five years, and cities would grow larger as the power of electricity expanded commuter range. Life would move more quickly, too, as the age of the horse waned. One New York City baseball team, the Brooklyn Dodgers, was named for the artful agility of its fans in ducking streetcars, which ripped along at a blurring twenty miles an hour. Other forms of horseless transportation were already in the works. In the United States, France, and Germany, inventors were tinkering with early models of the automobile, and within twelve years of Wounded Knee the horseless carriage would be on its way to revolutionizing transportation and turning the horse into a plaything.[28]

Even something as fundamental as the Euro-American diet was changing, and in the process creating a new impetus for farmers to cling ardently to plows. In the 1870s an American was likely to begin the day with a breakfast of steak, bacon, eggs, fried potatoes, pancakes, sausage, oatmeal, donuts, and fruit.[29] But late in the 1880s health-food faddists John Kellogg and C. W. Post began promoting cereals as the proper food for modern Americans, including such now-familiar products as Grape Nuts, Post Toasties, and Kellogg's Corn Flakes.[30] Critics mocked the new boxed cereals—dubbing them Eata Heapa Hay, Gripe Nuts, Shredded Doormats—but by 1915 the average American was likely to breakfast on a bowl of boxed cold cereal. With growing markets for grain, the farmer's yen for new land and the resolve for claiming it grew too.

How Americans related to these changes was summed up by Mark Twain, the era's most widely recognized celebrity writer, in an 1878 speech in which he urged his listeners to examine the century in which they lived: "Look at steam! Look at the steamboat, look at the railway, look at the steamship! Look at the telegraph, which enables you to flash your thoughts from world to world, ignoring intervening seas. Look at the telephone, which enables you to speak into affection's remote ear the word that cheers, and into the ear of the foe the opinion which you ought not to risk at shorter range. . . . Look at all these things, sir, and say if it is not a far prouder and more precious boon to have been born in the nineteenth century than in any century that went before it."[31]

Not every new thing under the Victorian sun functioned on the vast scale of steam power, but even the small changes suggested that life was growing more comfortable. In Pittsburgh, Pennsylvania, H. J. Heinz was founding a company that mass-produced canned goods, taking the canning process out of the home and nationally marketing factory-made and factory-packaged products such as beans and ketchup. In 1884 James Buchanan Duke, a twenty-eight-year-old manufacturer from North Carolina, developed a plan to mass-produce cigarettes, already rolled and neatly packaged, replacing the roll-your-owns that had been the vogue in America since the 1860s. Within five years his factories were responsible for half the country's total production, using machines that could turn out fifteen thousand packaged cigarettes each during a sixty-five-hour workweek.

Americans could enjoy their prefabricated cigarettes while sipping another new treat, a refreshing soda made of extracts of coca leaves and cola nuts by an Atlanta, Georgia, pharmacist named John Pemberton, who dubbed his concoction Coca-Cola. For Americans, one new thing after another seemed ready to pop up for their convenience. Until, that is, they took a notion to go west and develop a farm in Dakota Territory.

PLAINS PIONEERS BEGAN THEIR CAREERS on unbroken prairie with scarcely a rock under which to shelter.[32] Their first challenge was to stake a claim to potential farmland, no simple matter, as most pioneers were poor. Unable to buy the needed acreage, they generally took advantage of one of three federal programs—the homestead, preemption, and timber-culture programs—each of which sold land from the public domain in units limited to 160 acres per participant. Aspiring settlers usually made the claims in autumn, then went back to wherever they came from to await the spring plowing season.[33] During the Great Dakota Boom of 1878–87, settlers laid claim to most of the arable land in Dakota Territory, and offices in Huron, Aberdeen, Mitchell, and Watertown handled most of the claims. The busiest day ever for filing claims occurred in Huron on October 9, 1882, when the office there handled more than two thousand filings of one sort or another.[34]

Each of these programs required that the claimant improve the land and settle on it for a certain amount of time. In the case of the timber-culture program, claimants were supposed to plant a specified number of trees. All three approaches to claiming land were rife with corruption. Many claimants were mere speculators who had no interest in farming but simply wanted to buy and hold cheap land so they could sell it later as prices rose. They might attempt to meet the development requirements by putting out a packing crate and claiming it was a house, or digging a hole and calling it a well.[35] William Sparks, head of the federal land office in President Grover Cleveland's administration, was convinced that half of all land patents were frauds. After a study of timber-culture claims, Sparks's inspectors concluded that a quarter of the land in central Dakota had been taken without any real attempt to meet the requirements of the law.

Because of vagaries in land claims, the Homestead Act itself probably accounted for only 15 percent of all final patents to the total area on which claims were originally made. The historian Herbert Schell concluded: "Generally speaking, the actual settler who put permanent improvements upon his land and made it his home was a second- or even a third-comer, obliged to buy his farm on the market at a premium. The primary benefits from a government policy of free or cheap land thus accrued to the speculator. This was a perversion, if not an actual violation, of the spirit of the original homestead law."[36]

Prices rose rapidly as available public lands disappeared, and competition for land grew intense. Would-be farmers were pouring into the state. Entire communities—such as a group from Kankakee, Illinois, who shared a French-Canadian heritage—moved as units, re-creating their central-midwestern social life on the northern plains. The speculator who bought early and, by bending the rules, often, could rack up handsome profits.[37]

Although farming was the primary industry of the pioneer, the early settlers of Dakota Territory also felt the lure of a second calling: gold. The prospecting fields were centered in the territory's western reaches, particularly the Black Hills, and the men who made up the bulk of the population there were mostly single and mostly roughnecks. Western Dakota Territory soon became a haven for gunfighters, gamblers, gold seekers—people with a disdain for government and a belief in the equality bestowed by a six-shooter.[38] They contrasted sharply with the sodbusters of the eastern reaches of the territory, mostly family-oriented settlers more closely aligned with the civilizations of neighboring states and familiar with government largesse. So by the late 1870s the territory already had split into a conservative western portion and a more liberal eastern portion, a pattern that, in 1891, would affect the Plenty Horses trial.[39]

Another key economic endeavor in Dakota Territory was ranching. The

1880s lay in the era of the open range, when cattle were allowed to roam freely across unfenced prairie. Calves were branded with marks indicating who owned them. When the time came to round up the cattle for market, the ranchers could separate their stock by brand.

In 1884 South Dakota harbored nearly eight hundred thousand cattle. Then came the winter of 1886–87, which actually kicked off in autumn with subzero temperatures and heavy snow. By spring, ranchers in South Dakota had lost as much as half their stock. Farther north, in Montana and North Dakota, peak losses hit 90 percent.[40]

The ranchers realized that they had put too much stock out on the range, allowing the animals to graze the native grasses so heavily that they had no reserves for surviving a harsh winter. Moreover, farmers and sheep growers were moving into cattle range and putting up fences. The cattle interests knew they had to revamp their industry, a perception that would soon lead to fenced ranches. But meanwhile, still adhering to the old ways of doing business—not unlike the more conservative members of the Lakota community—the ranchers could see that they needed more land even as settlers were moving onto the plains. And they noticed that the Lakota people had millions of acres tied up in their Great Sioux Reservation.

CHAPTER 4

The Coming of the Ghosts

THE TREATY OF 1868 LEFT the Lakota holding a large portion of Dakota Territory, virtually the entire area west of the Missouri River in what today we call South Dakota as well as a small portion of south-central North Dakota.[1] Farmers, ranchers, and townspeople began turning covetous eyes toward that land by the early 1870s, leading to the last grab of Lakota lands. The confiscation began in 1874, when Congress, at the behest of the Dakota territorial legislature, sent army troops on an exploration of the Black Hills of western Dakota Territory. The project also enjoyed a little push from General Philip Sheridan, who wanted to set up a fort in the Black Hills to keep tabs on the Powder River Lakota.

In the mid-1770s an Oglala band led by the chief Standing Bull became the first Lakota to explore the Black Hills, which they called Paha Sapa.[2] Other peoples, notably the Crow, Kiowa, and Cheyenne, were already making use of the area, but the Lakota summarily pushed out the first two and, after a few battles with the Cheyenne, allied with them even while laying claim to the region. Essentially a spur of the Rocky Mountains named for their cloak of dark pines, the Black Hills became a sanctuary in which the Lakota could escape harsh winter winds and blistering summer heat and find the pines they needed for making lodgepoles. The hills also offered a reservoir of deer and other game that the Lakota could rely on when bison were scarce. The Black Hills were their meat pack, their special reserve, and hard-liners such as Sitting Bull contended that Paha Sapa should never be relinquished to anyone.

But the U.S. government was highly interested in the Black Hills. Rumors of gold there had echoed since at least the 1830s.[3] The U.S. Army had tried for years to suppress the reports in order to avoid a gold rush that would have triggered war with the Lakota. The army also may have been trying to keep soldiers with gold fever from deserting.

The congressional mandate for a military exploration of the Black Hills threatened the army's cautious handling of the region. It also raised ethical questions. Bishop William Hare, who founded missions among Indians throughout the West, protested to President Grant that the expedition would infuriate the Lakota and drive them to war as well as stand out as "a violation of national honor."[4] Grant ignored him.

The president's action may have been compelled in part by a financial crisis that struck the nation in 1873. The first of several banks collapsed on September 18, followed by a crashing stock market and the emergency closing of Stock Exchange doors. The Panic of 1873 had begun and would not end for four years. Everything seemed to go wrong all at once. Yellow fever swept down the Mississippi Valley, grasshoppers destroyed midwestern crops like a vengeful Egyptian plague, and a million urbanites—a fifth of nonagricultural workers—had no jobs. Factory wages fell 25 percent, but food prices dipped only 5 percent. A gold rush might be just the thing to make people feel better, especially as the politicians were committed to a gold standard that made money harder to come by. "The government's role in the economy, as they saw it, was to pour money into industry . . . but otherwise to keep hands off," wrote historian Stephen Ambrose.[5] "The nation's leaders were as hidebound about the functions of government as they were innovative about business." Their political views, Ambrose concluded, "remained stuck in the eighteenth century."

The Black Hills expedition began on July 2, 1874, when Lieutenant Colonel George Armstrong Custer rode out of Fort Abraham Lincoln, near present-day Bismarck, North Dakota, and moved southwest at the head of ten cavalry companies and two infantry companies—a total of about one thousand men that included geologists and other scientists as well as newspaper reporters and experienced miners.[6] In the Black Hills at the end of July, the miners panned for gold along French Creek. "The result was the discovery of a good bar, yielding from five to seven cents per pan, which could easily be made to pay if water were more plentiful here," reported the *New York Tribune*.[7]

At the end of August news of Black Hills gold broke nationwide. Miners began filtering into the mountains. The military at first turned them back, because the hills were Lakota land under the 1868 treaty. But the invaders whom soldiers escorted to nearby forts merely made a beeline back to the hills upon release. Local newspapers supported them. The *Yankton Daily Press and Dakotaian* for June 5, 1875, pronounced the theft of the Black Hills a matter of divine right: "That portion of Dakota occupied by the various bands of Sioux belongs not to them, but to the representatives of an advancing civilization. The romance of the Indian right to hereditary possession of all or portion [*sic*] of the domain over which the United States now claims jurisdiction is the veriest bosh. A power beyond that which takes to itself the right to make and unmake treaties between men long ago decreed that the American continent should be given over to the progress of enlightenment and the temporal advancement of those who are willing to make use of God's best gifts while they are on earth."[8]

Miners laid claim to the area by summer 1875, plotting out a town site on French Creek and naming it Custer. The Lakota were increasingly incensed. Spotted Tail and Red Cloud were among the leading chiefs who attended meetings in September with a federal commission sent to the reservation to buy the hills. No fewer than five thousand warriors from the northern plains, none of whom had signed the 1868 treaty, came to the meetings decked out in full war regalia. They were so menacing that the commissioners were forced to meet in a military stockade and limit their contact with the Lakota to twenty chiefs.[9] In the end, the commissioners offered $400,000 yearly to lease the Black Hills or $6 million to buy the area outright, and the Lakota turned them down.

In the wake of the Indians' refusal, a determined President Grant on November 3 held a secret meeting with his senior generals and officials in the Bureau of Indian Affairs and came to two conclusions: The government would maintain the ban on mining in the Black Hills but would not enforce it, and the army would demand that the northern Lakota give up life in the Powder River country and adjacent areas and come to live on the reservations. A month later, Edward Smith, the commissioner of Indian affairs, told his agents to order all the Lakota to go to the reservation by January 31, 1876. If the Indians ignored the dictum, they would be considered hostile and treated accordingly.

If ever a government policy was created purposefully to fail, this order was it. The Lakota were ensconced in their winter camps and were not about to journey across frozen, windswept prairies. The northern Lakota did not recognize the government's authority over them, anyway, and if they even deigned to heed the arbitrary deadline they would have seen it as a mere suggestion that they show up in, say, early spring.

When the northern Lakota failed to appear, the army launched attacks, one of which was Custer's charge into an encampment along the Little Bighorn River in what today is southeastern Montana. Custer divided his eleven companies of soldiers—about 450 men—into three groups and bore down on a combined Lakota and Cheyenne village that harbored as many as 1,800 warriors, who promptly wiped out Custer and the 200 some soldiers under his direct command.

That battle was a huge victory for the Lakota as well as a blow to American egos, if not to the military's strategic position. But the Lakota were on the anvil of civilization, and the hammer of American destructive power fell full force upon them. The battles of 1876 and 1877 led even Crazy Horse to give up. Only Sitting Bull, who had believed ardently in keeping the Black Hills under Lakota control, refused to surrender and live on a reservation. A tough but compassionate warrior, chief, and holy man, barrel-chested and round-faced, he slipped away and took his people into Canada, where he held on as the last wild Lakota. Four years later—abandoned by most of his people, unwanted by Canadian authorities, suffering a severe eye infection—he finally gave up and returned to the United States. Wearing a worn and dirty calico shirt and blanket, with a calico kerchief round his head like a turban, he led his equally threadbare tribal remnant to Fort Buford, Montana, where he surrendered on July 20, 1881. He handed his rifle to his four-year-old son, Crow Foot, and had him turn it over to the post commander. "I surrender this rifle to you through my young son, whom I now desire to teach in this manner that he has become the friend of the Americans," Sitting Bull said. "I wish him to learn the habits of the whites and to be educated as their sons are educated. I wish it to be remembered that I was the last man of my tribe to surrender my rifle. This boy has given it to you, and he now wants to know how he is going to make a living." A few days later, after reflecting on his fate, Sitting Bull wrote this song: "I have been a warrior. / Now it is all over. / I have a hard time."[10]

BACK IN DAKOTA TERRITORY, IN the fall of 1876 a new government commission came to the reservation and told leading chiefs such as Red Cloud and Spotted Tail that if they did not agree to sell the Black Hills, rations for the Lakota would be cut off, and the Lakota would be removed to Indian Territory (now Oklahoma). Neither proposition appealed to the agency Indians.

Sitting Bull, a leading Lakota chief and holy man. His death at the hands of Indian police set off events leading to the Wounded Knee massacre. *(Library of Congress)*

With the northern Lakota being trounced by the military, and with the military taking effective control of the reservations, the Lakota wavered and finally collapsed. They gave up the Black Hills as well as the unceded lands. As one chief, Standing Elk of the progressive Corn Brulé, complained to the commissioners: "My friend, your words are like a man knocking me in the head with a club. By your speech you have put great fear upon us. Whatever you white people ask of us, wherever we go, we always say Yes, yes, yes! Whenever we don't agree to what is asked of us in council, you always reply, You won't get anything to eat! You won't get anything to eat!"[11] The threats were effective. Red Cloud signed an agreement turning over the Black Hills to the white men, and Spotted Tail and the other chiefs, recognizing that they could no longer hope to resist, also signed.

The opening of the Black Hills triggered a gold rush. Three months after President Grant in November 1875 ended military enforcement of the ban on travel into the hills, the town of Custer mushroomed to six thousand residents where only eighteen months earlier no one had lived permanently. Some ten thousand people poured into the hills between November 1875 and March 1876.[12] "The country looks as though it had been settled ten years instead of three," wrote Zimri White, a *New York Tribune* correspondent who traveled in the Black Hills in 1879. "Good roads have been built in every direction over and around the Hills, and travel is as safe upon them as upon a New England or New York turnpike. Two years ago (in 1877) camping equipage was a necessity for the traveller, now there are comfortable wayside inns every twenty-five miles, and frequently at shorter intervals. The game that abounded in the hills has disappeared, and civilization has already gained the mastery."[13]

Miners scratched $3 million worth of gold a year out of the Black Hills in 1878 and 1879. In 1880 they dug out $5 million worth before the figure returned to about $3 million a year for several decades.[14]

The Lakota who did not sign the treaty giving up Paha Sapa continued to skirmish with the newcomers. The commissioners of the newly organized Lawrence County responded by offering a $250 bounty on any Indian brought in dead or alive.[15]

But the biggest land grab was still on the way.[16] In 1882 Dakota Territory's delegate to Congress, Richard Pettigrew, successfully sponsored a bill that called for sending a commission out to the Great Sioux Reservation to see if the Lakota would give up about half their remaining land, breaking their unified chunk of territory into disjointed reservations. The head of the commission, former Dakota Territory governor Newton Edmunds, subsequently claimed that he had worked out a deal with the Lakota, but in the end his bargain ran afoul of the 1868 treaty, which required that three-fourths of *all* adult

Lakota men sign an agreement in favor of selling before Lakota land could change hands. Edmunds had collected the signatures of only 384 chiefs. The deal fell through.

Four years later, Massachusetts senator Henry Dawes, who favored plans designed to turn Indians into land-owning farmers, shepherded through the Senate a bill called the General Allotment Act, or simply the Dawes Act. This law allowed the heads of Indian families all across the country to apply for allotments of 160 acres of reservation farmland, just like a homesteader. Single adult men could apply for 80 acres and minors for 40. Those who wanted grazing land would receive acreages twice the size of farmland. After four years the government would select land for any Indian who failed to apply for a plot, just to be sure that all the land was assigned. After twenty-five years the land would belong to the applicant, who then would be given U.S. citizenship. The "surplus" land left over after all the allotments had been made would be sold to settlers under the various homestead arrangements that had turned eastern Dakota Territory into a patchwork of farms.[17]

Even people working to protect Indian rights liked this plan. Herbert Welsh, head of the Philadelphia-based Indian Rights Association, a group that monitored the reservations and lobbied for Indian interests in Washington, D.C., said that in terms of moving the Indians down the path of civilization, the Dawes Act was the Magna Carta, Declaration of Independence, and Emancipation Proclamation all rolled into one.[18] The law would replace tribal ownership with individual ownership, get the Indians to farm, and solve the problem of what to do with them.

Dakota boosters jumped on this bandwagon with both feet, pushing through Congress the 1888 Sioux Act, which applied specifically to the Great Sioux Reservation. The bill also speeded the settlement of Lakota lands by calling for negotiations for the land even before it had been surveyed or Indian allotments made. According to government calculations, Lakota population figures indicated that land allotments to the Indians would leave more than half the reservation—some 9 to 11 million acres—up for grabs as "surplus." The government would buy the surplus for fifty cents an acre and open it immediately to settlement. The Lakota would receive clear title to the remaining land and would keep the proceeds of the sale, minus government expenses, for use in an interest-bearing account for educational programs. The land sale also would extend for another twenty years the educational benefits promised in the

1868 treaty and would provide the Lakota with livestock and farming equipment.[19]

The Lakota objected, contending they did not have more land than they required. In the future, they said, their children would need the land. And why, they asked, should the government buy the land for half a dollar an acre and sell it for a buck and a quarter? At Standing Rock, the proposal garnered only twenty-two signatures of approval from more than one thousand Lakota men, and it fared no better at the other agencies.[20]

The secretary of the Interior in October received a delegation of more than sixty Lakota chiefs and men of influence who demanded more money for their land. In a sense, the Lakota had blinked. By suggesting that they had their price, they made the selling of the reservation negotiable.[21]

And negotiate the government did. Congress enacted the Sioux Act of 1889, offering $1.25 an acre for any land sold to settlers during the first three years of the proposed agreement. Presuming that the best land would sell first, the bill called for a sliding scale in which land sold in the fourth and fifth years would go for seventy-five cents an acre, and the rest would go for fifty cents. In a further concession, the bill promised that the government would pay sale expenses, giving the Lakota all proceeds from the land. Heads of families would receive 320 acres—twice the originally proposed amount—and increased financing for improving the land. To safeguard Lakota property rights, the government would survey the borders of the six new reservations before opening the land to settlers and would find new sites for Lakota who lived on the land that was sold.

And so in 1889 another commission visited the Great Sioux Reservation, headed by General George Crook. A seasoned fighter known to Indians throughout the West, Crook, on the one hand, cajoled key Lakota leaders, unsuccessfully offering two hundred dollars each to Red Cloud, Young Man Afraid of His Horses, and Little Wound if they would sign. He threw big parties with food in bulk and lifted the 1883 ban on traditional Indian dances. On the other hand, he explained the matter bluntly. "Last year," he told the Lakota, "when you refused to accept the bill, Congress came very near opening this reservation anyhow. It is certain that you will never get any better terms than are offered in this bill, and the chances are that you will not get so good."[22] Those who failed to sign would miss out on the benefits that accrued to those who did sign. It was now or never, take it or leave it.

Nevertheless, at the Standing Rock agency, Sitting Bull opposed the allotment both to whites and to fellow Lakota. The Long Knives, he said, "will try to gain possession of the last piece of ground we possess. Let us stand as one family as we did before the white people led us astray."[23] Traditional Indians agreed with him, but other Lakota were prepared to sell out. Finally, Sitting Bull and twenty of his fellows mounted ponies and charged the commission, scattering the Lakota who had come to talk with Crook and his colleagues. The Standing Rock agent, James McLaughlin, however, had anticipated trouble and had on hand a unit of Indian police commanded by Lieutenant Bull Head, who once had fought beside Sitting Bull against the whites but who now was one of the most progressive of the progressives. When the riders were driven off, the commissioners resumed their work.

While Crook and his committee toured the reservations, the agents strong-armed the Indians. McLaughlin, for example, warned his favorite progressive chief, John Grass, and other progressive leaders at Standing Rock that if the Lakota did not take the money offered, they would lose the land anyway and receive nothing for it. Given their history of dealings with the U.S. government, the Lakota were easily persuaded by this argument.[24]

John Grass was among the first Lakota to sign the agreement, creating an avalanche of Lakota men eager to add their signatures. In the end, the land allotment was accepted by 4,463 Lakota, three-quarters of the 5,678 eligible voters.

Sitting Bull and other hard-liners believed the U.S. government would not keep its promises, and subsequent events appeared to prove these skeptics right. Shortly after the land sale, the beef ration was halved. However, this reduction was not an act of duplicity. During the previous two years, the government had conducted a census of the Lakota reservation and concluded that Indian numbers were fewer than previously believed. Although this conclusion was wrong—uncooperative Lakota skewed the results by avoiding the census takers—the data gave Congress an excuse to slash annual funding for Lakota rations by roughly $1 million, a cut that did not go into effect until after approval of the land agreement. The result was that on Pine Ridge alone, the beef ration was reduced by a million pounds a year. Frederic Remington weighed in on the subject: "We are year after year oppressing a conquered people, until it is now assuming the magnitude of a crime. . . . The short ration which is issued to them keeps them in dire hunger, and if starving savages kill ranchmen's cattle I do not blame them. I would do the same under similar circumstances."[25]

Then the other shoe dropped. President William Henry Harrison on February 10, 1890, announced that the "surplus" land would be opened immediately to settlers instead of being properly surveyed to protect the rights of Indians already living on it. The Lakota were furious, but there was nothing they could do.

In the wake of the land sale and the breakup of the reservation, Indians already suffering from cultural fragmentation suffered further from geographic fragmentation. Lakota from the Pine Ridge reservation, for example, could no longer ride exclusively on reservation land to reach kin and friends at Standing Rock. Now Pine Ridge and Standing Rock were separate reservations, and to get from one to the other, the Lakota had to cross lands claimed by settlers. And in order to travel off the reservation, they had to apply to the agents for permits.

The Lakota were utterly disheartened, their land gone, their bellies empty. Their troubles had been compounded when, late in 1889, South Dakota entered the Union as a state, giving land grabbers there an even stronger voice in Congress. One of the newly elected senators was Richard Pettigrew, who had been pushing to take Lakota land for a decade. Defeat was total, and hopelessness infused the reservation. As one bitter Indian said of the whites, "They made us many promises, more than I can remember, but they never kept but one; they promised to take our land, and they took it."[26]

For the Lakota, news out of Washington and on the prairie itself grew worse. Congress cut the $1 million usually earmarked for Lakota subsistence by $50,000. In addition, the Lakota who had attended the land-allotment discussions had been kept away from their farms so long that when they returned, they found their livestock in many cases had been stolen or killed. Problems mounted. Dakota Territory in the late 1880s was plagued with drought, so the Lakota's meager attempts to grow crops failed. Whooping cough and measles hit the reservation, especially children.[27] At Pine Ridge, disease killed as many as forty-five Lakota per month the year of the allotment sale, although Bishop Hare contended that they died "not so much from disease as from want of food."[28]

Even General Nelson Miles weighed in on the side of the Indians, declaring that their lack of sufficient food was especially onerous following a series of crop failures.[29] He added that the Lakota were forced to live on as little as half rations and that, to make matters worse, they were not paid for the surrendered

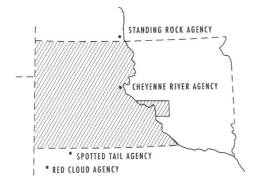

TREATY OF 1868

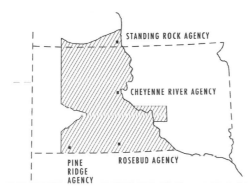

AGREEMENT OF 1876

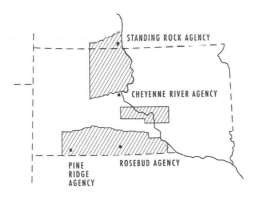

ACT OF 1889

Reduction of the Great Sioux Reservation, 1868–90. (Yale University Press)

lands. For the Lakota, the future looked as bleak as the present. Small wonder that one Indian complained that "their children [were] all dying from the face of the earth, so they might as well be killed at once."[30]

And then from the desert West came whispers of new hope for all Indians, a spiritual rebirth that would resurrect the old ways, and the Lakota were eager to listen.

FOR THE LAKOTA, THE SPIRITUAL world and the material world were virtually one and the same, and they believed that certain holy men—*wicasa wakan*—possessed supernatural powers. Sitting Bull, for example, believed that he could speak with birds and foresee the future. His people believed he could, too. This belief that individuals could have direct contact with the spiritual world would, in 1890, shake the Indian tribes of the West.

The tremors began on New Year's Day 1889, when a Paiute Indian, known as Jack Wilson to his white friends and as Wovoka among the Indians, fell ill with fever as he worked cutting wood in the desert near Pyramid Lake, Nevada.[31] He went to his wickiup, a domelike dwelling made of shrub branches, and lay delirious. In his fever he had a vision in which he went to heaven and talked with God and Jesus, who told him they were angry with the white men for killing Jesus the last time he visited the Earth. God told Wovoka that he was going to sweep the white man from the continent in spring 1891 and bring back to life all the dead Indians and all the vanished wildlife, and the old ways would return, and the Indians would be happy again. God told Wovoka to preach this new religion to the Indians, to tell them to be peaceful with the whites but to give up all white ways and materials. He showed Wovoka a special dance, the ghost dance, and told the Paiute that if the Indians did this dance, and kept peace with the Americans, and gave up the use of things from the whites, they soon would live again as they had before the arrival of the pale intruders.

Wovoka, who became known as the Messiah, preached ardently, and word of his new religion spread across the West. He was considered a spiritually credible source, a holy man well known to his people for his magical powers. It was said that he could make ice fall from the July sky over his desert homeland, that he lit his pipe merely by pointing it toward the sun, that he could make water appear in an empty container during a drought.[32] And so his word started a spiritual movement, the messiah or ghost dance religion (*wana'ghi wa'chipi* in Lakota).[33]

Religions such as the ghost dance often arise in cultures oppressed by outside forces and tottering toward collapse. A similar nativist religion had swept earlier through Indian tribes in the eastern United States, beginning with a dream that came in November 1805 to a Shawnee soon to be known as the Prophet.[34] In his dream he saw that most Indians after death were going to a place much like hell. He awoke determined to lead his people to the right path. He called on his followers to give up whiskey and other things from the whites, including livestock of any kind except horses. He urged them to go back to traditional Indian clothing, ornamentation, and grooming, such as shaven heads and painted faces for the men. He told them to "never think of war again" and to treat everyone with kindness.

The Prophet suggested that game animals, declining throughout the East, would recover if the people heeded his warning against the commercial hunting that the whites had initiated. In a record left by one of his disciples, the Prophet spoke from the persona of the Great Mystery: "My children, you complain that the animals of the forest are few and scattered. How shall it be otherwise? You destroy them yourselves for their skins only, and leave their bodies to rot or give the best pieces to the whites. I am displeased when I see this, and take them back to the earth that they may not come to you again. You must kill no more animals than are necessary to feed and clothe you."[35]

Speaking through the Prophet, the Great Mystery also touched on the subject of eastern woodlands: "I made all the trees of the forest for your use, but the maple I love the best because it yields sugar for your little ones. You must make it only for them, but sell none to the whites. They have another sugar which was made expressly for them. Besides, by making too much, you spoil the trees and give them pain by cutting and hacking them, for they have feeling like yourselves. If you take more than is necessary for your own use, you shall die, and the maple will yield no more water."[36]

Like the ghost dance, the Prophet's nativist religion was not the first to breathe hope into beleaguered Indian peoples. In the 1760s a Delaware Indian named Neolin had preached a similar creed and had predicted that the whites would be wiped out by spiritual powers.[37] Neolin had lived among the Shawnee in 1764, so the Prophet likely heard of this religion from his own people. A

Munsee Indian also had preached much the same thing up and down the Allegheny and Susquehanna valleys from 1752 to 1775. From 1740 to 1775 eight nativist prophets, including two women, had carried such beliefs around the East.

The Lakota heard about the ghost dance from nearby tribes farther to the west and in autumn 1889 secretly sent a delegation of eleven men to Nevada to learn about it.[38] The following March they brought back details of the new religion, just as representatives of other tribes spread the word in other parts of the West.

Not all tribes accepted Wovoka's preaching. The Navajo and Hopi, peoples of the Southwest, largely ignored it. The Kiowa, on the southern plains, and some other tribes adopted and then abandoned the religion after they saw the trouble that followed the dance to the Lakota reservations.[39] But the Lakota of the Pine Ridge, Rosebud, and Cheyenne River reservations proved a willing audience for ghost dance apostles. Many Lakota may have agreed with Little Wound's view of the ghost dance when he said: "My friends, if this is a good thing we should have it; if it is not it will fall to the earth itself. So you better learn this dance, so if the Messiah does come he will not pass us by, but will help us to get back our hunting grounds and buffalo."[40]

Chief among the Lakota apostles were Kicking Bear and Short Bull, who had visited Wovoka as part of the Lakota delegation. Kicking Bear had been born around 1849 and, as a young man, had earned a reputation as a fine warrior, taking many Crow ponies and fighting bravely in such key battles as the Little Bighorn.[41] A close friend of Crazy Horse, he also was married to a niece of Big Foot, renowned among the Lakota as a peacemaker. The Lakota knew Kicking Bear as something of a mystic with a hatred of whites and of the new life forced upon his people.

Short Bull, three or four years older than Kicking Bear, was a Brulé medicine man admired as a warrior and as a steadfast nonprogressive and esteemed for his kindness and generosity. Given the traditional warrior values of the two apostles, it is no surprise that in Short Bull's and Kicking Bear's hands, the ghost dance religion took on bellicose overtones. They reported that the Great Mystery had told them in dreams that if the whites fought the Lakota, the whites' gunpowder would not work, while the Lakota's would. Kicking Bear was credited with development of a belief in ghost shirts that would make wearers bulletproof. When Wovoka heard about the ghost shirts, he responded that they had no place in his religion.[42] But he had no control over what the

Lakota ghost dance prior to the Wounded Knee battle in December 1890. The dance was supposed to induce trances that took the dancer into the land of the dead for meetings with lost loved ones. *(George Trager, Minnesota Historical Society)*

Lakota chose to believe, and, as a people who had spent the past century or so running other Indians out of the northern plains, fighting whites, and even wiping out Custer, they were inclined to believe in ghost shirts.

Among the first Lakota bands to adopt the religion was that of Kicking Bear's in-law, Big Foot. Soon hundreds, perhaps thousands, were dancing. Believing that within a few months the whites would be gone—washed away by a flood or buried under fresh earth—the dancers took their children out of reservation schools. They abandoned crops and livestock. They danced, chanting special ghost songs, until they fainted from exhaustion and hunger. The songs they sang spoke of a return of the dead or of the buffalo. One of them went like this:

> *The father says so, the father says so.*
> *Over the whole Earth they are coming.*
> *The buffalo are coming, the buffalo are coming,*
> *The father says so, the father says so.*

Many who fainted reported that they had visited the afterworld and met dead wives, husbands, children, parents—the lost relatives of the lost world in which they had grown up. The Lakota found hope in this dance that mingled Indian aspirations with Christian religious symbols.

Meanwhile, the reservation agents and the residents of nearby towns and farms were increasingly alarmed by the dancing. Failing to understand that the religion preached peace, at least initially, the settlers saw a war dance in every step and chant. It probably did not help that Kicking Bear and Short Bull's preaching was becoming increasingly aggressive and hostile, not quite Wovoka's message of peace. At one point, Short Bull even said he was going to advance the date for the destruction of the whites to get the job done sooner.

Newspaper editors and local politicians exploited the dance as an excuse to call in the military, kill off the Indians once and for all, and take the rest of their land. A prime example was written by the owner and editor of the Aberdeen, South Dakota, *Saturday Pioneer*, Lyman Baum, who in ten years would become famous as L. Frank Baum, author of *The Wizard of Oz*. His paper was one of seven weeklies published in Aberdeen, along with two dailies—not an unusual number of papers for one town in a time when the periodicals were needed for land-claim legal notices. Baum, who ardently supported women's suffrage and other liberal causes, wrote about Indians with the belligerent bombast typical of the frontier journalist. On January 3, 1891, he opined: "The PIONEER has before declared that our only safety depends upon the total extermination of the Indian. Having wronged them for centuries we had better, in order to protect our civilization, follow it up with one more wrong and wipe these untamed and untamable creatures from the face of the earth."[43]

The Lakota did not need the wicked witch's crystal ball to know what was in the newspapers—Indian-school students kept even the illiterate abreast of the news. And so tension mounted on both sides.

One of Kicking Bear's key acts was to go in October 1890 to Standing Rock Reservation and win over Sitting Bull and his followers. Kicking Bear told Sitting Bull's people: "My brothers, I bring you the promise of a day in which there will be no white man to lay his hand on the bridle of the Indian's horse, when the red men of the prairie will rule the world and not be turned from the hunting-grounds by any man. I bring you word from your fathers, the ghosts, that they are now marching to join you, led by the Messiah who came once to live on Earth with the white men, but was cast out and killed by

Kicking Bear, who brought the ghost dance to Sitting
Bull and Big Foot. He was credited with originating
the idea of bulletproof ghost shirts. *(George E.
Spencer, Minnesota Historical Society)*

them. I have seen the wonders of the spirit-land and have talked with the
ghosts. I traveled far and am sent back with a message to tell you to make
ready for the coming of the Messiah and return of the ghosts in the spring."[44]

The great promise of the ghost dance, Kicking Bear said, came straight
from the Great Spirit, who had informed him:

> I have neglected the Indians for many moons, but I will make them my people
> now if they obey me in this message. The Earth is getting old, and I will make
> it new for my chosen people, the Indians, who are to inhabit it, and among
> them will be all those of their ancestors who have died, their fathers, mothers,
> brothers, cousins and wives—all those who hear my voice and my words
> through the tongues of my children. I will cover the Earth with new soil to a
> depth of five times the height of a man, and under this new soil will be buried
> the whites, and all the holes and the rotten places will be filled up. The new

Short Bull, a Brulé medicine man also admired as a warrior. He helped bring the ghost dance religion to the Lakota reservation. *(Denver Public Library, Western History Collection, B567)*

lands will be covered with sweet-grass and running water and trees, and herds of buffalo and ponies will stray over it, that my red children may eat and drink, hunt and rejoice. And the sea to the west I will fill up so that no ships may pass over it, and the other seas I will make impassable. . . . Go then, my children, and tell these things to all the people and make all ready for the coming of the ghosts.[45]

Sitting Bull remained skeptical about the ghost dance, but his people adopted it, so as a leader he felt obliged to sponsor dances. At this time he was involved in a friendship—some said a relationship—with a white woman from Brooklyn, New York. Her name was Catherine Weldon, and she represented the National Indian Defense Association in opposing efforts to force the Lakota to become farmers and laborers. She had first visited Standing Rock in 1888, returned in 1889 to fight the Crook Commission, and returned again in

1890 intending to live on or near the reservation. She befriended Sitting Bull and moved in with him, teaching his wives household skills and helping Sitting Bull pay for status-giving feasts for his people.[46]

Newspapers reported, and perhaps Standing Rock agent James McLaughlin believed, that Sitting Bull could not have supported the ghost dance without her money. In fact, she opposed Bull's participation in the dances, fearing it would get him killed.[47] She knew that McLaughlin—who blamed Sitting Bull for any management problems that arose among the Lakota—was looking for an excuse to arrest the aging holy man and that the dance was just what he needed. Such dances technically were illegal because the federal government had outlawed Lakota religious rituals in 1883. Sitting Bull contended that practicing the ghost dance was a matter of freedom of religion, which he knew whites considered a right. He also thought that if the religion were true, the people should dance. If it were false, the dancing would do no harm.

However, McLaughlin did consider the dances dangerous, particularly to the peace and tranquillity of Standing Rock. He sent a contingent of thirteen Indian police to throw Kicking Bear off the reservation, but the police came back to report that they had not ejected the apostle, because they feared his powers.[48] McLaughlin sent in another contingent, who proved less intimidated and escorted Kicking Bear off Standing Rock.

Weldon wrote to McLaughlin asking him to overlook the participation of Sitting Bull and his Hunkpapa people in the ghost dance and blaming the whole thing on Kicking Bear, whom she called by his Lakota name: "Please have pity on the Uncpapas & Sitting Bull, who has been under the evil influence of Mato Wanah Taka. Have pity on him & do not send the police or soldiers & I will induce him to come to you of his own accord. S. Bull will surely accompany me to the agency: but please do not detain him his brain has suffered; [sic] but his heart is good. He will be all right now that Mata [sic] Wanah Taka has gone. My heart is breaking when I see the work of years undone by that vile imposter. I will stay here of my own accord for several days & see what my influence can do."[49]

Failing to steer Sitting Bull and his band away from the ghost dance, and fearing she would see him killed if she remained on the reservation, Weldon packed up and returned to New York in November 1890.[50] She wrote on November 20 to Sitting Bull, telling him: "You are deceived by your prophets, and I fear some bad white men who are leading you into endless trouble. [By "bad white men" she meant Mormons, who she was convinced were behind the ghost dance.] I said enough when I was among you, you ought to remember my words. If I spoke harsh to you sometimes, forgive me; a true friends [*sic*] warning is not always pleasant to hear. I meant it for the best."[51]

Lakota allies also tried to dissuade Sitting Bull from holding the dances. Gray Eagle, who had been with Sitting Bull in Canada and was a brother of two of Bull's wives, told him: "Brother-in-law, we have settled on the reservation now and we are under the jurisdiction of the government, and we must do as they say. We must cut out the roaming around and live as they say, and must cut out this dancing."

But Sitting Bull would have none of this advice. "Yes, you are right," he replied. "But I could not give up my race as it is seated in us. You go ahead and follow what the white man says, but for my part leave me alone."[52] After Weldon's departure, Sitting Bull continued to hold dances at his compound in the broad valley of the Grand River, flanked by gentle prairie hills.

Meanwhile, from beyond the reservation, settlers listened to rumors about the ghost dance and managed to frighten themselves, corroborating one another's manufactured fears and becoming pawns in the game of national expansion. James Mooney, an anthropologist who investigated the ghost dance movement and its effects for the Bureau of American Ethnology and the Smithsonian Institution in the early 1890s, reported: "In view of the fact that only one noncombatant was killed and no depredations committed off the reservation" during the entire ghost dance scare, "the panic among the frontier settlers of both Dakotas, Nebraska, and Iowa was something ludicrous. The inhabitants worked themselves into such a high panic that ranches and even whole villages were temporarily abandoned and the people flocked into the railroad cities with vivid stories of murder, scalping, and desolation that had no foundation whatever in fact."[53]

The fright was compounded when a new agent, Daniel Royer, arrived at the largest of the Lakota reservations, Pine Ridge. A pharmacist and leading Republican citizen in Alpena, South Dakota, Royer knew nothing about administering a reservation or managing Indians. He was picked for the job by the newly minted senator Richard Pettigrew as payback for helping elect Pettigrew when Dakota Territory became two states in 1889. Royer lacked the personality for the job, but he had one quality that Pettigrew appreciated: He followed orders. While the Senate considered Royer's appointment, he received a letter from Pettigrew outlining in part the senator's plans for the reservation: "If you secure the appointment I shall want to clean out the whole force of farmers, teachers, and clerks as far as possible and put in Dakota men. You can not make an appointment until you consult Moody [Gideon C. Moody, the other South Dakota senator] and I about it."

Royer may have been up to the task of bringing in Pettigrew allies, but he was not up to the challenge of the ghost dance. He feared the Lakota, and they soon knew it, mockingly calling him Young Man Afraid of His Indians. Frightened by the dancing, he repeatedly demanded that the Indian Bureau request troops for the reservation.

Charles Eastman, a Santee Sioux who was the Pine Ridge medical doctor; Elaine Goodale, the superintendent of reservation schools and soon to be Eastman's wife; and American Horse and other progressive Indians tried to keep Royer steadfast by telling him that if he ignored the dance, the messiah movement would die out in spring, when the whites did not disappear. But Royer cracked on November 11, 1890, when an Oglala ghost dancer named Little fought back with a knife against a squad of Indian police who attempted to arrest him for cattle theft. The fight took place in front of Royer's office. While Royer watched from his door, a mob of two hundred Lakota armed with guns and knives surrounded and captured the police. One Lakota held a stone war club over a policeman's head.

"At this critical moment, a fine looking Indian in citizen's clothing faced the excited throng, and spoke in a clear, steady, almost sarcastic voice," wrote Charles Eastman, who witnessed this event as he would witness so many crises during the winter of 1890–91.[54] This man, American Horse, apparently had stepped from Royer's office at the start of the confrontation. "Stop! Think!" he said. "What are you going to do? Kill these men of our own race? Then what? Kill all these helpless white men, women and children? And what then? What will these brave words, brave deeds lead to in the end? How long can you hold out? Your country is surrounded with a network of railroads. Thousands of white soldiers will be here within three days. What ammunition have you? What provisions? What will become of your families? Think, think, my brothers. This is a child's madness."

Jack Red Cloud, son of the chief and a traditionalist who was hostile toward progressive Indians, put the muzzle of a cocked revolver up to American

Horse's face. "It is you and your kind who have brought us to this pass," Red Cloud said.

American Horse did not flinch, Eastman reported in his autobiography: "Ignoring his rash accuser, he quietly reentered the office; the door closed behind him; the mob dispersed, and for the moment the danger seemed over."

Eastman believed it likely that American Horse had saved everyone at the scene from death, "for the murder of the police . . . would surely have been followed by a general massacre." But in the end Little escaped, a free man. Royer panicked and began peppering the Indian Bureau with demands for troops, of which he said "nothing short of 1,000" could rescue him from "the mercy of the Ghost Dancers."[55] In mid-November Royer fled with his family in a carriage across the twenty-eight miles to Rushville, Nebraska, refusing to return to the reservation unless a military escort went with him.

In January 1891 at Pine Ridge, American Horse (left), a leading progressive, shakes hands with Red Cloud, a famous war chief who turned to conciliating the Americans. (Library of Congress)

And that was exactly how he did return, at dawn on November 20, with 170 cavalry troops, 200 infantry, and a Hotchkiss cannon and Gatling gun.[56] The horsemen were from the Ninth Cavalry, an African-American unit that the Lakota dubbed buffalo soldiers because of their hair. At the same hour, 110 buffalo soldiers and 120 infantry arrived at Rosebud, the Brulé reservation, the first time the Lakota had seen army troops lined up against them since the wars of the 1870s. And so the ghost dancers, who had expected buffalo to come, instead got buffalo soldiers, whose arrival frightened not only the dancers but also Lakota who were ignoring the new religion. Chaos ensued. At Kicking Bear and Short Bull's direction, many dancers retreated to the Stronghold, a triangular plateau a few hundred feet high, about three miles long, and two miles wide in the Badlands, north of Pine Ridge. There they could hold out for months, living on wild game and on livestock that they had driven up there. Access to the Stronghold was by a single trail only the width of a wagon, so the area was easily guarded. Here, followers of Kicking Bear decided to fight it out, if necessary, in a last stand to match Custer's.

CHAPTER 5

Death Comes for Sitting Bull

WHEN THE TROOPS RODE INTO Rosebud on November 20, 1890, about one thousand Brulé rode out, driven by fear. Within ten days, they had joined with other fleeing Lakota, forming a group that included some six hundred warriors, all headed for the Stronghold.[1] Along the way, they raided Indian homes and took cattle from Indian farms.

Once ensconced in the highland, the Lakota settled in to dance all winter and to fight to the bloody end if the army showed up.[2] Brigadier General John Brooke, commander of the Department of the Platte and the officer in charge of the troops at Pine Ridge and Rosebud, was under orders from General Nelson Miles to get the Indians at the Stronghold to surrender. Brooke knew that if the military approached the plateau, a bloody battle would ensue, so he sent in a one-man peace commission: Father John Jutz, a seventy-year-old Catholic missionary who had come to Pine Ridge two years earlier and had earned the Lakota's respect.

At the Stronghold, Jutz parlayed with several chiefs, including ghost dance apostles Short Bull and Kicking Bear. Among the chiefs was Two Strike—Nomkahpa in Lakota, a name that commemorated a battle in which he had, with a single swing of his war club, knocked down two enemies riding the same horse. For two decades he had been a hard-core opponent of U.S. encroachment on Lakota territory, leading raids against the Union Pacific railroad and fighting the army. He headed the Brulé band to which Plenty Horses' family belonged, so the young man probably was at the Stronghold.

By 1890 Two Strike was in his early seventies. Military and agency officials claimed he had become a bit erratic in his behavior, perhaps senile. When the military had first arrived at Pine Ridge, he had boasted that he personally would stab General Brooke. Among the Lakota he had attracted a considerable following and spoke with authority. During an entire night of discussion with Jutz, Two Strike was one of several chiefs who agreed to ride into Pine Ridge to talk with Brooke.

They set out the next morning. Fearing that Brooke was using the meeting as a ruse to capture them, the chiefs rode with an escort of twenty-four warriors. They spoke with Brooke, ate with him, talked over the situation, and returned to the Stronghold without making any promises.

Miles castigated Brooke for failing to work out an immediate surrender. Under pressure, Brooke dispatched to the Stronghold thirty-two friendly Lakota with a half-breed scout, Louis Shangreau, whom the Lakota knew well. Initially, the Stronghold leaders opposed any compromise. Short Bull, the first day, gave Shangreau a message for Brooke: "If the Great Father would permit us to continue the dance, would give us more rations, and quit taking away portions of the reservation, I would be in favor of returning. But even if you say that he will, how can we discern whether you are telling the truth? We have been lied to so many times that we will not believe any words that your agent sends us. If we return he will take away our guns and ponies, put some

The Brulé chief Two Strike (left) and Brulé leader Crow Dog surrender to the U.S. military in January 1891. *(Library of Congress)*

of us in jail for stealing cattle and plundering houses. We prefer to stay here and die, if necessary, to loss of liberty. We are free now and have plenty of beef, can dance all the time in obedience to the command of Great Wakan Tanka. We tell you to return to your agent and say to him that the Dakotas in the Badlands are not going to come in."[3]

Shangreau stayed two more days while the ghost dance went on without end. On the third day, when the chiefs sat down at about noon to talk over the situation again, Two Strike abruptly took the floor and shocked everyone by announcing his intention to take his people to the agency and surrender. Crow Dog, a Brulé chief in his late fifties who had once served as head of the agency police at the Rosebud Reservation, stood and agreed to do the same.[4]

Short Bull jumped up and urged everyone to stick together and remain true to their cause. He condemned Shangreau as a traitor and a liar and called upon the warriors to kill him.

As Short Bull's followers brandished their rifles like clubs, warriors who had arrived with Shangreau formed a shield around him, and Two Strike's men jumped in to help. The fight drew in more and more warriors.

Crow Dog responded with a masterly diplomatic move. While the Lakota clashed around him, he pulled his blanket up over his head and sat motionless and silent. His silence spoke loudly, however, and the combatants stopped fighting and turned their attention to him. After bemoaning that the Lakota were spilling one another's blood, Crow Dog declared that he would go to Pine Ridge and give up. "You can kill me if you want to, now, and prevent my starting," he said. "The agent's words are true, and it is better to return than to stay here. I am not afraid to die."

When he left, about half the camp went with him, and the rest soon caught up and joined them. As they rode toward the Pine Ridge agency, however, Short Bull and Kicking Bear unnerved themselves by reflecting on the likelihood that they would be sentenced to military prison.[5] With a few hard-core ghost dancers, they turned back to the Stronghold. Among those who continued on to Pine Ridge were Two Strike's people, Plenty Horses probably among them.

Two Strike's band straggled into the agency on December 15 and 16, some nine hundred Brulé in all.[6] Short Bull and Kicking Bear were still at large, but, with few followers, they were not likely to cause serious problems for the

A sentry guards horses watering in the White River outside a Lakota camp the U.S. military labeled "hostile." *(Library of Congress)*

army. And so there the whole "ghost dance trouble," as contemporaries called it, should have come to a close, and would have, had it not been for James McLaughlin's intractable hatred of Sitting Bull.

McLAUGHLIN WAS A FORMER BLACKSMITH who went from his native Canada to Minnesota at the age of twenty-one. He moved in 1871 to the Devil's Lake Dakota Reservation in southern Dakota Territory, where for five years he worked as an assistant to the agent. He took over as the agent of Standing Rock in 1881, the year Sitting Bull surrendered. Married to an Indian, McLaughlin ruled the reservation firmly. He held a high regard for his profession, and in an 1878 report to the Bureau of Indian Affairs he wrote: "To successfully manage Indians and conduct a large Indian agency requires a man of extraordinary ability. He must be a business man, a farmer and a mechanic, together with a good judge of human nature, have great patience and be endowed with practical common sense. Such a man, with his heart in his work, if left alone to manage the Indians, will succeed. . . ."[7]

McLaughlin may have had himself in mind when he wrote that description.

If so, independent sources corroborated his sense of self-esteem. In 1886 a representative of the Indians Rights Association wrote of McLaughlin's work at Standing Rock: "The liberal and intelligent support given to schools here, and the system of practical instruction in farming with teachers stationed in different settlements to direct and assist beginners, have produced effects which are already conspicuously interesting and valuable. I observed that some desirable things which are accounted impossible in other places are a part of the regular administration on this reserve and appear to be done without especial difficulty or friction."[8]

This particular Indian rights advocate seems to have missed the friction between McLaughlin and Sitting Bull. In fact, McLaughlin seems to have had an unreasonable disdain for Sitting Bull, who was in most visible ways making an effort to adapt to the new regime. In his fifties in 1890, the chief created one of the more successful reservation farms, including cattle and chickens, and urged his own and others' children to go to school to learn white ways. Perhaps McLaughlin simply

Sitting Bull (left) and reservation agent James McLaughlin at the 1886 dedication ceremony for the holy standing rock from which Standing Rock Lakota Reservation takes its name. Resembling an Indian woman and child, the rock can still be seen at the reservation. *(Denver Public Library, Western History Collection, B342)*

did not like dealing with a man whose resolve was as strong as his own despite years of defeat. Or he may have been siding with one of his favorite chiefs, John Grass, who allegedly was in a power struggle with Sitting Bull.[9]

Officials in Washington, like Pontius Pilate, failed to see what sins the accused had committed and rebuffed McLaughlin's request to arrest and remove Sitting Bull. McLaughlin persisted, and as tension over the ghost dance increased and fear of a Lakota outbreak escalated, Washington finally relented.[10]

Arresting Sitting Bull was a sensitive issue because of his high status among the Lakota as a warrior, chief, and holy man. He also was famous across the United States and its territories, perhaps the best known of all American Indians. Widely but erroneously credited with leading the Lakota in the battle that wiped out George Custer, he had traveled with Buffalo Bill Cody's Wild West show, where his autographed photos were much in demand. His arrest was likely to stimulate a certain amount of unhappiness and protest among the more conservative Lakota.

Consequently, although getting permission to arrest Sitting Bull had been a challenge, actually arresting him was even more difficult. General Nelson Miles, in charge of the army's Division of the Missouri, which ranged from Illinois to Colorado, from Canada to Texas and Arizona, wanted the military to arrest Sitting Bull. McLaughlin wanted his Indian police to do the job, fearing that military intrusion would lead to violence. He worked out an agreement with Lieutenant Colonel William Drum, the commander of nearby Fort Yates, to allow the police to make the arrest, with U.S. troops standing by to provide support if needed. McLaughlin hoped in this way to avoid the widespread panic that would result among the Lakota if the army showed up in force. Drum agreed, and so did Drum's immediate superior, Brigadier General Thomas Ruger, stationed in St. Paul, Minnesota.

Miles, stationed at his headquarters in Chicago, nearly demolished McLaughlin's plan by sending Buffalo Bill Cody, the former scout and famous showman, to Standing Rock to bring in Sitting Bull dead or alive. Cody, who had gotten to know Sitting Bull during the chief's year with the Wild West show, considered himself a friend of the holy man, leading Miles to believe that, despite the orders, Cody could complete the assignment without bloodshed.

Drum and McLaughlin immediately conspired to stop Buffalo Bill. As soon as he arrived at Standing Rock—according to some accounts, still decked out in the evening clothes he had been wearing when he dined with Miles back in

Chicago—McLaughlin and Drum took him to the post saloon and plied him with drinks. Cody had a reputation as an avid boozer, a reputation he apparently had earned honestly. Drum's officers drank in relays to keep Cody from single-handedly putting them under the table. Despite the impressive imbibing, the next morning Buffalo Bill was ready to hit the trail to Sitting Bull's compound far up the Grand River.

McLaughlin and Drum tricked Buffalo Bill into taking the wrong road, then tricked him into going back to the agency. By the time Bill realized what was going on, McLaughlin had a telegram from Washington rescinding Miles's orders to allow Buffalo Bill to make the arrest. The ball was back in McLaughlin's court.

On the night of December 14, 1890, McLaughlin made his play, sending Indian police under Lieutenant Bull Head to arrest Sitting Bull. Bull Head was an odd choice for command if the purpose was to avoid bloodshed, as he and Sitting Bull had been feuding for months and had long been on the verge of exchanging blows. Bull Head also had led the Indian police in quashing Sitting Bull's efforts to disrupt the Crook Commission meetings during the allotment conferences the previous year.

The police gathered at Bull Head's house, on the Grand River a few miles from Sitting Bull's compound. The night was cold and stormy. Snow and ice came down, the countryside froze, and the mood in the cabin was solemn. These men, who knew and had admired Sitting Bull, were saddened by what they were about to do. They offered a prayer to the white man's god and then headed into the night.

As they approached Sitting Bull's compound at around dawn the next day, owls hooted and coyotes howled. Even they, one of the policemen said, cried out warnings, so the police should beware.

The police descended on the sleeping compound and crashed into Sitting Bull's house. The old warrior, bleary from sleep, agreed to go with them peacefully. However, within moments a crowd gathered, and Sitting Bull's fourteen-year-old son, Crow Foot—who years before had handed over Sitting Bull's rifle at the time of his surrender—taunted his father for acquiescing. At these words, Sitting Bull balked. His followers threatened the police. Shots rang out, and instantly Lakota was fighting Lakota. Drum's soldiers, down the road but within earshot, rode to the compound and fired at Sitting Bull's people, driving them away. When the shooting ended, Sitting Bull and Crow Foot were dead, and Bull Head was dying. In all, at least fourteen Lakota died as a result of the fight. After the shooting had stopped, one of the Indian police used a wooden yoke to smash Sitting Bull's face.[11]

Sitting Bull's death reaped a variety of emotionally heated responses. It appalled the Reverend W. H. H. Murray, a New York minister opposed to making Indians into farmers. In the *New York World* for December 21, 1890, he wrote: "The land grabbers wanted the Indian land. The lying, thieving Indian agents wanted silence touching past thefts and immunity to continue their thieving. The renegades . . . among the Indian police wanted an opportunity to show their power . . . And so he was murdered."[12]

An observer at Fort Yates, Thomas Stewart, wrote in a January 9, 1891, letter to Herbert Welsh of the Indian Rights Association that McLaughlin had wanted Sitting Bull killed, which was why he sent a hardened enemy of the holy man to arrest him.[13] McLaughlin wanted Sitting Bull out of the way because prostitution was rampant near the military garrison, Stewart contended, and McLaughlin feared that an inspector from the Indian Bureau might visit, talk to Bull, and find out how bad the agent's management really was. McLaughlin, Stewart said, never tried to stop the ghost dances until Sitting Bull adopted them. Stopping the dances was merely an excuse for arresting Bull. "Sitting Bull never either by threats or other means mollested [*sic*] anyone," Stewart wrote, "and had he been left alone the dance would soon have been discontinued as the Indians were leaving everyday."

L. Frank Baum, in the December 20, 1890, issue of his newspaper, the *Aberdeen Saturday Pioneer*, weighed in with a different perspective.

> Sitting Bull, most renowned Sioux of modern history, is dead.
>
> He was an Indian with a white man's spirit of hatred and revenge for those who had wronged him and his. In his day he saw his son and his tribe gradually driven from their possessions: forced to give up their hunting grounds and espouse the hard working and uncongenial avocations of the whites. And these, his conquerors, were marked in their dealings with his people by selfishness, falsehood and treachery. What wonder that his wild nature, untamed by years of subjection, should still revolt? What wonder that a fiery rage still burned within his breast and that he should seek every opportunity of obtaining vengeance upon his natural enemies?
>
> The proud spirit of the original owners of these vast prairies inherited through centuries of fierce and bloody wars for their possession, lingered last in

Sitting Bull's son Crow Foot, who in 1890 was about fourteen years old when he was shot to death by Indian police during his father's arrest. *(Library of Congress)*

the bosom of Sitting Bull. With his fall the nobility of the Redskin is extermi-nated, and what few are left are a pack of whining curs who lick the hand that smites them. The Whites, by law of conquest, by justice of civilization, are masters of the American continent, and the best safety of the frontier settle-ments will be secured by the total annihilation of the few remaining Indians. Why annihilation? Their glory has fled, their spirit broken, their manhood ef-faced; better that they die than live the miserable wretches that they are. History would forget these latter despicable beings, and speak, in later ages of the glory of these grand Kings of the forest and plain that Cooper loved to heroism [*sic*].

We cannot honestly regret their extermination, but we at least do justice to the manly characteristics possessed, according to their lights and education, by the early Redskins of America.[14]

After the attempted arrest, Sitting Bull's people panicked and fled, some go-ing to the Stronghold to join the most militant ghost dancers and others going to the band headed by Sitanka, or Big Foot, one of the last traditional chiefs. On the day Sitting Bull was killed, Sitanka was leading his band down the Cheyenne River to the agency for their ration issue, slated for December 22.

CHAPTER 6

Gunfire at Wounded Knee

BY LATE DECEMBER THE MILITARY had been swarming into the reservations for almost a month in what eventually became the nation's biggest army deployment since the Civil War. The flight of Sitting Bull's Hunkpapa led General Ruger to order Lieutenant Colonel Edwin Sumner to arrest Sitanka, who Miles thought was a hostile cast from the same mold as Sitting Bull. Sitanka, a Miniconjou Lakota, was indeed a hard-core traditionalist who found hope in the ghost dance, but he was also known as a peacemaker, which was not a term much applied to the fiery Sitting Bull. Nevertheless, Miles wanted Sitanka and his band brought into the agency of the Cheyenne River Reservation—their homeland—where they could be monitored.

Sumner and his soldiers caught up with Sitanka on December 21.[1] Tension between the troops and Sitanka's warriors prompted Sumner—who repeatedly showed empathy for the Lakota—to allow Sitanka to lead his people to the agency on his own. But Sitanka was pondering another plan. Oglala chiefs at Pine Ridge had asked him to visit them and help settle differences among them concerning the ghost dance religion. In return for his advice, they would give him one hundred ponies. This offer, and the urging of some members of his band, led Sitanka to give Sumner the slip and head for Pine Ridge instead of Cheyenne River.

When Miles heard of Sumner's failure to bring in the wandering Miniconjou, he was furious. He mobilized nearly every army unit in the area to locate the band. Ironically, the soldiers closing in on Sitanka were from the Seventh Cavalry—Custer's old command—and among them were veterans of the Little Bighorn who had survived the battle under Major Marcus Reno. Commanded by Major Samuel Whitside, the Seventh soon located Sitanka and his band moving south along Porcupine Creek toward Pine Ridge. Sitanka contacted army scouts and told them he wanted them to surrender. Whitside, taking no chances, instead sent out his soldiers to end the chase on the spot without further discussion. When they met up with Sitanka's band west of Porcupine Creek, both sides set up skirmish lines. Whitside told Sitanka to surrender immediately and to camp along the banks of a stream the Lakota called Cankpe Opi, which the whites translated as Wounded Knee.[2] Sitanka, sick with pneumonia, complied.

When he got word of the surrender, General Brooke ordered Colonel James Forsyth to ride with the rest of the Seventh Cavalry to Wounded Knee and help Whitside disarm the Miniconjou. Forsyth was under repeated orders and warnings from General Miles not to let his men mingle with the Indians.

At about this time, Short Bull, Kicking Bear, and the militant ghost dancers who had returned to the Stronghold when Two Strike surrendered, started heading toward Pine Ridge to turn themselves in. But events surrounding Sitanka would soon cause them to turn back a second time.

AT WOUNDED KNEE CREEK, WHERE Sitanka lay half dead from pneumonia, Forsyth surrounded the Indian camp with soldiers, artillery, and machine guns. On the morning of December 29, 1890—two weeks to the day after the death of Sitting Bull—Forsyth ordered his men to disarm Sitanka's band. Forsyth made a serious error at this point, putting his men into the camp among the Lakota precisely as Miles had ordered him not to do. He even had soldiers searching tepees for guns. These men and the Lakota were both under the sights of the Seventh Cavalry's heavy guns. If the guns were fired, the soldiers in the camp were likely to be blasted by friendly fire. Among those soldiers was Captain George Wallace, who had survived the Battle of the Little Bighorn. His command, Troop K, was only a few paces from Indians clustered in the center of the camp.

As the disarmament was taking place, a shot rang out, and then a general melee ensued. The soldiers had the Indians in a cross fire, but likely shot one another as well. Wallace was hit in the head and died at the outset. Sitanka, too—lying sick on a cot in the center of the camp—was among the first killed, riddled with bullets.

Indians, mostly unarmed women and children, fled on foot, and mounted

Wounded Knee just after the December 1890 battle, with bodies in the foreground backed by the skeletal remains of tepee frames abandoned on the frozen plain. *(Library of Congress)*

soldiers rode them down and killed them. When the shooting stopped, as many as 200—some sources even say 350—Lakota were dead.[3]

Some survivors sought refuge at Pine Ridge, where Elaine Goodale and other schoolteachers were decorating a church for Christmas, which they were celebrating late that year. Hearing the distant shots at Wounded Knee and fearing that the Lakota had gone on the warpath, they fortified the church and kept the Indian students inside for their own safety. Instead of warriors, wounded women and children soon were filtering in. Goodale helped turn the church into a hospital, covering the floor with straw for bedding, and Dr. Charles Eastman tended the injured. One girl, brought in battered and bleeding, begged for the removal of her ghost shirt now that it had "wholly failed to protect her from the storm of flying steel," Goodale wrote.[4]

"Our patients cried and moaned incessantly, and every night some dead were carried out," Goodale recalled. "In spite of all we could do, most of the injuries proved fatal. The few survivors were heartbroken and apathetic, for nearly all their men had been killed on the spot. The [Christmas] tree was dragged out, but joyous green garlands still wreathed windows and doors, while the glowing cross in the stained glass window behind the altar looked down in irony—or in compassion—upon pagan children struck down in panic flight."[5]

THE SHOTS AT WOUNDED KNEE were heard for miles around the battleground, and among those who heard them were Short Bull and Kicking Bear as they led the last of the militant ghost dancers to the Pine Ridge agency. The shooting panicked them, and they reversed course. At the agency itself Two Strike's people, among them Plenty Horses, believed they were about to be attacked by the army and started to exchange gunshots with Indian police. They set fire to houses and captured Red Cloud, aging and infirm but still a powerful symbol among the Lakota, and took him with them as they fled.

The violence that Royer had feared had finally arrived, primarily thanks to measures he had taken. Dr. Charles Eastman described the shooting at Pine Ridge. "General Brooke ran out into the open, shouting at the top of his voice to the police: 'Stop! Stop! Doctor, tell them they must not fire until ordered!' I did so, as the bullets whistled by us, and the General's coolness perhaps saved all our lives, for we were in no position to repel a large attacking force. Since we did not reply, the scattered shots ceased, but the situation remained critical for several days and nights."[6]

The alarmed "hostiles," as the army called them, moved into the valley of White Clay Creek, perhaps 4,000 people in all, as many as 1,000 of them warriors. General Miles had about 3,500 of his own blue-coated warriors nearby, amounting to half the army's infantry and cavalry, plus scores of enlisted Indian scouts.[7] He had 2,000 more ready to enter the fray as needed—in all, a fifth of the U.S. Army was at his disposal on the reservations.[8] By shifting these forces around, Miles blocked the route to the Stronghold and kept all the fleeing Indians in the White Clay Valley, where they camped.

Shooting erupted at other places on Pine Ridge, however, as the warriors under Two Strike and from other bands made forays in the wake of Wounded Knee. They attacked a Ninth Cavalry wagon train that was bringing supplies to the agency and also burned houses along the road to the Drexel Mission, the Catholic church that was Father Jutz's home. The day after Wounded Knee, Brooke ordered Forsyth to take his troops to the mission and drive off any hostile Lakota. Jutz and his colleagues had taken refuge in the church, but the priest had been assured by the Lakota that they would not attack him.

Forsyth reached the church, assured himself that all was well, and then proceeded north along White Clay Creek, where he led his men into a deep valley. The Lakota, who in all likelihood were mostly Two Strike's Brulé and included Plenty Horses, quickly took a position along the steep valley walls and trapped Forsyth and his troops. He had to be rescued by the Ninth Cavalry's buffalo soldiers.

Snow had begun to fall the day of Forsyth's battle in the valley near Drexel Mission, and it continued to fall and pile up for the next two days. On New Year's Day a burial party of about one hundred or so civilians, including ten or fifteen white men, went to the Wounded Knee battlefield to bury the dead in a mass grave for two dollars per body. Among the party was Dr. Charles Eastman, who hoped to find and help survivors. A photographer and several reporters also joined the group. "Fully three miles from the scene of the massacre we found the body of a woman completely covered with a blanket of snow," Eastman wrote, "and from this point on we found them scattered along as they had been relentlessly hunted down and slaughtered while fleeing for their lives."[9]

The bodies lay under the snow, scores of still and silent mounds. Indians in the party began to cry or to sing their death songs. Miraculously, one old woman from Sitanka's band, an American flag sewn onto her hat, had survived the days and nights of freezing cold that followed the shooting. So had a girl, only about a year old, who would be adopted by a white officer and his wife. An old man also was brought in alive, found his wife and daughter at Goodale's chapel, and died a day or two later. "All this was a severe ordeal for one who had so lately put his faith in the Christian love and lofty ideals of the white man," Eastman wrote. "Yet I passed no hasty judgment, and was thankful that I might be of some service and relieve even a small part of the suffering."[10]

The burial crew dug a pit sixty feet long and six feet deep and threw in Big Foot and more than 140 of his people, stripping jewelry, clothing, and ghost shirts from many of the bodies. Later, anonymous Lakota would smear the posts erected at the burial site with red paint that had been sent to them by Wovoka and that was supposed to have ghost dance powers.

Black Elk, a young warrior who would be a noted holy man in later life, took an overtly dimmer view of Wounded Knee than did Eastman. Recognizing that the shooting at Wounded Knee killed the ghost dance, he wrote in his autobiography: "And so it was all over. I did not know then how much was ended. When I look back now from this high hill of my old age, I can still see the butchered women and children lying heaped and scattered all along the crooked gulch as plain as when I saw them with eyes still young. And I can see that something else died there in the bloody mud, and was buried in the blizzard. A people's dream died there. It was a beautiful dream."[11]

As with Sitting Bull's death, white response to Wounded Knee ranged from compassion to satisfaction. Philadelphia resident Sarah Dickson wrote to Herbert Welsh of the Indian Rights Association shortly after the battle, alluding to Helen Hunt Jackson's seminal book on Indian issues, *A Century of Dishonor:* "Alas that the dishonor still clings to the Century & this dreadful war is partly the fault of our so called Christian nation."[12]

The *Chadron Democrat* took a view more familiar to residents of the recent frontier, editorializing on January 1, 1891:

> For once it has occurred that more Indians than soldiers have been slain, and we doubt not but that either Gen. Miles or Brooke will be cashiered from the service as was Gen. Harney for such pitiless bloodshed. Nothing will be done about the poor soldiers who were slain, but the Indian department [*sic*] is undoubtedly already getting in its work upon some crank of a congressman to present a bill before that august and wise (?) body to investigate the cause that led to the late massacre (?) and uncalled for (?) slaughter of such dear, good Indians. . . . We glory in the revenge of the Seventh, although they sustained a heavy loss, and notwithstanding there may have been but a few in the late fight left who belonged to the Seventh during Custer's life. . . . We predict that the killing of Big Foot and his warriors will have a telling effect on the messiah craze, and will civilize more reds who are yet alive than all the power of God and education that has been pumped into them for the past 16 years.[13]

General Nelson Miles, rumored to be interested in running for president, said, "I have never heard of a more brutal, cold-blooded massacre than that at Wounded Knee."[14] He immediately ordered an investigation into the shoot-out.

CHAPTER 7

Casey's Last Ride

WHEN LIEUTENANT EDWARD WANTON CASEY arrived at the Pine Ridge reservation in mid-December 1890, his orders required him not to fight the Lakota but to keep an eye on them and to avoid conflict. Restraint was General Nelson Miles's way of dealing with a people who knew they had been defeated and just needed to be reminded of it. By keeping his troops from attacking, Miles hoped to succeed in demonstrating the power of the military without having to unleash it. Miles's approach struck old Indian fighters as a touch peculiar. Frederic Remington, who traveled with Casey during the Wounded Knee crisis, quoted one seasoned soldier who pointed out that neither he nor Casey's Cheyenne scouts understood Miles's limited warfare: " 'This is a new kind of war. Them Injuns don't understand it, and to tell you the truth, I don't nuther. The Injuns say they have come all the way from Tongue River, and are going back poor. Can't get Sioux horses, can't kill Sioux,' and in peroration he confirmed his old impression that 'this is a new kind of war,' and then relapsed into reveries of what things used to be before General Miles invented this new kind of war."[1]

One of Casey's assignments was to reconnoiter the Stronghold, the natural fortress in a remote part of Pine Ridge that several thousand Lakota had occupied at the height of hostilities. Recent reports indicated that the Indians had abandoned the Stronghold, and Casey was supposed to find out if the reports were true. The officer and his Cheyenne scouts rode there through twelve miles of Badlands, rugged, barren country cut up with ravines and arroyos. Remington described the Stronghold: "All about the plain were strewn the remains of dead cattle (heads and horns, half-butchered carcasses, and withal a rather impressive smell), coyotes, and ravens—all very like war. These Brules [*sic*] must have lived well. There were lodge poles, old fires, and a series of rifle pits across the neck of land which the Sioux had proposed to defend, medicine poles, and near them sacrifices, among which was food dedicated to the

Lieutenant Casey (center) leads his Indian recruits prior to their assignment to Pine Ridge during the ghost dance panic. *(Christian Barthelmess, Montana Historical Society, Helena)*

Great Spirit, but eventually consumed by the less exalted members of Casey's command. I vandalized a stone pipe and a rawhide stirrup."[2]

Soon, on the plain below, Casey's group spotted the dust of retreating Lakota, who fired at them. Casey had a hard time keeping his Cheyenne warriors from attacking—the scouts feared they would go back to Fort Keogh without the Lakota horses they expected to take as war booty. "The Cheyennes were uneasy, and not at all pleased with this scheme of action," wrote Remington. "What could they know about the orders in Lieutenant Casey's pocket?"[3]

Soon Casey was confronted with a large body of Lakota warriors. The Cheyenne wanted to fight, but Casey held them back. Resting his hand on his revolver, he told them, "I will shoot the first man through the head who falls out of the ranks."[4] Leaving the scouts in the command of another soldier, Casey rode out to speak with the Lakota. The sun was setting, and darkness came while Casey talked. "The daring of Casey in this case is simply an instance of a hundred such," Remington wrote. "By his prompt measures with his own men, and by his courage in going among the Sioux to powwow, he averted a bloody battle, and obeyed his orders." Three or four Brulé from the hostile group visited Casey's camp that night, resulting in uneasy rest for the troops and scouts.

The next day white troops from Casey's unit had to make a running retreat when the Lakota opened fire on them. Strictly obeying Miles's orders against fighting, the troops rode hard, some of them on horseback and some—including Remington—in a wagon pulled by a laboring team of horses. "Above the pounding of the horses and the rattle of the wagon and through the dust came the cowboy song from the lips of Mr. Thompson [a Civil War veteran who rode in the wagon]: 'Roll your tail, / And roll her high; / We'll all be angels / By and by.' "[5]

But in fact they survived, after making a run of ten miles "at a record-breaking gallop," Remington wrote. "We struck the scout camp in a blaze of excitement. The Cheyennes were in warpaint, and the ponies' tails were tied up and full of feathers. Had the Sioux materialized at that time, Mr. Casey would have had his orders broken right there."

That night Casey and the scouts slept outdoors and woke with frozen sleet on their faces. It was the last day of 1890. The sleet that glazed them fell likewise on the dead at nearby Wounded Knee.

PERSISTENT HOSTILITIES BETWEEN THE ARMY and Two Strike's White Clay encampment of some one thousand warriors did not keep Casey's Cheyenne troops from daily contact with the hostiles, allowing Casey to invite a few Lakota warriors to drop in and talk at the nearby army camp on White River where Casey was stationed.[6] The evening of January 6, 1891, perhaps half a dozen hostiles palavered with Casey and his men.[7] Casey sensed that they wanted the shooting to end. Pondering this potential, Casey apparently decided to ride the next morning to Two Strike's camp to see if he could meet with a chief or two and talk peace. Officially, he hit the trail to check out the camp in a reconnaissance mission, as he was authorized to do. He was not authorized to set up discussions with chiefs, but his actions on January 7 suggest that is what he intended to do, and his second in command of the scouts, Lieutenant Robert Getty, corroborated this view later when he wrote, "Casey started out with the intention of penetrating the hostile Camp to have a talk with the principal chief, and thought he could accomplish his object by boldness."[8] And if negotiations failed, riding out to the camp for a look around was still an important part of Casey's duties.

Two Strike and Crow Dog's camp in 1890. Lieutenant Casey was trying to visit these people when Plenty Horses shot and killed him. *(Nebraska State Historical Society Photograph Collections)*

Casey took only two Cheyenne scouts. Had he shown up at the Lakota redoubt with more men, he would have been perceived as out for blood. He may have been taking his cues from a similar effort completed successfully in Arizona almost five years earlier, when Lieutenant Charles Gatewood had ridden with two Apache scouts into the camp of one of the fiercest Indians ever to carry arms: Geronimo. This warrior chief of the Chiricahua Apache had surrendered to the military a few months before Gatewood's ride, then had changed his mind and run off into the Sierra Madres with about two dozen warriors. When Gatewood rode in, he flatly told Geronimo to surrender. Geromino's jaw may have dropped at Gatewood's sheer audacity, but the warrior actually had little choice. He was being hunted by U.S. soldiers, civilian militiamen, Mexican soldiers, and Apache scouts. Weary of war, facing destruction, Geronimo gave up.[9]

Casey may have figured that what worked for Gatewood would work for him. After all, Casey knew that, like Gatewood, he had a persuasive argument on his side: The Lakota camp was surrounded by U.S. soldiers, and the Indians knew their backs were against the wall.[10] Casey probably also thought that he had one other important factor on his side: justice. Like many officers, he believed that the Indians had been wronged. Throughout his almost twenty-year career in the West he had seen again and again the same sorry scenario in which whites provoked Indians to violence and then called in the military to punish them.[11] As a just man, Casey wanted to set things right with the Lakota and restore peace and security, such as they were, to the reservations. He would meet the Lakota halfway. More than halfway. He would ride all the way into their camp and talk it over.

Despite similarities between Casey and Gatewood, important differences also should have been apparent. Geronimo knew and trusted Gatewood, while Casey was riding toward a village of strangers—armed, dangerous strangers conditioned to respond negatively to white men in blue uniforms with brass trim. Moreover, the two scouts who rode with Gatewood were related to members of Geronimo's band, while the scouts with Casey were Cheyenne— sometimes allies, but lately enemies, of the Lakota.[12]

LIEUTENANT CASEY MOUNTED HIS BLACK horse at 9 a.m. on January 7, 1891.[13] The two Cheyenne soldiers he had selected to go with him were twenty-nine-year-old White Moon (Is-she-wo-go-mi-ast in Cheyenne) and twenty-five-year-old Rock Road (O-ni-me-o). Both had enlisted in May 1890, and both were married. Probably neither had fought in battle before.[14]

By midafternoon Casey and his men, according to some reports, were within a mile and a half of the Indian camp, although some witnesses put them four miles away. The trio stopped along White Clay Road to greet a group of perhaps forty Lakota who were watching cattle and perhaps butchering beef.[15] At about this point Casey told Rock Road to go back to check on three Cheyenne scouts somewhere in the area. Rock Road left Casey to carry on the mission with White Moon.[16]

Two Lakota, both in war paint, then joined Casey and White Moon as they headed toward Two Strike's camp. One of these was an Oglala called Broken Arm. The other was the Brulé named Plenty Horses, who had been riding the edges of the camp that day, keeping watch for approaching enemies. Plenty Horses had been at Pine Ridge the day of the shooting at Wounded Knee and had fought against the army in the days that followed. He was in no mood for fraternizing with U.S. soldiers. "Of course I was in a bad frame of mind," he would say later. "Our home was destroyed, our family separated, and all hope of good times was gone. There was nothing to live for."[17]

Nevertheless, when Casey and Plenty Horses first met, Casey had extended a hand, saying, *"Hau, Kola"*—hello, my friend. Plenty Horses shook hands and, as the two rode side by side for a mile or so, talked in English.

At some point along the way, the four riders met a Lakota named Bear Lying Down, who had just ridden out of the camp. Although he was not a hostile and had a travel pass from General Miles, he had spent the previous night with the warriors because they would not let him leave. Casey asked Bear Lying Down to return to the camp and request a meeting with a chief. At that moment Casey exceeded his authority. He was not supposed to seek contacts with Indian chiefs, although he was permitted to speak with them if they initiated a discussion.

The chief on whom he pinned his hopes was probably Red Cloud, the old warrior who had first won fame in the 1860s when he led the Lakota in fighting the U.S. Army to a standstill. In January 1891 Red Cloud was about seventy years old and had traded in his war lance for more peaceful means of persuasion. He lived on the Pine Ridge reservation in a two-story house that was more comfortable than that of the reservation agent, and he had avoided any participation in the ghost dance.[18] Nevertheless, Red Cloud had tremendous symbolic value to both whites and Lakota, so much so that the hostiles had kidnapped him from his house during the brief shoot-out at Pine Ridge headquarters. "I being in danger of my life between two fires I had to go with them and follow my family," Red Cloud explained a few days later to Thomas Bland, of the National Indian Defense Association, who was investigating the Lakota ghost dance conflict. "Some would shoot their guns around me and make me go faster."[19] He would never have received such treatment during his days as a warrior chief, but then a chief had more status than did a waning cultural symbol. Casey, counting on the old diplomat to work out yet another peace, may not have known that Red Cloud was a virtual prisoner.

While waiting for Bear Lying Down, Casey told Plenty Horses that he wanted to visit the Lakota camp. Plenty Horses later said that, thinking of the vulnerable women and children living there, he told the officer to go no closer. And so Casey, Plenty Horses, White Moon, and Broken Arm settled down to wait for the messenger's return.

Bear Lying Down, meanwhile, talked with Red Cloud, who was instantly alarmed at the news that an army officer was nosing around on the outskirts of the Lakota camp.[20] Red Cloud wanted an end to the hostilities, but he knew

Plenty Horses, the young Brulé who killed Lieutenant Casey, during his imprisonment at Fort Meade. *(Library of Congress)*

that several hundred young warriors beyond the confines of his tepee were eager to gun down a U.S. soldier, particularly one with brass on his shoulders. Given what had happened at Wounded Knee, Red Cloud feared that an assault on the officer would lead to a large Lakota body count that would include women and children. The safety of this soldier was as important to him as it was to the army, perhaps more so.

Red Cloud gave Bear Lying Down an immediate answer and sent him back to Casey along with Pete Richard, Red Cloud's half-white son-in-law. The two riders did not bring Casey the message he had hoped for. Red Cloud, Richard said, was planning to slip out of the camp and go to the Pine Ridge agency soon, and he would talk then. Red Cloud also sent a warning: Leave immediately. "I told him [Casey] he had better go home at once," Richard would later relate, "for the young fellows were just the same as if they were drunk or crazy."[21] Chiefs always had trouble controlling hot-blooded young warriors.

Accounts differ on Casey's reaction to Red Cloud's message.[22] Plenty Horses would insist that Casey threatened to return with more soldiers and capture the chief. Other witnesses reported that Casey simply said he would come back later. In any event, as Casey prepared to leave, Broken Arm said in Lakota that he wanted to go with Casey to retrieve horses of his that he thought were near the army camp. With Richard as interpreter, Casey agreed. "My horse and the Lieutenant's were facing each other, and we both turned to go," Richard would later report during official questioning.[23]

Plenty Horses, looking at Casey's retreating figure, shouldered his Springfield rifle, aimed down the heavy muzzle, and fired a bullet that crashed through the back of Casey's skull and exited below his right eye. Casey's horse reared, and Casey fell to the ground, instantly dead. Plenty Horses turned his horse and rode slowly back toward camp. He ignored White Moon, treating Casey's scout as if he weren't there.

White Moon was in fact no threat. Even if he had been a seasoned fighter, he would have seen the odds against him if he shot Plenty Horses in plain sight of a hostile encampment bristling with warriors. He started to ride off, but Pete Richard called him back and told him to take Casey's gear to the army camp. Speaking in signs, White Moon refused, and asked Richard, "Why don't you shoot Plenty Horses?"[24]

"Why don't you shoot him yourself?" Richard replied. Broken Arm, apparently interested in more practical matters, got off his horse and took Casey's two revolvers, one of which the lieutenant had carried in his boot, and a belt of cartridges. Another Lakota, No Neck, rode up about then, and he and Richard urged White Moon to take everything else belonging to Casey, but White Moon refused. "I told him then to take Lieutenant Casey's horse and we would go home and he did this," Richard later told military authorities.[25]

And so Casey was left dead on the chill prairie, as Lakota dead had been left at Wounded Knee. The decades of Indians and soldiers killing each other ended with his abandoned corpse.[26]

WORD OF CASEY'S DEATH TRAVELED quickly. The following day, not fifteen hours after Casey had turned away from the Lakota camp, his oldest brother, Thomas, was preparing to start his day in Washington, D.C. He came downstairs from his bedroom for breakfast and found a military colleague talking solemnly with his wife, Emma. The two turned to Thomas, and, as he would write later that day in his diary, he learned that his "dear brother Edward Wanton has been killed by the Sioux."[27]

That evening the *Washington Star* reported Secretary of War Redfield Proctor's reaction to the shooting: "I don't know when I have heard anything that has shocked me more than the news of Lieutenant Casey's death. He was here in the spring, and I grew very fond of him, he seemed so bright and energetic and enthusiastic, and he had such excellent plans and ideas about the Indian troubles. . . . I regarded him as one of the most promising men in the service."[28]

An officer of the Twenty-second Infantry wrote from Fort Keogh to Thomas Casey the day after Edward's death, "Everyone throughout the service who knew him liked him so thoroughly admired [*sic*] him as a man and as a soldier while we of the 22nd thought that no one was like him before and now feel as if no one could ever take his place."[29]

Nettie Atchison, the woman Casey had wanted to marry, was in Paris, France, when she learned that he was dead.[30] In a January 9 letter to family friend Mrs. N. W. Mason she described her reaction when she first read of Casey's death in the newspaper: "It seemed at first as though I should go crazy."[31] She added that she had recently inherited money and that she and

Ned, as she called Casey, were finally going to marry. "I am not afraid to let the whole world know that Ned has had my whole heart all these years," she wrote. She asked if the family would let her have his class ring.

General Nelson Miles labeled the killing a crime and forged ahead with intentions to arrest the warrior responsible. His reaction may have stemmed as much from a sense of personal interest as from a sense of justice. He had known the lieutenant well. Just the previous spring, Miles had reviewed Casey's scouts and had promised that the officer could soon expand his unit from 100 to 200 Indian soldiers. Miles was even familiar with Casey's family. He had served under Casey's father briefly during the Civil War, and he had competed aggressively against Edward's brother Thomas for the position as the army's chief signal officer (the job went to a third man). He would continue to hold Casey respectfully in mind.[32] In any event, Miles likely did not stop to think that if he jailed an Indian for shooting Casey, he might at the same time be indicting every soldier who fired on the Lakota at Wounded Knee. However, others would soon make this connection and see its potential effects.

Elsewhere, life and death went on: As Casey was being lowered into his grave, another murder was unfolding on the western prairies that would have profound implications for any attempt to punish Lieutenant Casey's killer.[33]

CHAPTER 8

Ambush or Self-defense?

ABOUT A WEEK AFTER CASEY'S death, area newspapers began covering another shoot-out between whites and Indians, although from the very beginning reporters expressed doubts about the information they were receiving. The Rapid City, South Dakota, *Black Hills Weekly Journal* gave readers a front-page story based on information from an allegedly reliable source: an interpreter named Henry Kirkham, who had spent the past five months at Camp Cheyenne, an army outpost at the junction of the Cheyenne and Belle Fourche rivers not far from the site of the shooting.[1] Kirkham, whose veracity was vouched for by the camp commander, told the *Journal* that a hunting party of "two bucks and two squaws" had been joined along nearby Alkali Creek the previous Saturday evening, January 10, by about twenty warriors on horseback. The warriors had with them some forty horses, including several belonging to three local ranchers, the Culbertson brothers.

The next morning, according to the newspaper, the Culbertsons and their friends rode up and cut out their horses, whereupon the Indians fired at them. "Two bucks, a squaw and two horses were killed on the ground," the *Journal* erroneously reported. In fact, only one Lakota, a middle-aged man named Few Tails, had been killed. "A buck and a squaw started north with one of the teams and wagons and five wounded Indians followed," and the Indians "made good their escape." Only one white man was injured: Pete Culberston, the palm of one hand grazed by a bullet.

The anonymous reporter, however, remained skeptical, even though Kirkham said his story came "from the lips of those who participated in it." Perhaps that was *why* the reporter was skeptical, because the Culbertsons' reputation was less than spotless. At any rate, the story concluded, "It will strike the average reader as somewhat peculiar that Indians bent on horse stealing or on the warpath should be encumbered with wagons, or, supposing the wagon Indians to have had nothing to do with the stolen horses, that the others should, while having the horses in their possession, join them at a place so near the ranches where the stock belonged."

The *Journal* was not the only paper to express doubt. The *Sturgis* (South Dakota) *Weekly Record* reported that a "large number of citizens here seem to think it a cold blooded murder."[2] The paper added, "It seems very strange that [the Culbertsons] could not see, that Indians with wagons and women were not on the war path. They camped in a neighborhood where they were certain to be seen, when they could go a few miles further and be quite safe." The *Sioux Falls Argus-Leader* was less measured in its reaction, calling the shooting of Few Tails "one of the most cold-blooded and unjustifiable murders ever committed on the frontier."[3]

Immediately after the shoot-out, General Nelson Miles had sent out from Camp Cheyenne a dozen troops and three scouts under Second Lieutenant F. C. Marshall to investigate the battle site. Marshall and his men arrived at around half past eight on the evening of January 12 at the Quinn ranch, where soldiers of the Eighth Cavalry were stationed on courier duty. Soldiers from the ranch had been in on the shooting, and Marshall grilled them for information. One private told Marshall that on Sunday morning, the eleventh, a cowboy—one of the Culbertson brothers—had ridden into the army camp in great alarm and reported that "Indians were driving off his stock."[4] He had said his brothers were shooting it out with the Indians. "I wish you fellows would come and help us," he had pleaded.

The troopers rode out and joined the melee, but only briefly, because the Indians soon escaped on horseback. Sergeant Frank Smith, stationed at the Quinn Ranch, told Marshall that he had gone out later to examine the site of the shoot-out, which lay near the junction of Alkali Creek and the Belle Fourche River, and had found an abandoned wagon with two dead horses lying in front of it, their harness stolen. The wagon seat was occupied by Few Tails's corpse, shot below the right eye and in the chest. As Smith examined the body, he heard hoofbeats and turned to see a lone rider coming toward him, a tough-looking cowboy with long hair and pearl-handled pistols who introduced himself as Pete Culbertson, owner of a ranch only half a mile away. He spoke bluntly, there by the wagon with Few Tails's body. "I have shot one of those damned Government pets," Culbertson said, "and if any more of them want to be fixed, let them come this way."[5]

Pete Culbertson worked his ranch with his two brothers, Andrew and Nelson, and all were infamous hard cases. One newspaper later would point out, cryptically, that the brothers had been warned "last fall if they did not mend their ways and turn over a new leaf something would be done."[6] Two of the brothers had been indicted in Bon Homme County in 1882 for horse stealing but had been acquitted on a technicality. According to local legend, Pete Culbertson, sometimes called Indian Pete, slept with a holstered gun hanging above his bed and had a paranoid sense of hospitality—he designed a contraption that kept a pistol aimed at the head of anyone who knocked at his door. Pete raised spotted horses on his ranch, running some twenty-five or thirty head. He also looked after some 250 horses belonging to a neighboring rancher, James Juelfs.[7]

Pete told Smith that he had caught the Indians stealing several of his horses and that when he had tried to reclaim the animals he had been met with gunfire. He and his brothers fired back, wounding several of the marauding Indians and killing the one in the wagon. He showed the sergeant where a bullet had grazed his right hand during the fight.

Before daybreak on the thirteenth, Marshall rode out to inspect the abandoned wagon, with Few Tails's corpse—for reasons veiled by history—still in the seat and the horses still lying where they had fallen.[8] Marshall had his men fan out to collect evidence while he studied the earth for clues. Wagon and horse tracks indicated that the Indians, traveling toward Pine Ridge, had had about sixteen horses with them, including six for pulling their two wagons. Regardless of Culbertson's claim that the Indians had been driving away his horses, the shape and small size of the hoofprints indicated that all had been made by Indian ponies. "I do not think there was an American horse in the lot," Marshall concluded in the report he later wrote summarizing his investigation.[9]

Judging from the tracks etched into the prairie, Marshall surmised that on the morning of the shoot-out, the Indians had broken camp and proceeded only about three hundred yards when they were fired upon. The belly of one of the dead horses had been grazed by a bullet shot from the front, but the shots that killed the horses and Few Tails had come from the right, from the direction of the sagebrush-shrouded banks of Alkali Creek. Judging from the trajectories of the bullets, Marshall guessed that the first shot had been made while the wagon was going straight toward men lying in ambush. Few Tails presumably had turned his horses to the left to flee and had then been hit from the right.

Inspecting the creek bank, Marshall and his soldiers found nineteen rifle shells scattered in three spots. Two of the shells were Winchester .45s, and thirteen were Winchester .44s. Four were from what Marshall called a U.S. or American rifle, meaning a firearm of the type recently distributed by the federal government to state officials, who turned them over to citizens for defense in case of an Indian outbreak. "There was no indication that the Indians returned the fire or did anything but attempt to escape," Marshall wrote. "No shells were found, although every part of the ground was carefully searched." He added that tepees, mattresses, and other supplies abandoned in the wake of the second wagon as it bolted across the prairie suggested that the Indians had been taken by surprise and "thoroughly scared."[10]

Tracks showed where the cowboys chasing the Indians were joined by the soldiers from the Quinn ranch. Marshall and his men also backtracked the gunmen, starting at the ambush site on Alkali Creek, and found that a trail left by three riders led to the Culbertson ranch. That came as no surprise, since Pete Culbertson had admitted killing an Indian. But the rest of his story did not jibe with Marshall's evidence.

The investigators proceeded down the Belle Fourche and for the next couple days interviewed ranchers along the way. No one had any complaints about stolen horses. "On the whole, it was the general opinion of all parties with whom I talked that no depredations had been committed by Indians during the past year in the section visited," Marshall wrote.

According to Marshall, "Pete Culbertson told such contradictory stories of the affair to me, to Sergt. Smith, and to one Franz, a rancher, that I could put no faith in any of them, and am inclined to discredit his statement to me that these Indians were stealing his horses, but to believe that the Indians were fired on in a spirit of purest bravado, with no cause or provocation whatever."[11] Nevertheless, Marshall gave the cowboy the benefit of the doubt. "In justice to the Culbertsons it may be said that they have always been most friendly towards the Indians, often feeding them," he reported.[12] "On the other hand, they are known as hard characters, one of them recently returned from the penitentiary. Pete, the one whom I talked with, said that he would shoot an Indian on sight, now that they were so stirred up. He regarded it as almost necessary to do so, to protect his property and life."

*   *   *

WHEN GENERAL NELSON MILES RECEIVED the reports of the Alkali Creek investigation, he readily agreed that the shooting was unprovoked murder and promptly demanded the arrest of the Culbertsons, who fell under civilian jurisdiction because the shooting had occurred off the reservation. But civilian officials waffled, in part because they did not want to arrest a white man for killing an Indian.

The army had put Miles in charge of the Division of the Missouri just the previous summer. After spending years in the West fighting Indians—bringing down Chief Joseph and the Nez Percé in the Pacific Northwest, Geronimo in New Mexico, and Crazy Horse in the northern plains—he had been glad to move with his wife to division headquarters in Chicago. He relished the city nightlife, the plays and music, the exquisite dinners. And now here he was in South Dakota, at the coldest time of year in one of the coldest parts of the country, once again struggling to hammer out peace agreements with armed Indians.[13]

Miles was furious over what he interpreted as the insubordination of his officers in handling Sitting Bull's arrest and disarming Lakota warriors at Wounded Knee. Sitting Bull's death was being called an assassination by some Indian advocates in the East, and Wounded Knee a mass murder. Outraged that women and children who had fled from the battleground, escaping up ravines and hiding behind shrubs, had been hunted down by soldiers on horseback and slaughtered, Miles set his sights on a court-martial for the officers who had been in command at Wounded Knee.[14]

On top of all this, Miles now had to deal with Casey's murder and the killing of Few Tails, a well-liked man among the Lakota and also among whites. The Deadwood, South Dakota, newspaper, the *Pioneer*, would soon refer to Few Tails as "a kindly-hearted and peaceable old man."[15] Following the shooting of Few Tails, the Lakota Indians, who had been settling down after Wounded Knee, were once again close to panic, particularly on Pine Ridge. They had begun bringing horses into camp for instant flight at the first hint of an attack.

Miles was determined to see it all through—from Wounded Knee to Plenty Horses to the Culbertsons—and his determination was steeled by a will that balked at nothing.[16] He had once spent a full day in battle at Fredericksburg, Virginia, during the Civil War despite a bullet wound he had taken in his throat that morning. His aggressiveness had been admired by his superior

Major General Nelson A. Miles, a Civil War hero and self-made military man. He commanded the forces that occupied the Lakota reservations during the ghost dance panic of 1890–91. *(Library of Congress)*

officers, winning him rapid promotion: He ended the Civil War as a brigadier general, though he was only twenty-five years old. In an exchange of letters with General George Meade just prior to Robert E. Lee's surrender in April 1865, General Ulysses S. Grant wrote, "Miles has made a big thing of it and deserves the highest praise for the pertinacity with which he stuck to the enemy until he wrung from them the victory."[17] Miles in 1892 would receive the Congressional Medal of Honor for his Civil War exploits.

His gutsy determination materialized during the war in a high body count, and not just for the enemy. He bragged that his own division suffered the highest casualties of any in the Second Corps, which in turn had more men killed and wounded than any other corps in the Army of the Potomac. His men were proud of their fighting reputation, too, but also complained that Miles was a glory seeker who would risk their lives to build his own reputation and win promotions.

Born in 1839, Miles grew up on a Massachusetts farm near Wachusett Mountain, where he hunted, skated, and played military games with other boys.[18] One school chum said, "The study in which he seemed to take the most delight was fighting."[19] When the Civil War broke out in 1861, Miles was working as a clerk in Boston, first in a fruit market and then in a crockery shop. A Republican strongly opposed to slavery, he formed a military drill club with some friends. After the North lost the First Battle of Bull Run in July 1861, Miles used one thousand dollars his father gave him and two thousand dollars borrowed from an uncle to organize and outfit an army unit that became Company E of the Twenty-second Massachusetts Infantry Regiment. Although his men elected the twenty-two-year-old Miles captain, the governor of Massachusetts turned down his commission because he was too young, making him a first lieutenant instead. By December 1861, however, his bravery had earned him a promotion to lieutenant colonel.

After the Civil War, the army reduced his temporary wartime brevet general's rank to colonel and put him in command of Fort Monroe, on the Virginia coast. There he took charge of the most important political prisoner of the War Between the States: Jefferson Davis, formerly president of the Confederacy. Although Davis was ailing and under heavy guard, Miles clapped him in leg irons, winning himself some bad press and the enmity of many southerners. Shortly after his service at Fort Monroe, Miles took command of the Fortieth Infantry Regiment, made up of black enlisted men and white officers. Subsequently, he served on the Freedman's Board, set up by Congress to guide reconstruction in the South, where freed slaves were under attack as former Confederates returned to power. He led efforts to register black voters, educate former slaves, and find employment for them.

Perhaps Miles's work with freed slaves helped him see the perspective of other races. In any event, although the bulk of his career by January 1891 had been spent fighting Indians, Miles did not blame the Indians for the hostilities. He believed that the government's bad faith and mismanagement were at fault. Chief among the problems, in Miles's view, was the corrupt Indian Bureau, whose reservation administrators commonly stole supplies intended for the Indians and sold them for personal profit. Miles wanted to cure this ill by placing the bureau in the War Department so it could be cleaned up under military control. In an 1880 speech before the New England Society, a literary and philanthropic group, Miles said, "With [the military] it is not a question of destroying [the Indians] or being at war with them perpetually, but whether we are competent and able to govern them not only with a strong and firm hand, but also with entire justice."[20]

While dealing with Wounded Knee and its aftermath, Miles successfully urged Congress to meet its treaty obligations and to give the military control over the reservations. In January 1891 Congress appropriated $465,000 for rations, horses, and education for the Lakota, as outlined in federal treaties, and provided $1.4 million for the Lakota for the next fiscal year as well as $100,000 to compensate "friendly Sioux" for damages incurred during the Wounded Knee period.[21] The military also took temporary control of the Lakota reservations as the army's ghost dance campaign ended. Federal costs came to about $2 million. Forty-eight soldiers and one shepherd on Pine Ridge had lost their lives during the conflict, and scores of Lakota had died.[22]

As peace was restored, Miles turned his attention to Plenty Horses' arrest. The 1868 treaty required the Lakota to turn over for trial under U.S. law any of their people who committed a crime against an American citizen.[23] The U.S. government also agreed in the same treaty to bring to court any American citizen who committed a crime against the Lakota. The cases of Plenty Horses and the Culbertsons would test both sides of this agreement. Because prosecuting the Culbertsons was a civilian matter, Miles turned over to the governor of South Dakota the records of the military investigation of the Few Tails shooting. Before returning to his Chicago headquarters in late January, the general told Colonel William Shafter to arrest Plenty Horses as soon as it could be done without inciting any trouble among the Lakota, who were still skittish after the battering at Wounded Knee and during subsequent events.

The Lakota by this time had presumed that the cessation of hostilities had let Plenty Horses off the hook. After all, Casey had been killed in the midst of war. Under those circumstances, how could Plenty Horses be charged with murder? In raising this question, the Lakota anticipated an issue that would haunt the prosecution of the young Indian. Even some army officers thought that if Plenty Horses were guilty of murder, perhaps quite a few soldiers were too, given the events of the past few weeks.[24] Certainly, the mounted soldiers who had run down and killed fleeing women and children at Wounded Knee would have been vulnerable to prosecution if Plenty Horses were found guilty, a verdict that would lead to a cascade of other charges, investigations, courts-martial, and trials.

When it became clear that Miles intended to arrest Plenty Horses, the Lakota balked, angry that Few Tails' killers had not been arrested. They also refused to turn over another Lakota, Young Skunk, whom the military wanted for murdering a shepherd named Henry Miller. The Lakota would not give up either man until the cowboys who had ambushed Few Tails were arrested. Young Man Afraid of His Horses, a highly influential progressive chief who had helped talk militant ghost dancers into surrendering, put the issue succinctly: "No, I will not surrender them. But if you will bring the white men who killed Few Tails, I will bring the Indians who killed the white soldier and the herder, and right here in front of your tepee I will have my young men shoot the Indians, and you have your soldiers shoot the white men, and then we will be done with the whole business. They were all bad men."[25]

When Miles made it clear that he would do all that he could to see Few Tails's killers prosecuted, the Lakota relented. The way was opened for the army to track down and bring in Plenty Horses and Young Skunk.

ABOUT TWO WEEKS AFTER THE slaying of Few Tails a major break arose in the case as victims of the shooting began drifting in to Pine Ridge. The first of these, her clothing stained with her own blood, staggered up to a reservation corral where cattle were kept for slaughter. As she tottered on the verge of collapse, a soldier spotted her. He shouted to the men in a nearby camp, and within minutes about fifty soldiers were gathering around her.

Her name was Clown, and she was Few Tails's widow. Shot twice, she had walked alone almost one hundred miles back to Pine Ridge in the dead of winter. "They got a blanket and took me to a tent," she later told military officials. "I had no blanket and my feet were swelled, and I was about ready to die. After I got to the tent, a doctor came in, a soldier doctor, because he had straps on his shoulders, and washed me and treated me well."[26]

At midday a Lakota named Knife came for her and took her to the church near the headquarters of the Pine Ridge Reservation, where victims of Wounded Knee had been treated. By late February she had recovered enough to tell her story to military officials, who also interviewed two other survivors of the shoot-out: Red Owl and her husband, One Feather, who arrived at Pine Ridge in Clown's wake.

According to the three survivors, on the morning of January 11, 1891, Few Tails's and One Feather's families were camped at the confluence of the Belle Fourche River and Alkali Creek in western South Dakota.[27] During the past two months they had been hunting near Bear Butte, one of the sacred sites of the Lakota, and their two wagons were loaded with about a ton of meat. They had visited with Crow Indians, erstwhile enemies of the Lakota, and received gifts from them. They were now about one hundred miles from Pine Ridge— only a few more days, and they would be home.

The youngest member of the party was only an infant, the daughter of One Feather and Red Owl. Their thirteen-year-old daughter, Otter Skin Robe, also was there, helping that morning to take down the party's four tepees.

The oldest member of the group was Few Tails, who had seen some forty winters and was a close relative of Young Man Afraid of His Horses. Few Tails himself was liked by whites who knew him. The *Sioux Falls Argus Leader* would report that he was "one of the most reliable and progressive Indians" of Pine Ridge.[28] His wife, Clown, rounded out the hunting party.

Despite the shooting of Sitting Bull in mid-December and the events at Wounded Knee two weeks later, Few Tails and his friends had found themselves on good terms with everyone they met during their travels, including whites. Only the night before the ambush, as the Lakota prepared dinner, Sergeant Frank Smith of the Eighth Cavalry had stopped in while on his way to his duty station at the Quinn ranch, about seven miles distant. When he asked the Indians what they were doing off the reservation, Few Tails showed him a pass that had been written by the federal agent at Pine Ridge. A letter of recommendation indicated that Few Tails was a friend of the whites.[29] Seeing that they had permission to hunt near Bear Butte and that they had apparently done so, Smith rode on.

Smith wasn't the only visitor that evening. Andrew Culbertson—Pete's brother—rode into the camp and talked awhile, walking into the tepees and nosing around. Clown would later recall him as a short man with a light-colored mustache who rode a yellow horse and wore cowboy garb.[30]

That night, Andrew Culbertson returned to the family ranch, where it is likely that he told his brothers about the Indians and the various goods in their tepees and wagons. The brothers almost certainly conspired at that time to raid the Indians the next morning, ambushing them outside their camp.[31] Although what the brothers discussed that night in regard to Few Tails and his hunting party is speculative, archival records indicate that Andrew Culbertson returned to the Few Tails camp the morning of January 11, 1891, wearing a fur cap and clothing that led Clown to conclude he was a soldier.[32] He soon departed.

After packing up their gear and rounding up the eight to ten saddle horses they had used for hunting, the Indians climbed aboard their wagons and moved out, with Few Tails and Clown in the lead. The two families had scarcely left camp when rifle fire blasted them from a sage-covered knoll ahead of them. "My husband had a gun and ammunition, but had no chance to use them," Clown would say with forlorn simplicity in the final words of her testimony.[33]

Hit in the leg and breast, Clown fell to the ground and feigned death, lying beside the wagon in which her husband already had died. She looked in the direction of the gunfire and saw two men in fur caps riding toward her on black horses. When they passed, she saw four more men coming up behind them. Among the four she recognized Andrew Culbertson. She continued to lie by the wagon while the shooting continued.

At the opening volleys, One Feather had spotted three men on horseback and one on foot shooting at the hunting party from the nearby hill covered with sagebrush.[34] When he saw Few Tails shot dead, he instantly turned his own wagon to retreat. His wife, Red Owl, was shot at about that moment. One Feather, with his two daughters cowering under a blanket in the back of the wagon, headed down the Belle Fourche, but three horsemen cut him off, forcing him to retreat back to the site where Few Tails lay dead. There a man on foot fired at him from a stand of trees.

Thinking fast, One Feather drove past Few Tails's wagon, abandoned the road they had been traveling, and cut uphill across the prairie. On the hill he found one of his saddle horses running loose and jumped from the wagon to catch it. He put a rope around the horse's nose and told his injured wife to drive on ahead.

As Red Owl fled, One Feather fired back at the attackers, holding them off and catching up with his wife. One Feather took over the reins and drove as fast as his four horses would go, aiming for a ford on nearby Elk Creek. But just as he reached the crossing, another gunman opened fire and was soon joined by two others. The firing intensified after the trio dismounted and fired from the ground.

One Feather drove on. When he had put some prairie between his family and the gunmen, he returned the reins to his wife and remounted his pony. Firing at the cowboys, he covered his wife's retreat. In the direction Red Owl was headed, One Feather saw what he thought was a small white house—actually, the Viewfield post office. As the wagon drew near, someone inside shot at Red

Owl. One Feather galloped up and saw two men shooting from the post office. Jumping from his horse, he returned fire until his wife was able to withdraw. He then mounted and rode after her as four or five more horsemen came charging toward him.

He had no way of knowing that, in addition to the cowboys who had launched the ambush, he was now fighting U.S. soldiers from the Quinn ranch, who had joined the melee at Andrew Culbertson's request. One of them, Adolph Rundquist, would later report that he had found about five Indians and their wagon at the gunfight. "I tried to head them off and they fired on me and I returned fire, but did not hit any that I know of. I fired 5 or 6 times." Two more soldiers rode up, but the fight was ending, and they returned to Quinn's. Rundquist noticed that some of the cowboys carried .50-caliber army rifles, given to state officials shortly after Wounded Knee for arming a militia to fight Indians. By the time the soldiers departed, One Feather and his family had been chased, under fire, for at least eighteen miles.

The fight came to an end when One Feather, with his harness horses played out, abandoned his wagon. He caught another saddle horse and put his two daughters on it. He and Red Owl rode double on the other horse, fleeing as fast as the horses would carry them.

Meanwhile, the gunmen closed in on the wagon, firing at the retreating Indians but abandoning pursuit. "That was the last I saw or heard of them," One Feather later testified.

The cowboys lost interest in fighting once they had possession of the two wagons. At some point—records are inexact—at least one of the wagons was taken first to the Timmons ranch, near Viewfield and the post office, and then to the army's Camp Cheyenne, where soldiers and citizens divided up the Indian property among them as trophies of the "Sioux war," including harnesses, ponies, clothing, and even the gifts from the Crows.[35]

One Feather and his family arrived at Pine Ridge two weeks later. During that period, exposed to freezing cold, shelterless, One Feather and Red Owl's infant daughter died.[36]

Meanwhile Clown, after pretending to be dead, endured her own agonizing fight for survival. She would later tell military officials, "I got up and saw that one horse was not killed, and I got on him and came to a house on Elk Creek, and I knew the people living there, and they opened the door for me."[37]

When the door opened, Clown saw inside two men who "got their guns and one of them loaded his gun, and they pointed their guns at me, and the white girl inside said something, I don't know what it was, and they took their guns off me. One man came to me and motioned to me to go away." Her horse balked, however. "I could not get him away," she would later say—perhaps the horse was ready for a barn or corral and some grain. Anyway, in her haste she left the horse.

Dusk was falling as she trudged across the plains. She found a track she recognized as coming from One Feather's wagon. But behind it were the tracks of horsemen, which she took as a warning to stay away. In the evening she came to a store at the mouth of Rapid Creek, where she had traded frequently, but avoided it now. "I was afraid I would cause trouble again," she would report, "so I did not go in the store."

Instead she walked all night across the snow-shrouded landscape, resting now and then. She made it to the foot of the Badlands, and there she heard the rattle of wagons. Too frightened to seek help, she hid as the wagons passed close by. After that, she traveled only at night, resting by day.

While she struggled to reach safety, the Culbertsons and their allies were spreading the word about the shoot-out. Soon, a report was sent east by wire that "the bloody Sioux were devastating the Black Hills country and murdering helpless women and children, etc."[38]

The killing of Few Tails was big news on the reservations, too, frightening Lakota already on edge in the wake of Wounded Knee and the killing of Sitting Bull. The state of mind of the Lakota is exemplified by a conversation with a Lakota who in late January visited a shop in Sturgis, South Dakota, after peace was restored. A reporter for the *Sturgis Weekly Record* asked the Indian why the Lakota had not surrendered sooner.[39] He replied, "They were afraid they would be treated as were Big Foot's people; disarmed, stood up in a line and killed like so many cattle." With palpable frustration, the paper observed, "So strangely were the Indians impressed with this belief that it was with the utmost difficulty that they could be made to believe otherwise."

CHAPTER 9

The Last Battle

THE ARMY CLOSED IN ON Plenty Horses on February 18, 1891, when Lieutenant S. A. Cloman and a contingent of fifty Indian scouts visited a Lakota encampment on a tributary of White Clay Creek.[1] Cloman stopped at the lodge of Corn Man, Plenty Horses' grandfather, and found Plenty Horses with two other young warriors. All refused to come out or even to talk, and Cloman decided to move on discreetly and camp for the night.

The next morning, Cloman returned and found that most of the men in the Indian camp had gone to the agency to pick up their government beef ration. In fact, only about half a dozen Lakota men were there, including the two wanted men. Cloman had arrived at the perfect time to take his prisoners. First, he arrested Young Skunk.[2] Then, stationing his troops close to a group of five tepees where he expected to find Plenty Horses, he dismounted and searched the lodgings, accompanied by two other men on foot and four on horseback. They found Plenty Horses in the last tepee, seized him, and took him outside, "telling him that [they] had to arrest him, but that he would not be hurt in any way if he would submit quietly," Cloman would later report.

Cloman left Plenty Horses with two of his men and started to remount his horse. Plenty Horses at that moment broke loose and bolted for his tepee. "We ran after him and caught him as he was going through the door," Cloman wrote. "He was then mounted on a horse belonging to one of the scouts, and brought with us to Pine Ridge Agency, where I turned both men over to the Camp Commander." The army immediately sent off Plenty Horses by train to a jail cell at Fort Meade, near Deadwood, South Dakota, about 125 miles from Pine Ridge. There he would stand at the center of the last confrontation of the Indian wars, a battle fought with law and word on the cloistered fields of justice.

* * *

MANY DAKOTANS IN SPRING 1891 must have thought it remarkable that, after decades of Indians and whites killing one another with abandon, the shooting of a single soldier by a lone Indian had resulted in a burgeoning courtroom drama making headlines across the United States. The idea that the Culbertsons might be put on trial for killing an Indian was doubtless off the sociopolitical charts, the stuff of satire and parody. White men simply were not arrested for killing Indians. Only a few years before, in northern California, Indians literally had been hunted for sport. But in South Dakota, the brothers *would* be arrested, eventually, and made to stand trial.

The trials were the product of a nation experimenting with and expanding the boundaries of its way of life. In New Orleans Charles Buddy Bolden's band was pioneering a new American music that would be called "jazz." Not long before Plenty Horses' trial, Emily Dickinson's first book of poems rolled off the press, setting the stage for spare, twentieth-century poetry. While the trial was in progress, a physical education instructor at a Massachusetts college was inventing a new ball game that would soon sweep the nation. He was calling it "basketball." During summer 1891 Thomas Edison patented the motion-picture camera and, on the first anniversary of Wounded Knee, the wireless telegraph.

Change was barreling down on South Dakota, too. Farmers busted virgin sod for crops, producing around 30 million bushels of corn and 40 million of wheat yearly as well as oats, barley, flax, and various vegetables. Where wild grasses did still grow, they no longer nourished vast numbers of bison but increasing numbers of domestic cattle.

The changes coming to the West were personified in the residents of Rushville, Nebraska, a typical prairie town just south of the Dakota border. F. H. Carruth, a man of uncertain identity who left for posterity his account of a visit to Rushville in 1886, recalled that the town's one thousand inhabitants were "at the time a queer combination of Eastern and Western civilization."[3] Founded on a Fremont, Elkhorn & Missouri Valley railroad line, Rushville was only a year old when Carruth visited.[4] Farmers plowing the rolling, outlying country had settled in only recently, but cattle ranchers had been working the area for several years. Both groups were seasoned westerners, carving a living out of the wild prairie. Local businessmen, on the other hand, were newcomers from the East.

The streets of Rushville chimed when cowboys rode in. "Every man from outside the town—and they made up probably three-quarters of those on the streets—wore big, jingling Mexican spurs," Carruth wrote. "Indeed, it is part of the religion of every man connected with a Western stock ranch to never remove his spurs on any occasion whatever, with the possible exception of going to bed . . . Besides their spurs the men also wore big felt, or buckskin hats, with the wide leather bands which are also peculiar to stockmen, and many of them leather or goatskin chaparejos, or leggings. The businessmen wore the ordinary attire observed in any American city; but it was considered among them that some concession should be made to their newly-made Western friends and patrons in the matter of dress, so they hit upon the happy plan of wearing the wide, heavy leather bands on their ordinary stiff or soft Eastern hats. To see a promising young physician start out on his professional rounds wearing a derby hat of the latest New York shape, with a thick, embossed leather band two inches wide, is a sight only occasionally afforded to mortals."

The southern boundary of the Pine Ridge reservation lay only a few miles from Rushville, so the town also attracted a few Lakota. "Most of them were genuine wild Indians," Carruth wrote with palpable relish, "slightly tamed by the use of cigarettes, and with the murderous eyes and cruel mouths of full-fledged cut-throats. . . . They lounged about all over town, and lent a picturesqueness [sic] to the scene. They went a step further than the businessmen in their costume, and combined elements of the savage, the cowboy, the United States soldier, and the man of fashion. Some of them had succeeded in giving up everything of the savage except the buckskin moccasins, with elk-hide soles and bright porcupine quill-work on the insteps and toes." Carruth also noted—though with what factual liberties is hard to tell—that the Indian of Rushville invariably had "one thing about his make-up in the cleanest and best possible condition—namely, his Winchester, fifteen-shot, forty-five caliber rifle."

The town hustled with a businesslike atmosphere, Carruth wrote, although "it was hard to tell exactly what kind of business was going on. Judging from appearances only any one [sic] would have said that the leading industry was the buying and shipping of buffalo bones. Across the railroad tracks there are great heaps of buffalo, deer, elk and antelope bones, which had been gathered in the surrounding country and brought to town and sold to dealers, who shipped them to fertilizer factories to be ground up. A half-dozen freight cars were being loaded with them." Nothing better symbolized the changing West than those railcars carrying away the bones of vanished plains creatures so they could be turned into fertilizer for crops planted on newly plowed prairies.

In a world of such amalgams—and hardly a town sprouting on the plains of South Dakota would have been any different—authorities stalled on taking any action against the Culbertsons and their allies in the ambush. Consequently, the Plenty Horses case led the way: Plenty Horses was indicted for murder in federal court in Deadwood, South Dakota, on March 3, 1891.[5]

Deadwood was a drab little town in the Black Hills, established during the gold rush of the 1870s. Its main attractions were its many saloons and the grave of celebrity gunman Wild Bill Hickok, who on August 2, 1876, had been shot in the back of the head in Deadwood while playing cards in Saloon Number Ten.[6] J. W. Buel, in his 1886 book *Heroes of the Plains*, described Deadwood with memorable piquance: "Deadwood, like every other big mining town that has yet been located in the West, was full of rough characters, cutthroats, gamblers and the devil's agents generally. Night and day the wild orgies of depraved humanity continued; a fiddler was an important personage, provided he would hire out to saw all night in a saloon, and the concert singer was a bonanza, especially if the voice were clothed in petticoats. The arbiter of all disputes was either a knife or a pistol, and the graveyard soon started with a steady run of victims. Sodom and Gomorrah were both dull, stupid towns compared with Deadwood, for in a square contest for the honors of moral depravity the Black Hills' capital could give the people of the Dead Sea cities three points in the game and then skunk them both."[7]

Participants in the Plenty Horses case presumed that after the grand jury indictment, the trial would begin immediately. But U.S. judge Alonzo Edgerton had other ideas. An attorney and politician in his midsixties who had earned a reputation in South Dakota for honesty and erudition, Edgerton feared that the prejudice against Indians that permeated the Black Hills would weigh against a fair trial for Plenty Horses in Deadwood. Consequently, he changed the venue to the federal court in Sioux Falls. "This announcement came like a thunderclap on both the United States officials, the litigants, witnesses and jurors," reported a local newspaper, adding that all had expected to spend the next three weeks in Deadwood for the trial.[8] Now they would have the additional expense of traveling to Sioux Falls. They were, the paper said, "much surprised at the sudden freak of Judge Edgerton." Edgerton set the trial date for April, with himself and Judge Oliver Shiras presiding.

But in early March a fundamental matter about the trial had yet to be settled. The federal prosecuting attorney, William B. Sterling, still had not taken legal control of Plenty Horses, and there the case stalled. Sterling had issued a warrant for the Brulé's arrest by U.S. marshals, but General Nelson Miles, who had been holding Plenty Horses as a prisoner of war at Fort Meade under the command of Lieutenant Colonel Edwin Summer, refused to give up the young Lakota until Few Tails's alleged killers were arrested.[9] As early as March 7 Sterling began a series of letters to the U.S. attorney general in Washington, D.C., W. H. H. Miller, complaining about the refusal to give up Plenty Horses. On March 16 Sterling still had not succeeded in bringing Plenty Horses under civilian control and wrote to Miller asking him to obtain from the War Department orders for Miles to give up the prisoner.

Miles was not alone in pushing for arrests in the Few Tails case. On February 23, 1891, Colonel William Shafter, who at Miles's orders had overseen Cloman's arrest of Plenty Horses, wrote to Miles with gentle sarcasm: "So long as Indians are being arrested and held for killing armed men under conditions of war, it seems to me that the white murderers of a part of a band of peaceful Indians should not be permitted to escape punishment."[10] Dr. Valentine T. McGillycuddy—a much-respected former agent of the Pine Ridge reservation—agreed. As foreman of the grand jury that had indicted Plenty Horses, he persuaded the other jury members to support Miles in a letter to Edgerton, urging the federal government to "spare no expense" in prosecuting the men who had ambushed Few Tails. An ex–Army surgeon with a massive handlebar mustache and the hard, level gaze of a remorseless gunfighter, McGillycuddy also wanted the Department of Justice to assign Sterling to assist in the prosecution.[11]

McGillycuddy had been pushing for prosecution of Few Tails's killers almost since the day of the shooting. On the letterhead of the Lakota Banking and Investment Company, of which he was president, McGillycuddy in a January 24 letter had provided the federal Bureau of Indian Affairs a list of the suspects in the killing: the three Culbertsons and three other cowboys or ranchers. "Affairs like the killing of Few Tails, who was always as I knew him a peaceable Indian, do not tend to make good feeling between settlers and Indians," McGillycuddy wrote. "The citizens generally of this region desire a thorough and searching investigation, and if the parties as charged are guilty, they should be punished."[12]

Plenty Horses under arrest at Fort Meade, South Dakota, in spring 1891. He is wearing the blanket he wore when he killed Casey and which he continued to wear through the trial. *(Library of Congress)*

McGillycuddy saw the Few Tails case as a matter for federal action. Sterling, however, took a different view. Concluding that Few Tails's killers should be tried under state law—because Few Tails and his friends were not on the federal reservation when attacked—Sterling turned the case over to the authorities of Meade County, site of the killing. Meade County officials were in no hurry to get involved, complaining that the case was just too expensive. Alex McCall, the state attorney for Meade County, wrote a letter on March 18 to the U.S. commissioner of Indian affairs in which he referred to the Lakota as "simi-barbarous [*sic*] offenders against the peace and dignity of the nation" and said that Meade County officials were "strongly opposed, considering all the circumstances, to burden our County with all the costs of so expensive a trial as this one in all probability will be, if determinedly prosecuted."[13]

McCall went on to blame the killing more on the agent who gave Few Tails permission to leave the reservation than on the gunmen who shot him. "Permit me to say in all earnestness that in giving these Indians passes to leave the Reservation and go out on a hunting expedition, at such a time of great public danger, and consequent fear and excitement amongst the settlers, cannot be characterized in a term so mild as to merely style it a blunder."

McGillycuddy backed McCall's claim about the expense in a March 19 letter to Morgan, writing that the county "is financially in bad shape, and for that reason I fear that it will be difficult to procure an indictment before the county grand jury."[14] He suggested that the federal government cover some expenses.

His idea apparently was a good one, or at least acceptable. In late March the U.S. attorney general ordered Sterling to assist McCall with the prosecution, and the Indian Bureau agreed to pay travel expenses for Indian witnesses. At the same time, even though the Culbertsons had not been arrested, the secretary of war ordered Sumner to turn over Plenty Horses to civilian authorities.[15]

U.S. Deputy Marshal Chris Mattheison, a powerful-looking man with an open, clean-shaven face, took Plenty Horses from the Fort Meade guardhouse and clapped him into shackles for the train ride to Sioux Falls—a portentous name for a town in which a Sioux would be tried for a capital crime. Once in Sioux Falls, Mattheison had a blacksmith remove the shackles, then locked Plenty Horses away in the county jail. In a small, dingy cell with a single, tiny window, Plenty Horses waited for the court to deal with him. He presumed he would hang, and although he showed no emotion while imprisoned— observers remarked on his stoicism—he did sink into a noticeable depression. One of his key preoccupations was finding legal aid. He was poor in a way only Indians could be poor: bereft of their hunting lands, locked away on reservations, unable to fend for themselves, lacking jobs, forced to farm in a region too arid for crops, and fed and supplied by meager government handouts. He had nothing, and a lawyer would cost hundreds of dollars.

PLENTY HORSES SOUGHT HELP FROM John Burns, an attorney and well-known Indian sympathizer who lived in Deadwood, the town that Judge Edgerton believed too prejudiced to give the Brulé a fair trial. From his cell in the Fort Meade guardhouse, Plenty Horses wrote pleading letters to Burns almost every day. Plenty Horses' father, Living Bear—who had met Burns in January when the lawyer had visited the Stronghold to talk peace—also sent several letters begging Burns to serve as his son's defense attorney. Burns answered Living Bear in a March 27 letter addressed to Pine Ridge military authorities. He warned Living Bear that although he was "anxious to befriend" Plenty Horses, the case would be expensive, in part because the trial required travel across the state to Sioux Falls.[16] He told his "Red brothers" that as "a poor man" he would need five hundred dollars in cash to mount a defense, with a three-hundred-dollar down payment.

The day he wrote to Living Bear, Burns visited Plenty Horses at Fort Meade. He thought the young Brulé was "a handsome fellow."[17] Plenty Horses must have taken heart when Burns showed up, but when they discussed the attorney's fees, Plenty Horses' face fell. Five hundred dollars. Burns might as well have said a million dollars or one hundred thousand ponies. By the time Burns left, Plenty Horses had become so transparently despondent that Burns feared he might try to kill himself. Speaking softly and carefully, Burns made him promise to "bear his fate whatever it may be, like a brave Indian."

Although Living Bear, nearly sixty years old, was a headman among the Brulé and had many ponies—newspapers referred to him as a rancher—he had no cash. Recognizing this, Burns wondered if perhaps they could get the money from Herbert Welsh, a wealthy Philadelphian who had helped fund reservation schools and who fronted the Indian Rights Association.

Welsh had traveled widely in the 1880s on behalf of the Indians, visiting reservations from Dakota Territory to the Southwest as well as Indians at military prisons in Florida.[18] He helped shape federal Indian policy by meeting personally with incumbent presidents. He penned so many letters in support of his cause that he sometimes lost the use of his writing hand. In 1889 his doctor urged him to take a two-week vacation to recover from exhaustion, but even on vacation he wrote letters, editorials, and other correspondence.

The Indian Rights Association, which in January 1891 had helped raise $1,200 for the victims of Wounded Knee, could easily have solved Plenty Horses' financial woes. But because Burns did not know Welsh personally, he worried that his appeal for help would fall flat. However, Burns did know Valentine T. McGillycuddy, whom Welsh greatly admired for the way he had worked with the Lakota as agent at Pine Ridge. McGillycuddy gave Burns a letter of introduction to Welsh. The attorney then wrote to Welsh, outlining cryptically but with emotion his interest in defending Plenty Horses: "[The Lakota] seem somehow to think that because I have stood by them, or up for them, in the past, they have only to call upon me, overlooking entirely the question of compensation. This would be under the present circumstances, a question of absolutely no weight if I was financially so situated that I could spare the time and means. The case of the defendant appeals strongly to me, as his father was one of the chiefs present at the council in the bad lands [*sic*], which I held with them, and so I may say that to some extent at least I owe my life to him."[19]

Burns explained that he had interviewed army officers he knew as friends, all of whom agreed that Casey was a war casualty, not a murder victim. Whoever defended Plenty Horses, Burns contended, would have to persuade a white jury to accept that view. Recognizing that the outcome of the Plenty Horses trial could affect or be affected by the Culbertson case, Burns also assured Welsh, "I am doing everything in my power to induce the Meade Co. authorities to proceed against the men who killed Few Tails, but so far without results."

Burns asked Welsh if the Indian Rights Association could pay Plenty Horses' legal fees. Living in an era in which an attorney might be castigated for trying to drum up business, Burns added, "These miserable people are so utterly helpless, that I think it my duty to write this." As Plenty Horses would soon be taken from Fort Meade by civilian authorities, Burns ended by urging Welsh to cable his response quickly.

Welsh was becoming the focal point for those who sympathized with Plenty Horses' plight. Lieutenant Colonel Edwin "Bull" Sumner, the Civil War veteran who commanded Fort Meade and who had played a leading role in tracking down Sitanka prior to Wounded Knee, also wrote to Herbert Welsh about Plenty Horses. His letter probably arrived only a day or so after Burns's. "The trial commences early in April and this poor d——l has no one to defend him," Sumner wrote, "and although his deed was horrible I still feel that something should be done in his behalf for the sake of justice if for no other reason."[20] Reminding Welsh that the two of them had met a few years earlier, when Sumner commanded Fort Robinson in Nebraska, Sumner concluded, "Knowing of your kindly feeling for the helpless I now ask that some steps be taken to help this man 'Plenty Horses.'" The pressure on Welsh to do *something* for Plenty Horses was steadily mounting. The Indian Rights Association held Plenty Horses' fate in its hands.

* * *

UNFORTUNATELY, THE ASSOCIATION AND GROUPS like it, though composed of well-intentioned people distressed by the treatment of the Indians, could be as deadly as cannon fire to the survival of Indian culture.

The Indian Rights Association could trace its beginnings to May 17, 1882, the day Herbert Welsh and another well-dressed Philadelphia gentleman, his friend Henry Pancoast, stepped from a train at Chamberlain, a small town in southeastern Dakota Territory.[21] The duo looked out approvingly on the broad, green stretch of Dakota prairies rushing off to all horizons. An aspiring artist who had studied painting for a year in Paris, Welsh was about thirty, lean, mustached, with piercing eyes and a resolved set to his jaw. He looked like a man accustomed to wealth and authority, and in fact Herbert Welsh was on his way to becoming a leader of Philadelphia society. He and Pancoast had come to the West at the urging of another Philadelphian, Bishop William Hobart Hare, who was leading an effort to establish missions among the Lakota. Deeply religious and active in the Episcopalian church, Welsh believed that it was the responsibility of "good men" to determine what needed to be done to reform the world and then to do it.[22] He wanted to investigate the status of the Indians and what might be done to help them.

Welsh liked the vast prairie, but he thought the little pioneer towns that punctuated the plains were blots on the landscape. He and Pancoast also disdained the pioneers they found eking out a living on the frontier, personifying these "border whites" as gamblers, convicts, and emigrants and describing them as the "scum of many nations, complacently taking claims on land wrested" from the Indians.[23]

The two Philadelphians toured eastern Dakota Territory and crossed the Missouri River into northeastern Nebraska. As they traveled, they encountered the more traditional Indians, who immediately struck in them a romantic chord. Pancoast described them "on ponies, dashing and wheeling over the hills with a peculiarly Indian recklessness and grace."[24] The Indians' "brilliant costumes and strange ornaments sparkled in the sun," dazzling both men, who also remarked on the Lakotas' marked dignity of bearing, "the faces of many showing great character and intelligence."

But these straitlaced eastern gents had traveled to Dakota Territory not to praise the Indians but to save them. As Welsh said, he and Pancoast were not "sentimentalists" but practical men trying to plan a future for the Native American in the United States. They were convinced that the new nation had no place for traditional Indians, however picturesque they might be. The traditional way of life was over. A buffalo-hunting culture, or a hunting culture of any kind, would not survive the onslaught of towns, ranches, and farms. The Indians would be wiped out *unless* . . .

That *unless* was the void which Welsh hoped to explore and map.

Much as Welsh liked the look of the traditional Indians, he disapproved of their traditions. He particularly despised the sun dance, the central celebration in Lakota religious life. Held in June, sun dances were a chance for bands of Lakota to gather, socialize, and reinforce their religious beliefs. Anyone could dance, but only male dancers engaged in ritual sacrifice of their own flesh and blood to the sun, the most powerful force of God, in return for God's goodwill for all Lakota. The dancer's skin on chest and back would be pierced with skewers, and he would be tethered to a pole or to bison skulls, blood streaming from his wounds as he danced until he tore himself free. His skin might not tear loose for many hours. Sometimes, bits of flesh were cut from a dancer's body as a sacrifice. The dancer might collapse from exhaustion or become entranced and experience visions. Just days before Custer's famous last stand, Sitting Bull during a sun dance saw a vision of myriad soldiers cut down in a great battle.

More accustomed to the symbolic blood sacrifices of Christianity, Welsh thought the dance was barbarous and that the giving away of gifts that played an important part in the ceremony was a waste of material wealth on people less fortunate or lazier than the giver. He wanted to ban the whole ritual, to "discourage a baneful generosity on the part of those whose labors had won success, and entirely prohibit the degrading spectacle of self-torture."[25] A practicing philanthropist of inherited wealth, he failed somehow to understand a culture in which status was conferred by giving and in which the sharing of food and other goods with the old, disabled, or incapable was a vital underpinning of society. Generosity was one of the virtues most admired by the Lakota.

On the Santee Reservation in northeastern Nebraska, Welsh found the kind of Indians for which he was looking, the type who provided hope for his concept of Indian survival.[26] They wore "citizen's dress," as European-style clothing was called when donned by Indians. They lived in wooden houses instead of tepees. They did not dab paint on their faces or practice traditional dances and other Indian rituals. These people were models for all Indians—farming, getting jobs, merging, blending in, disappearing as a separate culture.

After four weeks in the West, Welsh and Pancoast returned to Philadelphia, full of ideas for improving the lot of the Indian. Without doubt Welsh talked over his plans with John Welsh, his father and a former ambassador to England who was highly regarded in Philadelphia for public service and for donating to good causes. More to the point, he would have sought the advice of his uncle William Welsh and his aunt Mary.[27] William was involved deeply in Indian matters. President Ulysses S. Grant in 1869 had appointed him the first chairman of the Board of Indian Commissioners, a body of philanthropists assigned to monitor the purchase of supplies for Indian reservations. Mary had founded a group for Episcopal women, the Indian Hope Association, to support the church's missionary work. She also had encouraged Herbert Welsh to help the Indian cause.

Welsh had the time and energy to devote to this cause, as well as to several others, as he emerged as a civic leader. Wealthy merchants and businessmen, his father and his maternal grandfather had bestowed on him enough money that he could spend his life as a gentleman philanthropist without ever having to work to support himself, his wife, and their four children.[28]

Convinced that he knew what the Indians needed, Welsh outlined his ideas in a pamphlet he wrote and published, called *Four Weeks Among Some of the Sioux Tribes*. In a nutshell, Welsh wanted to turn the Indians into white people and thus save them from being hunted down by the military and shot into extinction, even if his plan meant wiping them out as a culture. He thought of this as a vast improvement for everyone concerned.

These ideas were nothing new. They had been bandied about by various other Indian rights groups and by government officials for years. Because they were popular among the eastern social and political establishment, Welsh found a ready audience for his message as he laid out several specific goals.[29] First, he wanted to turn the reservation system inside out. In 1882 Indian tribes held their reservation lands as a group. He wanted the land to be allotted to the Indians *in severalty*, meaning that individual Indians would be given ownership of land allotments, preferably in the form of farms that could be self-supporting. He saw "in severalty" become a byword of the Indian allotment movement that burgeoned in the 1880s and that came to fruition in 1889 despite the opposition of Sitting Bull and other conservatives.

Welsh hoped that allotting the land in severalty would destroy the tribal system, leading to his second goal: development of new laws to keep order among the Indians as they adjusted to the new pattern of life, work, and property. To help with that legal development, the reservations would need better agents, and getting better agents for the reservations was in fact his third goal. In the 1880s agents were political appointees. As such, some were good agents, while others were just good Republicans or Democrats who knew nothing about Indians but plenty about currying favor with politicians. Welsh wanted the appointments based on qualifications measured by civil service testing.

Fourth, he wanted Indian children to be educated, preferably in Christian boarding schools that would keep the students away from traditional cultural influences, such as their parents. Finally, he wanted to end the ration system, in which the federal government, through the Bureau of Indian Affairs in the Department of the Interior, distributed food and clothing periodically to reservation Indians. He contended that the ration system undermined Indian self-sufficiency and made the challenge of turning Indians into farmers even more difficult by forcing the Indians to settle near government distribution points rather than on the best farmlands. Moreover, Indians who did settle farther out on the plains spent most of their time traveling to and from the distribution points rather than tending to crops.

Welsh spoke widely, mostly to church groups, and promoted his ideas in the press. He and his allies, he would later say, "determined to do all in our power to make the situation known to the public, especially to the Christian public which is at all times anxious to carry out the ideals of Christianity into public as well as private life."[30] On at least one issue he achieved quick results. Shortly after Welsh distributed his pamphlet, the secretary of the Interior initiated plans to establish Courts of Indian Offenses on most reservations to punish Indians who practiced traditional rituals, such as the sun dance.

Before 1882 came to a close, Welsh determined to call together the cream of Philadelphia society to create an organization that would pursue his Indian agenda. He lacked the social clout to attract the prestigious people he sought, but his father, John, had all the stature necessary. John issued invitations to a December meeting at his house.[31] Those who attended included ministers of leading churches, the publisher of the *Philadelphia Inquirer*, a railroad and oil baron, and the dual president of the Midvale Steel Company and the Edgemoor Iron Company.

Developments at the meeting moved with a speed which suggests that every step had been orchestrated in advance. Pancoast and Welsh both spoke, describing their experiences in the West and charting plans for the Indians. When the roster of speakers came to an end, Welsh, Pancoast, and N. Dubois Miller, an attorney and friend of Welsh, produced a constitution for their proposed organization, the Indian Rights Association. The meeting adopted the constitution and appointed a committee to choose officers and set up the organization. Three of the five committee members were Welsh, Pancoast, and Miller.

Within two weeks the committee selected a panel of officers, and Welsh became the functional leader of the group. By 1891, when Welsh was being dunned with letters about Plenty Horses' need for money, the association had about 1,200 members and was raising about eleven thousand dollars yearly from such donors as John Jacob Astor, a social leader in New York City, and J. Pierpont Morgan, one of the leading capitalists of the day.

Helping Plenty Horses should have been a minor-league activity for the Indian Rights Association, something done at the flick of a pen across a check. But the association was not sure that it could or even should spend money on Plenty Horses' defense. Instead of offering funds, Welsh urged the Bureau of Indian Affairs to help out, arguing that as a ward of the government, Plenty Horses should be provided with an attorney. But the Department of Justice, to whom Welsh also appealed, declared that it was not clear that the government legally could provide defense attorneys for accused Indians and, in any event, could not do so without a congressional appropriation.[32]

Eventually, Welsh adopted a halfway measure. He pledged $325 to help cover Plenty Horses' legal expenses but not his lawyer's fees. Before the trial ended, however, Welsh would amend his decision, allowing the attorneys to keep any money left over after expenses.

ATTORNEY JOHN BURNS DROPPED OUT of the picture as the case moved to Sioux Falls, where two local attorneys came to Plenty Horses' aid.[33] One was thirty-three-year-old David Edward Powers, who grew up on a farm outside Oneida, New York, studied at Niagara University, and was admitted to the New York bar at twenty-three. In 1889 he formed a partnership with an attorney in Rome, New York—which, ironically, was the hometown of Judge Alonzo Edgerton, who had moved west years before.

A lean man with high forehead, bushy mustache, and steely eyes, his hair parted in the middle in keeping with the latest fashion, Powers had moved to

South Dakota only the previous December, arriving in the midst of the troubles on the Lakota reservation. After that baptism in the ways of the Old West, he was now at the center of a trial that could have happened nowhere else.

He was partnered with George P. Nock, an older lawyer with a reputation as a brilliant defender in criminal cases. Shorter than the lean Powers, he was round-cheeked and double-chinned—almost cherubic—with hair slicked back and mustache worn in the popular walrus style. He had begun practicing in South Dakota at least ten years earlier.

Of the lawyers involved in the case, the man who had the most at stake in winning was William B. Sterling, the U.S. attorney for South Dakota. Affable, clean shaven in an era in which most men sported heavy mustaches, with a receding chin and large nose, Sterling was cut from the same cloth as the businessmen that Carruth described in Rushville, one of those suit-wearing pioneers given to long, Prince Albert coats. He would serve as a fulcrum in the trials of Plenty Horses and the Culbertsons, because he would prosecute both cases.

Sterling was both typical of the professional on the plains at the end of the frontier and an exception whose life shows how quickly success could come to young men who went west to find fortune and fame.[34] Although scarcely twenty-eight years old in 1891, he was already a well-known figure throughout South Dakota. The state had about four hundred thousand residents then, and he was one of the most prominent.

Sterling was a product of the restlessness and ambition that drove nineteenth-century Americans from hearth and home, friends and family in the hope that greater prosperity lay just beyond the western horizon. "Hope, indeed, was the *sum totum* of our wealth—bounding, buoyant hope—and health!" wrote a friend of Sterling about those early years in Dakota Territory, before South Dakota was even a state. "Not much else did we possess."[35]

When Sterling moved with his parents, two brothers, and two sisters in 1881 from Dixon, Illinois, to the territory, the region was home to about one hundred thousand residents. He was only eighteen years old, but—a high school graduate at sixteen—he had already studied law and taught school in Dixon, where his grandfather had settled in the 1830s. Like Herbert Welsh, he was overwhelmed by his first sight of the limitless Dakota prairie—the waving, green flow of untrammeled land stretching to all horizons. He also was eager to lay claim to his family's share of it, to put it to plow and seed. It was soon done when the Sterlings settled on a farm near Huron, in the east-central part of what would be South Dakota. At that time Huron was only a collection of "weather beaten square-fronted stores, tar-paper covered shacks with one way roofs, sod houses, tents, wagon camps, saloons galore, no churches or schools, and streets hub deep in mud most of the time," according to a record left by an anonymous settler.[36]

People who knew Sterling during his first years in Dakota Territory recalled an amiable young man, with a constant smile, who was frequently seen around town with a group of friends. He spent the summer of 1881 working the family farm—a profession he would remember with pride in later years, saying, "There is no more useful or honorable calling among men."[37] But the hardship of that life is apparent between the lines of a speech he gave commemorating Dakota pioneers: "It is easy enough for the sanguine to say in their letters home, that our Beadle County soil was so rich that it needed but to be tickled with the hoe to laugh with an abundant harvest; but I will venture the assertion that the pioneers of Grant Township, found this tickling process anything but a holiday pastime."[38]

The difficulties of farm life may have contributed to his decision in September 1881 to take a job as a clerk in a Huron clothing store, earning thirty-five dollars a month. During the next year, he resumed studying law, this time with a local attorney. He also saved enough money to enroll in law school at the University of Wisconsin in Madison. The law program was supposed to take two years, but Sterling could afford only one. So he asked permission to crowd two years' work into twelve months. Although his professors thought it impossible that he could succeed, within the year he had finished with high honors. He then entered private practice in Huron, working with William T. Love, an attorney for the Chicago & Northwestern Railway Company.

Working for the railroad—which Sterling called "the greatest invention and blessing of modern times"[39]—gave the young attorney a place in one of the most powerful commercial interests of his time. In 1890 railroads were the nation's principal employer, with 749,000 workers,[40] and had created a vast new market for other industries, shaping U.S. commerce. Railways needed iron and steel for locomotives, cars, rails, bridges, and other equipment. They needed coal and wood for power. They changed the nature of agriculture, creating railheads to which cattlemen drove herds of livestock for shipment east and to which farmers brought crops. Towns and cities grew up around rail lines. The rail companies were also a bottomless source of jobs as they insatiably ate up manual laborers. Sterling was in a position to build a successful career at only twenty-one years old.

Love, a busy man with many businesses to attend to, turned over many of his practice's important assignments to Sterling. Working on a large share of Chicago & Northwestern's business affairs in territorial courts required Sterling to travel widely around the state, enlarging his circle of friends and contacts.

People found him easy to like. H. S. Mouser, an attorney who first met Sterling when the latter was a law student, said, "There are some people whose friendship, although they desire to be friendly with you, results in stirring up your nerves, but *his* friendship was restful as the touch of an *infinite calm*."[41] Another old friend said that knowing Sterling somehow gave his friends more respect for themselves.[42] He won a reputation for being loyal and generous, always willing to help out.

Sterling's skill at building social and professional contacts paid off while he was still young. In 1886 the Republican Party nominated him as a candidate for Beadle County district attorney, and he won. He was only twenty-three. Two years later he was reelected. Huron was the county seat for the district, so the number of cases passing through, including criminal cases, was large, giving the young lawyer wide experience.[43] He prepared for cases meticulously and usually covered his courtroom table with stacks of references to related cases.[44] He seldom lost a case, even though, as one colleague put it, he was "frequently pitted against the ablest and brightest attorneys of the territory."[45]

Although friends said that Sterling showed no evidence of desiring political power, he was an unabashed booster for the Republican Party. In a campaign speech during the 1888 presidential election, he drove home his high regard for the GOP: Between 1860 and 1885, "that grand party of noblemen had, by the sacrifice of precious lives, crushed out the greatest rebellion the world has ever known; and had preserved inviolate for you, for me and for countless generations unborn, the blessing of liberty enjoyed under the freest, most philanthropic and most beneficent Government, the world has ever known. . . . Its foreign and domestic policies were so wise that they caused an era of prosperity to thrill the Nation's pulse with health and vigor. Its policy concerning the public lands, was so just and liberal that hundreds and thousands flocked from the overcrowded cities, towns and farms of the East, to the broad and fertile acres of these Western prairies."[46]

Sterling's support for all things Republican caught the attention of politicians in Washington, D.C., and before 1889 came to a close, the newly elected president, Benjamin Harrison, named Sterling U.S. district attorney for South Dakota, making the twenty-six-year-old lawyer the youngest man ever appointed to a U.S. district attorney office up to that period. At about the same time, the Chicago & Northwestern Railway Company named him their attorney for the entire state.[47]

On January 7, 1891, the day Plenty Horses pulled the trigger on Lieutenant Edward Wanton Casey, Sterling was just short of his twenty-eighth birthday. Despite his busy schedule, he had found time in June 1890 to marry a woman who had been his childhood playmate: Olive Snow Underwood of Dixon, Illinois. The coupled lived in Huron near his family. He traveled frequently on business throughout the state—especially to the district courts in Pierre, Deadwood, and Sioux Falls. He had accumulated some debts, but his career was meteoric, and everyone expected him to reach the loftiest heights of politics and business.

Sterling must have believed that convicting Plenty Horses would be an easy matter. The young Lakota had spent five years in a government school, then had returned to the reservation, grown his hair long, painted his face, and fought U.S. soldiers. A white jury would see him as backward and hopeless. He shot Casey in the back of the head rather than face-to-face, assassinating a well-intentioned officer who for weeks had kept his own Indian troops from fighting the Lakota, who had gone to Plenty Horses' camp in peace. Sterling thought the shooting was inexcusable and cowardly.[48]

The same sentiment had been expressed by illustrator Frederic Remington in his eulogy of the dead officer, "Casey's Last Scout," in the January 31, 1891, issue of *Harper's Weekly*.[49] "A nasty little Brulé Sioux had made his *coup*," Remington wrote, "and shot away the life of a man who would have gained his stars in modern war as naturally as most of his fellows would their eagles. He had shot away the life of an accomplished man; the best friend the Indians had; a man who did not know 'fear;' a young man beloved by his comrades, respected by his generals and by the Secretary of War. The squaws of another race will sing the death-song of their benefactor, and woe to the Sioux if the Northern Cheyennes get a chance to *coup*!"

CHAPTER 10

A Fractured Life

FOR MANY OF THE TOWNSPEOPLE of Sioux Falls, South Dakota, the Plenty
Horses trial was a welcome distraction from the grind of frontier life. A practical farming town developed by businessmen expressly to make money, Sioux
Falls had not produced much in the way of local diversions—"In the West, a
man's goal was to get rich, not to exploit latent artistic abilities, to entertain or
to seek intellectual stimulation," wrote Sioux Falls historian Wayne Fanebust.[1]
Despite those shortcomings, the capitalist urge had created a town that had
grown from 2,500 residents in 1880 to more than 10,000 in 1890.[2] Around the
time of the Plenty Horses trial, Senator Richard Pettigrew was promoting
plans to create an industrial complex on the southern end of town, an area already being called South Sioux Falls in anticipation of the great boom that
would accompany the opening of such businesses as an axle-grease plant and
an oatmeal factory.[3] Town leaders also looked forward to other new industries
proposed by eastern investors who had bought 350 acres in South Sioux Falls,
doubtless with Pettigrew's urging.[4] As prices for land exploded, speculators
were laying out subdivisions on paper. Pettigrew, who had run the town's
horse-drawn streetcar line in the 1880s, opened an electric line in 1890, reaching out to the east side of town, which land speculators expected to grow
quickly. The leading local newspaper, the *Argus-Leader*, predicted the town
would boast 100,000 residents in no time at all.[5]

The town indeed was booming. The newspaper reported that county farmers were raising more than $100 million in crops.[6] Local granite quarries were
providing paving stones and building blocks for cities all over the nation.[7] The
town's thirty-two saloons were producing twenty thousand dollars yearly in
tax revenue. About a dozen Sioux Falls businessmen were making solid profits
from the Mint, the biggest and most opulent of the town's twenty or so gambling halls. Winning gamblers could retreat for the evening to Willowdale
Mansion, a prosperous brothel just west of town.

Sioux Falls also was mopping up money in another arena: quickie divorces. When South Dakota law set residency requirements for divorce proceedings at only ninety days, Sioux Falls became a mecca for the divorce trade, attracting clients from all over the world and supporting not only lawyers but hotels, restaurants, and housing rentals. More than four hundred marriages came to an end there between 1890 and September 1892 alone.

Despite some businesses of ill repute, Sioux Falls struggled to maintain an image of decorousness. Consequently, the town required homeless transients—called tramps and widely disdained and abused in late-nineteenth-century America—to register with the city clerk and pay a dollar for an identification tag to be worn around the neck. Failure to do so landed tramps in jail.

A crackdown on transients came on July 1, 1890, with enactment of an ordinance that defined a tramp as anyone ten years or older without a "calling or business to maintain himself."[8] For this crime of unemployment, even a ten-year-old could be sentenced to five days' solitary confinement and ten days' hard labor. And the city meant business: If the sheriff or a jailor took pity on a poor vagrant, letting him have tobacco, cards, newspapers, or other privileges allowed to most prisoners, the lawman could be fined $125.

On the other hand, the townspeople could see the positive side of an alleged murderer like Plenty Horses. With an eye always on community interests, the *Argus-Leader* did not fail to notice that his case as well as other court activities produced revenue. "The United States court is worth more to Sioux Falls than the capital is to Pierre," an unnamed official declared to one reporter. "Every day the court is in session, Uncle Sam pays out over $500 in witness and juror fees. So far during this session over $3,000 has been paid out to witnesses alone. Practically all of this money is spent here. A witness gets $2 per day for attendance and over three fourths of this is spent for board and incidentals. . . . Not only this but the court will grow more valuable as time goes on. The business will constantly grow and the sessions will be longer and longer. I want to commend the foresight of your Sioux Falls rustlers who slipped off with the United States court while the rest of the towns were fighting for the capital."[9]

In a town where entertainment was limited to drinking, gambling, and visiting the local zoo to see animals that had been captured on nearby prairies, a murder trial offered not just profits but also entertainment. "Everyone turned his attention to the act, the accused and his fate—particularly his fate," Fanebust wrote of trials held in prairie communities.

Crime, especially homicide, ignited community curiosity instantaneous with the discovery of the victim. Interest was heightened by apprehension of the accused. His arrest and incarceration were cheered. His trial was watched in the newspapers and in the courtroom, the later [*sic*] often became a circus of clamoring, curious onlookers. Trials frequently became spectacles, great sport for the common man.

All of this was but a prelude to the big event, an appetizer for the main course: the punishment. It was the climax, the fulfillment of public expectations, or sometimes the subject of deep disappointment. If the penalty was death, the impending execution attracted the attention of everyone as nothing else could. . . . People looked forward to the day of death and then turned out in droves to commemorate the destruction of a fellow human being and watch the hangman do his duty.

Sometimes the hanging came replete with food vendors, as at a carnival. The hangman's rope might even be cut up into small pieces to be sold as souvenirs.[10]

Crime certainly won its share of space in the newspapers covering Plenty Horses' trial. The *New York World* reported on a Jack-the-Ripper imitator who mangled a woman he killed in New York, an attempt by an army officer's wife while at a ball to stab a woman she thought was a rival for her husband's affections, a shoot-out and stabbing involving two jealous men in love with the same woman, a tragedy in which the wife of a destitute and unemployed man apparently burned herself and her three children to death in a suicide-murder, an abused wife killed when her drunken husband hit her on the head with a thrown brick ("Drink Made Him a Murderer" read the headline), and a soldier who apparently did not know what to do with himself when he was honorably discharged after twenty years of service and so overdosed on morphine, leaving a note that read, "Bury me where you please; nobody cares, I least of all." The *Argus-Leader* even reported lightly that three or four pairs of trousers belonging to the Sioux Falls chief of police had been stolen from his clothesline one night and that "the whole force [was] quietly working on the case."[11]

BY THE TIME THE OPPOSING parties were gathering in Sioux Falls to battle over Plenty Horses' fate, he was the talk of the town, although most of the talk

concerned how soon he would be hung. He was also a topic of discussion elsewhere. Before the trial, he received more than 150 letters of support, mostly
from the East.[12] His trial, reported the *New York World*,

> promises to be the most sensational case in the annals of border history.
> Among the Indians at Pine Ridge, Rosebud and Fort Keogh, the feeling over
> the matter has reached a fever heat, while the whites all over the West are even
> more deeply interested. The Winter lethargy was shaken off in this region as
> soon as the importance of the trial dawned on the little town. The dullness of a
> week ago is forgotten and an electrical change has come over the old sleepy
> condition of affairs. Every man interested in the town feels pleased to point to
> the Masonic block, where court is in session, and then explain with unfeigned
> pride that two United States District Judges, Edgerton and Shiras, were
> deemed necessary to sit at the trial of the Indian who killed the daring Casey.[13]

In response to the insatiable curiosity, a crayon portrait of Plenty Horses
appeared in the window of Lowry's drugstore.[14] But a much wider audience
than could be mustered on the streets of Sioux Falls longed for the Plenty
Horses story. The *New York World,* established in 1860 and owned since 1883
by Joseph Pulitzer, sought both to meet and to inflame that interest, sending
reporter J. J. McDonough to Sioux Falls.[15] When on April 24, 1891, McDonough became the first journalist to interview Plenty Horses after his arrest,
the Lakota was "confined in the rather humble brick annex to the imposing
county building, where he has fared much better than he would at any of the
agencies, although cornmeal mush is here the chief article on the bill of
fare."[16] McDonough found that "though he evidently regards all white men as
his natural enemies, it required very little persuasion to get him to talk for THE
WORLD." Plenty Horses spoke to him in halting English, as if afraid that he
might make a serious error in his speech, and sometimes used an interpreter.

McDonough described Plenty Horses as lost and pensive. "He stood back
from the iron door in the little cell and reflected fully five minutes before utter-
ing a word, presenting a picture simple, silent, sad—for he was alone in a
strange country, without a friend to cheer him or any one [*sic*] to whom he
could speak in confidence; a barbarian still in spite of a little education, the
only one of his band ever brought before a tribunal on a charge so serious.
There was something pathetic in the spectacle.

"He looked out of the tiny window that lets in an occasional ray of sunlight, folded his arms low under the faded blue blanket, standing so still that the silence was oppressive. He gave no sign that he was anxious about his fate; he spoke no word that he was being persecuted; made no plea that it was the act of another."

In depicting Plenty Horses, McDonough mixed that strange brew of admiration and condescension that marks the reporting of many journalists of the time when covering Indian activities. The young Brulé was athletic, about five feet ten inches tall in his moccasins, "with broad shoulders and deep chest," McDonough told his readers. "His face bears the stamp of a higher intelligence than one ordinarily sees among the Sioux, and when it lights up with a smile there is something of winning melancholy in the expression. . . . He is a very bright Indian, although there is in every word and action that peculiar desire of all Sioux to impress one with the idea that they find it difficult to comprehend your meaning."

Condemning Casey as a spy, Plenty Horses described how he had shot the officer. He added that the killing was justified and his arrest an injustice. "We were at war," he told McDonough, "and the Indian style of fighting to the bitter end is just as fair as the white man's. Besides, we were only fighting for our rights." But now he was in jail for doing what others had done in that brutal winter at Pine Ridge.

He took pains to explain to McDonough that the Lakota were brave warriors: "No man can say we are not fair fighters. The Sioux never laid in ambush to slaughter soldiers, but met them in open day and battled man to man." He blamed the fighting, and by implication his imprisonment, on the whites. "The white man came and we were his friend," he said, "until the time arrived when our people could no longer stand his treacherous ways of treating with them. I know all these things, for my forefathers have told the story in council and by the fireside. They report our people as fighters and it is true, for we have been driven to it."

HOWEVER INTERESTED PEOPLE BECAME IN Plenty Horses, much about him would remain unknown. Although no written record of his childhood exists, much about the accused man's younger days can be understood through

the autobiographical writings of Luther Standing Bear, a Brulé born about the
same time as Plenty Horses.[17]

Standing Bear remembered his childhood as idyllic. The Lakota, he recalled, lived in a "beautiful country. In the springtime and early summer, the
plains, as far as the eye could see, were covered with velvety green grass. Even
the rolling hills were green, and here and there was a pretty stream. Over the
hills roamed the buffalo and in the woods that bordered the streams were lus-
cious fruits that were ours for the picking. . . . Life was full of happiness and
contentment for my people."[18]

The Lakota lived directly off the wild species of a wild land. A basic
knowledge for doing so was shared by all Lakota, from Sitting Bull and Crazy
Horse to Luther Standing Bear and Plenty Horses, as were the tools of the
trade. Among the first gifts Standing Bear remembered receiving from his father were a bow and some arrows, all painted red to signify that his father had
been wounded in battle.[19] In those days of hunting and almost constant warfare, a boy grew up learning the importance of making good bows and arrows.
The short bow—never more than five feet long, making it efficient for stalking
through tall grass and for shooting from horseback—"was the one weapon
that preserved us from starvation and defeat, so it would have been unpardon-
able for a Sioux boy to grow up without knowledge of this useful article,"
wrote Standing Bear.[20] "It was with him at all hours, even at night. At the
slightest noise his hand was on the bow and arrow that lay by his side."[21] The
importance of the bow was so ingrained in the Lakota mind that when he was
in his sixties in the 1930s, Luther Standing Bear wrote, "Even today I like once
in a while to make a nice bow and to feather some pretty arrows." Like Standing Bear, Plenty Horses would have learned that the branches of cherry trees
made the best arrows, the wood of ash trees the best bows, and turkey feathers
the best fletching.[22]

Equally important was knowledge of horses, critical to the dangerous work
of war and hunting. "To ride side by side with the best hunters of the tribe, to
hear the terrible noise of the great herds as they ran, and then to help bring
home the kill was the most thrilling day of any Indian boy's life," wrote Standing Bear.[23]

Living Bear likely gave a pony to Plenty Horses as a youngster, just as
Luther Standing Bear's father matched him with a young horse before the boy

was big enough to mount on his own. From then on, Standing Bear trained constantly, he and the horse growing up together. By his teens, Standing Bear could charge into battle pressed against the side of the horse, firing arrows under its neck. If a horse fell while running at full tilt, Standing Bear, even if thrown clear, was supposed to remount by the time the horse was back on its feet. "Even if we were injured, it was part of our training never to stay down," wrote Standing Bear.[24] "It was not with the idea of doing 'fancy' riding, but the thought of safety first was always in our mind. There could be no more dangerous place for a hunter than to lose his horse in the midst of a buffalo herd."

The horse, too, received an education. "We trained our pony to walk or run right up to anything we wanted him to," recalled Standing Bear.[25] "We picked out a good-size bush, shrub, or trunk of a tree. Our pony was trained to run up as close as he could to the object without dodging. Our pony must learn to go wherever he was told. Even if there was shooting, yelling, and great noise and much confusion, a well-trained pony would go anywhere he was told to go by his rider. So boy and pony trained together for warfare."

Standing Bear was only eight years old when he plunged for the first time into a herd of bison, one of the most important trials of his life. He left behind an eloquent account of his earliest buffalo hunt.

> Soon I was mixed up in the dust and could see nothing ahead of me. All I could hear was the roar and rattle of the hoofs of the buffalo as they thundered along. My pony shied this way and that, and I had to hold on for dear life. For a time I did not even try to pull an arrow from my quiver, as I had all I could do to take care of myself. I knew if my pony went down and one of those big animals stepped on me, it would be my last day on earth. I then realized how helpless I was there in all that dust and confusion, with those ponderous buffalo all around me. The sound of their hoofs was frightening. My pony ran like the wind, while I just clung to her mane; but presently we came out of the dust. . . . When I looked at those big animals and thought of trying to kill one of them, I realized how small I was. I was really afraid of them. Then I thought about what my stepmother had said about bringing her a kidney and a skin, and the feeling that I was a man, after all, came back to me; so I turned my pony toward the bunch which was running north. There was no dust now, and I knew where I was going.[26]

Buffalo gave the Lakota more than meat. The Indians tanned hides for tepees, clothing, and carrying bags. Untanned hides, which dried hard like
wood, were used for bowls and drumheads. Water and hot stones were put into
empty bison stomachs, suspended on tripods, to boil meat. Bones were used
for tools. Horns could be made into utensils such as spoons or into weapons
such as war clubs.

The buffalo was the basis of life for nomadic Plains Indians, but the Lakota
also hunted other animals: elk, deer, pronghorn. "The hide of the elk is very
strong, so we used it for wearing apparel, such as moccasins or leggings, but
never for tipis," wrote Standing Bear. "Deer hide when tanned is soft and pli-
able and also durable enough for tipis. Because of its pliability, deer hide was
used mostly for women's and children's dresses, being white and soft as a vel-
vet fabric. However, the elk provided teeth for decoration on the clothing.
From every elk we saved two teeth and used these on dresses and shirts long
before the Elk Clubman used them for a watch-charm. A woman who could
afford a dress trimmed with elk teeth was considered very beautifully and ex-
pensively dressed."[27]

The Lakota also were expert in prairie plant life, from roots to berries. The
cottonwood, according to Luther Standing Bear, was the most useful of all
trees. The Lakota used its bark for fires in which coals were needed and for
tanning hides.[28] Children chewed the thin, juicy, and sweet layer just under the
bark. The Lakota used the wood for ceremonial objects, such as the central
tree in a sun dance; for saddle frames, which they covered with bison hide; and
for toys, such as dolls and spinning tops. In winter they cut down the trees so
ponies could feed on the bark, leaving behind the wood used to warm the tepees. They filled pillows with fleecy cottonwood seeds. Remembering in later
years the plants and animals that had so abounded on the plains, Standing Bear
wrote, "It seemed that everywhere we went there was food waiting for us. In
those days the Indian led a happy life."

If Plenty Horses did experience that happy life, it came suddenly to an end
for him, just as it did for Luther Standing Bear. When Plenty Horses was about
fourteen years old, and Luther Standing Bear about eleven, they were sent off
to live at a federal school for Indians in Carlisle, Pennsylvania. Standing Bear
in his later years would recall the day he left the reservation: "These are all
glad memories that I have told you, but I have one sad memory and that was
when I went away to Carlisle School and had to leave my little pony behind. I

still remember how sad I was because I could not take him with me. . . . I was only a little boy of eleven and the first part of the journey was fifty miles away from home, where we got the boat that was to take us to the railroad station. I rode my pony for that fifty miles and there had to say good-bye, for I was going East and thought at that time that I would never be back."[29]

The Carlisle school, which stood in the vanguard of the movement to transform Indian children into farmers and factory workers, was founded by a former military officer, Richard Henry Pratt, in the late 1870s. By then the predominant Indian rights advocates believed that all Indians were doomed unless they learned to live in family units and work at regular jobs. Pratt was a top proponent of this approach, and he bluntly said that the goal of those who wanted to "civilize" the Indian was cultural extinction, or, as he put it, to "kill the Indian [and] save the man."[30]

The idea that the nomadic, bison-hunting Lakota could be "saved" by forging them into laborers and farmers was officially espoused as early as 1851 by Superintendent of Indian Affairs D. D. Mitchell after he attended treaty talks at Fort Laramie, Wyoming. In his report on the event he wrote: "Humanity calls loudly for some interposition on the part of the American government to save, if possible, some portion of these ill-fated tribes; and this, it is thought, can only be done by furnishing them with the means, and gradually turning their attention to agricultural pursuits. . . . Fifty years it was thought would be time sufficient to give the experiment a fair trial, and solve the great problem whether or not an Indian can be made a civilized man."[31]

Richard Henry Pratt was in a position to carry out such ideas. In 1875 he was a thirty-five-year-old army lieutenant in Indian Territory assigned to escort a group of seventy-three Cheyenne Indian prisoners by train to Fort Marion, Florida, where they would be jailed for three years for their part in frontier warfare. On the way he was disgusted by local people who peered into carriage windows to gawk at the Indians during station stops. Pratt had worked with Indian scouts of various tribes, including Cherokee who had been educated in tribal schools and whose "intelligence, civilization and common sense was a revelation" to him. Watching how his prisoners were treated, he concluded that somehow "we must get [the Indians] out of the curio class."[32]

At Fort Marion, he required the Indian men to cut their long hair and wear army uniforms. The warriors opposed these measures, but within a few months they had done a complete turnaround, taking pride in their new look.

They adapted to Pratt's ways and by 1876 were making a living by selling polished seashells for the tourist trade. "They have polished 10,000 seabeans for curio dealers," Pratt reported to the War Department. "They have made canes, bows and arrows and painted fans. They have glutted the market."[33] Apparently the prisoners were pleased with their new lives: At the end of their sentence they asked to send for their families and live in the East, rather than return to Indian Territory. "We want our wives and children to come," they said, according to Pratt's account. "Then we will go any place and settle down and learn to support ourselves as the white men do."[34]

The Indian Bureau did not like the plan but in the end agreed to let twenty-two of the younger Cheyenne stay in the East as long as it cost the government nothing. Pratt found a place for seventeen of the former warriors at the Institute for Freedmen (also called the Hampton School) in Hampton, Virginia, created originally to educate African-Americans. The other five men were sent to live in private homes.

The popular press soon latched on to Pratt's story. A scribe of no less stature than Harriet Beecher Stowe—author of *Uncle Tom's Cabin*, the book Abraham Lincoln only half jokingly credited with starting the Civil War—published a magazine article about Pratt and the Cheyenne. Within short order, Indian rights advocates were suggesting that Pratt, too, go to Hampton to teach Indians. Instead, Pratt set out to start his own school, talking with various Washington bureaucrats and political appointees about his plan. General Sherman advised him to open his school out west, but Pratt was determined to locate it in the East, where the students could be isolated from their native land and people. "To civilize the Indian, put him in the midst of civilization," Pratt said. "To keep him civilized, keep him there." Still a military officer, Pratt soon found himself also headmaster of a school housed in an old army barracks in south-central Pennsylvania. He opened the school in October 1879 with eighty-four boys and girls from the Lakota tribes and fifty-two from Indian Territory. Among his first teachers were Cheyenne from Fort Marion. Among his first students was Luther Standing Bear.

Pratt ran his school with military discipline. Students were required to wear uniforms and to cut their hair. Cutting the hair was onerous to the Lakota, for whom short hair was a sign of mourning. Even their names were changed. The first word of a student's name would be combined with his or her father's name to create a new, presumably "whiter," name, since the father's name functioned as a surname. Thus, Plenty Horses became Plenty Living Bear.[35]

For the Lakota, this loss of name must have cut deeply, because names were not bestowed lightly. In the Carlisle school's weekly newsletter, the *Indian Helper*, a Lakota girl described the pains the Lakota took in naming their children.

> When a child is born it is not immediately named, and when it is, it is named after an ancestor—a grandfather or grandmother or grand aunt or some other relative. If not named as above it is named whatever the father or mother or uncle wants to name it. It is mostly the father or uncle of the child who names it. Whenever a great or good thing has been done or a brave act performed the child is named by the action, the name meaning whatever the deed has been done [*sic*] by the father or uncle, or grandfather. . . . The child is taken to the sun-dance and dressed very gay and fine in beads and red paint and highly trimmed moccasins, and oftentimes with a buckskin dress with beautiful designs made with beads of different colors. Taken then by the parents the father [*sic*] of the child brings three or four ponies and rides around the camps. He prepares a feast for the people. The feast consists of meat and bread and soup of some kind. And then the child is taken by the old chief who talks awhile and tells the people the name of the child and why it has been given this name. This is the way the Sioux name their children.[36]

All students were crippled socially by the ban on speaking their native tongue. The ban was strictly enforced. Pratt would whip infracting students with a leather strap. Carlisle gave Lakota children, whose parents never struck them, their first experience with corporal punishment. Other punishments were applied, too. Boys who got into fights or were caught drinking might be locked in a guardhouse. One boy who tried to sneak food out of the cafeteria was made to stand on a chair in the middle of the room during dinner, and a girl who wet her bed was ordered to carry her mattress wherever she went for a day. Those who could not take this treatment might try to run away—children under the age of ten tried walking cross-country or hopping trains to get home. Two girls attempted to burn down their dormitory and ended up in the Pennsylvania women's prison.[37]

So many students died of disease while at the school that Lakota parents often believed they would never see their offspring again after sending them away. However, as reservation agents sometimes threatened to withhold rations if a certain number of children were not sent, parents felt compelled to deliver at least portions of their broods.

Carlisle and other boarding schools were not all bad for all students. Girls learned sewing, housekeeping, and laundering, boys farming, carpentry, and printing, among other trades. They also participated in school athletics. Jim Thorpe, from Indian Territory, was a Carlisle athlete who went on to win Olympic medals and to become a top-notch football and baseball player. Charles Eastman attended schools in Wisconsin, where, he wrote in his autobiography, "my eyes were opened intelligently to the greatness of Christian civilization, the ideal civilization, as it unfolded itself before my eyes." He went on to medical school at Dartmouth before going to the Pine Ridge reservation to treat his fellow Indians.[38]

But Carlisle was not a success for students like Plenty Horses who later went back to the reservation. "Five years I attended Carlisle and was educated in the ways of the white man," he told a reporter. "When I returned to my people, I was an outcast among them. I was no longer an Indian."[39]

No better-informed voice could have supported Plenty Horses' view than that of Charles Eastman. Speaking to the Congregational Club in Chicago in early 1891, he sympathized with Indians in Plenty Horses' predicament. "If you were to send me back to the reservation, and make me stay there with nothing to do, I think I would go back to the old form of life," he said. "I would take up my blanket like my ancestors. What is wanted for the graduates from the Indian schools is work, not money. If they don't get work they naturally sink back into their old manner of living. The young Indians are taught to make shoes, to do carpenter work and tailoring, and then they are sent back to the reservation, where they have little, if any, chance to put their knowledge into practical use."[40]

While traveling the West, writer and artist Frederic Remington met graduates of the Carlisle school who recently had completed enlistments as military scouts, and he also agreed with Plenty Horses' assessment: "I talked with some Carlisle school-boys who had lately been discharged from the corps in order to make room for others of the tribe, and they were full of regrets, as they had liked soldiering, and now had nothing to do but draw rations at the agency. They were very bright young fellows, fairly educated, and each had a trade, I

Dr. Charles Eastman, a Dakota Indian, attended U.S. schools to become a medical doctor and an advocate for Indian education. He helped collect the dead at Wounded Knee in January 1891. (*The Sophia Smith Collection, Women's History Archive, Smith College*)

believe. There was no possible way for them to earn a living. They were not allowed off the reservation, and so they must sit calmly down and do nothing. Idleness is fully as bad for an Indian as a white man, and is always the godfather of folly and crime."[41]

Carlisle officials admitted the problem in the pages of the *Indian Helper*. The June 18, 1891, issue reported: "Citizens of Norfolk, Nebr., protest against the employment of Indians in the beet fields at that place, on the ground that the Indian is a foreigner. The reports that some of the Indian boys from the school at Genoa were to be employed, was the cause of a meeting in which a set of resolutions were drawn up declaring it detrimental to the interests of the country to give the Indian work."[42] With perhaps false bravado, the newsletter writer added: "Carlisle can find employment for a THOUSAND Indian boys immediately in this Eastern country at good wages. The Indians are WANTED here, on account of their true worth."

Plenty Horses, however, went back to a reservation in the West. He had been trained as a farmer, an occupation seen as the most promising for Indian boys. He had arrived at the school on November 14, 1883, as a fourteen-year-old standing five feet tall and weighing only ninety-four pounds.[43] He had had no previous schooling, so he was enrolled in the first grade. When released in 1888, he was in the fourth grade but had spent nearly three of his four years at Carlisle in the "outing" program, in which students were sent to work on farms, in print shops, and so on. In 1890, for example, Pratt reported that more than five hundred students served in the outing program, earning an aggregate of fifteen thousand dollars, which apparently they were permitted to keep.[44] Plenty Horses was outed to farms in Bucks County, Pennsylvania.

Although Pratt claimed with pride that few students returned to the old way of life when back on the reservation, Pratt's figures are suspect. He tended to shut his eyes when students did things he did not like. No example of this practice is better than Pratt's response to inquiries about Plenty Horses after the Casey shooting. In the Carlisle school publication, the *Red Man,* Pratt reported that a Chicago newspaper had suggested that Casey's killer—whom the paper erroneously identified as the son of No Water—had been a Carlisle student. Pratt responded that No Water's son had never attended the school, which was technically correct but evaded the fact that Plenty Horses, though no son of No Water, nevertheless was a Carlisle man.[45]

WHEN THE PLENTY HORSES TRIAL opened at 9:45 a.m. on Friday, April 24, 1891, the street outside the courthouse thronged with women dressed to the nines in colorful finery and with "rough and hardy frontiersmen, with broad-brimmed slouch hats and revolver belts."[46] All wanted into the courtroom, which had, for Sioux Fallsians, become the center of the universe. Few were motivated by interest in justice or in a legal inquiry. The citizenry was incensed against Plenty Horses and eager for revenge. "Everybody is talking about the Casey tragedy and the opinion that the prisoner will be hanged is unanimous," reported the *New York World.* "The situation, as the poplar [*sic*] mind views it, is this: 'A white man has been murdered by an Indian. The Indian must be hanged.' "[47]

Witnesses had been filtering into Sioux Falls for days, and the Indians among them drew particular interest as they paraded down the street, led by a U.S. marshal. Among them was Broken Arm, a broad-faced, middle-aged man who parted his long hair in the middle and highlighted his suit with a kerchief at his throat. He had ridden with Plenty Horses the day of the killing and witnessed Casey's death. Jack Red Cloud, the son of old Red Cloud, was there as well, decked out in a fine suit. Always grasping for acclaim—throughout his life he would long for the mantle of his father, but it would never fall on his shoulders—he had declared at one time that he, too, had seen the lieutenant killed, but in town, the courthouse looming near, he denied this and offered no recorded explanation for either his original statement or his retraction.

While Plenty Horses was languishing in jail—he would grow paler and thinner throughout the course of the trial—his comrades from the reservation stayed in a hotel. One morning they entertained themselves by going to see the seventeen buffalo penned in the park on the edge of town. Broken Arm and another witness, He Dog, climbed into the enclosure with the bison and tried to hug the animals, which warned them off with threatening shakes of their horned heads. The Lakota nevertheless ran around in the enclosure, and the bison watched them warily—"as though dazed at the proceedings," wrote one observer.[48]

A singular distraught figure caught the town's attention—an older man, "as fine a specimen of the Sioux Indian as one could find," neither tall nor stout but athletic.[49] This outstanding individual was Living Bear, Plenty Horses' father. Once he was in town, Plenty Horses' stoic but dour demeanor relaxed a little, and he allowed himself a few rare smiles, according to one observer, even "on occasions when an ordinary person in his position would at least pretend to be serious. This is understood to be the Indian way of expressing entire satisfaction with the proceedings."[50] When father and son first met in Sioux Falls, they embraced, and although Plenty Horses, as vaguely described in the *New York World*, remained as "unmoved as though he were a statute of bronze," his father revealed "that deep affection Indians always show for their offspring." Plenty Horses, according to the newspaper's cryptic account, "partially gave way to his emotions" when his father had to leave him.[51]

Throughout the trial, at the end of each session, Living Bear, head bowed and eyes lowered, would follow his son and two escorting deputies back to jail. When the door closed behind Plenty Horses at the jail steps, Living Bear would stand and gaze at the spot where he had last seen his son, then walk to his hotel. In the morning or after the lunch break, the first thing the deputies saw when they stepped outside was Living Bear, waiting for them, "and thus he goes on day in and day out, without a murmur of discontent, solemn, silent, sad."[52]

Chief among the frontiersmen who drew the public's attention was Philip Wells, a scout and interpreter from Pine Ridge who had been in the thick of the opening fire at Wounded Knee. He wore his hair cut close and his mustache waxed to hold it straight out, extending past his jawline. In hand-to-hand combat at Wounded Knee, a Lakota warrior had slashed Wells's nose, cutting it from the bridge to his lip and leaving it hanging by the skin. After shooting and killing the warrior, Wells left the battle hastily, found a doctor, had his nose plastered into place, and returned to the fight. The next day he joined the fray at the Drexel Mission battle, in which Plenty Horses also had taken up arms. By the time of the trial, Wells's nose had healed but was scarred. He was to serve the court as a witness and as a translator for Lakota participants. Another translator would handle the Cheyenne witnesses, such as Casey's scout White Moon, who spoke little or no English.

The trial was staged in a room warmed by the prairie spring and by a sweltering horde of humanity eager to see the goings-on. For them, the trial may have served as entertainment, but for Plenty Horses' as-yet-unpaid attorneys, George Nock and David Edward Powers, it was a fight to save the Brulé's life. As the *Argus-Leader* put it: "There is no such think [*sic*] as life imprisonment for murder, under the United States statutes. The jury can only acquit, convict for murder, and hang the defendant, or convict of manslaughter."

Those with an opinion about the trial and about Plenty Horses' innocence or guilt divided into two uneven camps.[53] The larger one held that Plenty Horses was an assassin who had shaken Casey's hand, talked with him as a friend, and then shot him from behind. This group believed Plenty Horses should hang. The other side, which at the outset of the trial was probably a tiny minority, believed Plenty Horses was a troubled young man driven to distraction by the ghost dance and by events surrounding and including Wounded Knee, where, according to newspaper accounts, he had lost a cousin. Casey, they believed, had threatened verbally to attack the camp in which Plenty Horses was living, and the young man had done what any soldier would do to a threatening enemy. This argument, however, was weak because only Plenty Horses had heard the alleged threat.

The pro–Plenty Horses camp nevertheless did have a couple of things working in its favor. One was the defendant's demeanor, the controlled calm of a man facing death with courage, a stoicism that the press portrayed with open admiration. He may not have killed bravely, but apparently he knew how to die bravely. Another was the pathetic look of the young Indian, dressed in his cheap shirt and pants and wrapped up in the weathered blue blanket he had been wearing when he shot Casey. Pitifully, he made an effort to conceal his left hand, from which he was missing fingers. In every photo taken of Plenty Horses at the time of the trial, his left hand is hidden, as if he were determined to conceal his flaws. The *New York World* reported that Plenty Horses in court "looked rather lonesome there, and, though he pretended that it was all satisfactory, it did look severe to see the semi-savage on trial before a court which he did not understand and under laws the nature of which he was not able to comprehend. He knew not whether the defense was properly conducted, or even whether it was conducted at all, but contentedly he bowed to the governing power and made a show of satisfaction."[54]

Plenty Horses' conduct in court may have turned a few heads, but it provided no legal defense. For that, his lawyers had only a single arrow in their quiver: They had to prove that on the day Plenty Horses shot Lieutenant Casey, the Lakota nation was at war with the United States and, therefore, the killing of Casey was not murder but just another wartime slaying. Given the battle of Wounded Knee and the subsequent fights, as well as the huge military buildup on the reservations, the idea that the reservations were at war seems a given, and yet opinions differed sharply on this point.

It almost goes without saying that Plenty Horses believed that what he had done was a guiltless act of war. After the ghost dancers had surrendered, neither he nor any other Lakota had thought he would be arrested for murder. In an interview with the *New York World* reporter, published also in the *Argus-Leader*, he said of the shooting: "I do not deny that Lieutenant Casey came to his death at my hands, and whatever the fate the court decrees I am ready and willing to suffer. He was killed, yes; but not murdered, and I shall go to my grave in that opinion."[55] He also made the point that would be central to the defense strategy. "We were at war with the whites. If we had sent a spy into their camp with the expressed intention of getting points to use against them for an attack, they would not have hesitated to kill him if captured."[56]

It is not surprising that among those who agreed with Plenty Horses' position was Red Cloud, who said that though the killing was an unfortunate act of war, it was not murder. But Plenty Horses also had an unexpected ally: General Nelson Miles. Richard Henry Pratt wrote in the February–March 1891 issue of the *Red Man* that "General Miles is reported to have said that if any of the ghost dancers had come as near to the military camps as Lieut. Casey went to the ghost dancers' camps, they would have been justifiably shot."[57]

Plenty Horses alluded to another issue in the subtext of his trial. "If they are going to punish every man who shot another when not engaged in actual fighting, then why not arrest the soldiers who killed poor old Big Foot? He was lying before his tepee dying of fever, unable to raise his hand, and yet a dozen bullets were fired into his body. And look at the six Indians found long after the battle—one man and the rest women and children, all shot down within eight miles of Pine Ridge by scouts or soldiers! Why not investigate that? I suppose they say it can't be done, but it can. There are many similar cases to mine. We were at war."

Here, Plenty Horses introduced a theme that would crop up in subsequent newspaper coverage of his trial. Why not arrest the soldiers? And if Plenty Horses were convicted, would the soldiers, or at least the officers in charge, be arrested for murder? Or at least investigated as potential murderers? Especially vulnerable on these charges, as Plenty Horses pointed out, were the soldiers who on horseback had ridden down fleeing women and children and killed them even miles from the battle.

BY APRIL 1891 GENERAL MILES had in fact already investigated the events at Wounded Knee.[58] He wanted to hold Colonel James Forsyth responsible for botching the disarming of Sitanka's warriors and particularly for disobeying Miles's order that the colonel avoid mixing soldiers with the Indians during any action. This disobedience, Miles believed, reflected badly on himself.[59]

Miles also contended that Forsyth's deployment of troops among the Indians would have disgraced even a second lieutenant fresh out of officer's training. The colonel had had 500 troops against the Lakota's 100 warriors, who were encumbered with about 250 women and children. He should have been in complete control if he possessed any measure of military competence.

After removing Forsyth from command, Miles put Captain Frank Baldwin—for many years a Miles ally—and Inspector General Jacob Ford Kent of the Missouri Division in charge of an investigation into the Forsyth case. Their report would move up official channels to Washington, D.C., making recommendations for Forsyth's punishment. In Washington, the military took a mere measured view of Wounded Knee. The retired but still influential Civil War general William Tecumseh Sherman, to whose niece Mary General Miles was wed, told Miles via a letter written to Mary on January 7, "If Forsyth was relieved because some squaw was killed, somebody has made a mistake, for squaws have been killed in every Indian war." To Miles directly he said in regard to Wounded Knee, "Say little and write less."[60]

Baldwin and Kent examined the troop deployments that so rankled Miles, but Forsyth's junior officers offered only measured criticism of their colonel's actions, contending that if none of them had foreseen a fight, they could not hold their commander accountable for failing to do so. When Baldwin and Kent investigated the killing of women and children, the junior officers maintained that smoke and confusion had led to the unfortunate deaths. The two investigators on January 13, 1891, gave Forsyth only a slap on the wrist, censuring him for his troop deployments and dropping all other charges. Kent called the situation at Wounded Knee "unavoidable and unfortunate," but nothing more.

Miles, outraged, three days later ordered the case reopened. The investigators were assigned specifically to determine whether Forsyth had disobeyed Miles's order about mingling. Kent still sided with Forsyth, reporting, "It seems impossible to me that he could then calculate that the Indians would deliberately plan their own destruction."[61] In effect, he was blaming the Indians for being slaughtered.

This time Baldwin harshly concluded that Forsyth had "entirely disregarded" Miles's order about keeping the troops separate from the Indians. Miles heartily agreed with the tougher judgment, writing in his endorsement that Forsyth had left Miles's order "unheeded and disregarded" and concluding, "It is in fact difficult to conceive how a worse disposition of troops could have been made." He also wrote of Forsyth to the adjutant general, "I have no hesitation in saying, that I would not jeopardize the lives of officers and men in the hands of such an officer."

But Miles's superiors, including the secretary of war, wanted Wounded Knee to vanish into the past and be forgotten. They put Forsyth back in command, ignoring Miles's recommendation for a court-martial. At the time of Plenty Horses' trial, however, Miles was still not willing to drop the issue of Wounded Knee and Forsyth's culpability, although his interest was primarily in Forsyth's failure to follow an order rather than in punishing mortal crimes.

The killing of fleeing women and children at Wounded Knee had more in common with the charges against Plenty Horses than did the exchange of fire between soldiers and warriors, and Miles did not neglect this issue. During the Wounded Knee inquiry, Miles had Baldwin investigate the shooting of a Lakota woman, two Lakota girls (ages seven and eight), and one boy (about ten years old) whose bodies had been found together about three miles west of the Wounded Knee battle site on the day of the battle. The Seventh Cavalry officer who had tracked down these Indians testified at the Forsyth hearings that his men had fired on the group when they were hidden in shrubs, fearing they were warriors, and had hit them randomly but fatally. Baldwin, however, examined the bodies and reported that "each person had been shot once, the character of which was necessarily fatal in each case. . . . The shooting was done at so close a range that the person or clothing of each person was powder burned."[62] If any outright murder occurred because of Wounded Knee, this killing of four people was it. But this issue, too, was swept under the rug, and no punishment was meted out. Perhaps the case would be reopened in a future investigation, if Miles were able to initiate one, but if Plenty Horses were found innocent, justice for these four dead, as well as others, would be impossible to achieve.

Miles's effectiveness in reopening the investigation could have been enhanced by the Plenty Horses trial. If Casey's killer were found guilty of murder, Indian rights groups certainly would raise the issue of murder at Wounded Knee. Miles could use the groups' outcry as a wedge for pressing further charges. On the other hand, he might see murder charges at Wounded Knee as a blemish on his record and seek instead to clear the soldiers of any guilt. It is doubtful anyone feared that either the army as a whole or individual soldiers would face prosecution, but everyone also knew that if Plenty Horses were held accountable for killing Casey, his guilty verdict would raise the specter of culpability for the army.

In addition to establishing that the reservations had been at war during the shooting, Plenty Horses' attorneys had one other potential means for winning acquittal. If they could show that Plenty Horses' motive in killing Casey was self-defense—or, an even larger cause, the defense of the Indian camp with its women and children—then the jury might let him go home unharmed. Unfortunately, although Plenty Horses did tell the grand jury in Deadwood that he had shot Casey to protect the camp, he also added another rationale: "I shot the lieutenant so I might make a place for myself among my people. I am now one of them." He knew the whites would make him pay, but he did not care. "I shall be hung," he had said, "and the Indians will bury me as a warrior. They will be proud of me. I am satisfied."[63]

IF SHOOTING HIS ENEMY IN the back of the head, instead of bravely charging him head-on, was a far cry from Lakota concepts of warfare and bravely, the killing itself was not. In fact, winning prestige through homicide was a well-traveled road in Lakota culture. Leaders among the Lakota gained status in part—and it was a large part—by fighting and killing enemies, actions that demonstrated bravery and fortitude, not to mention skill in the art of death, a form of prowess highly regarded by the Lakota and necessary to their survival. All the great chiefs took lives. Red Cloud and Spotted Tail won their status in part by taking more than one hundred lives apiece. Red Cloud could be ruthless in battle. He once led an attack on peaceful Arapaho, killing all the men but letting the women and children go. In another fight he charged into a river to capture an enemy on the verge of drowning. He dragged his opponent out of the water by the hair and scalped him as soon as they reached shore.[64]

Sitting Bull, one of the greatest Lakota chiefs of the nineteenth century, first won acclaim when, at fourteen, he chased down a mounted Crow Indian and struck him with a war club, knocking him from his horse.[65] Soon his renown in battle was so great that enemies could be thrown off their game when he simply shouted out to them, *"Tatanka Iyotanka he miye,"* which means "I am Sitting Bull."[66] His horse was famous too, so fast that it generally carried him ahead of all others into battle. Crazy Horse, whom the Lakota considered their finest warrior-chief of the mid-1800s, also aimed always to be in the lead when attacking enemies.[67] He was only sixteen when he faced two Arapaho in battle and killed them both, launching his career as a great warrior.[68] Killing breathed prestige into a man's life.

Killing in the name of status was not always reserved for warfare. Red Cloud won prestige early among the Oglala after he helped kill an arrogant and troublesome chief named Bull Bear.[69] Within Lakota society, Plenty Horses' assassination of Lieutenant Casey, although without valor, was still not a criminal act. It fell within the acceptable bounds of taking enemy life.[70]

However, killing by itself was not a point of pride. The real issue was bravery, a cardinal virtue among the Lakota, who relished courageous deeds and
were constantly looking for new ways to exhibit their boldness. For example,
during a battle with the army in the 1870s a younger warrior mocked Sitting
Bull, then nearing his forties, for keeping back from enemy fire. Sitting Bull
promptly awed his war party by sitting down on a hillside in full view of enemy soldiers and calmly smoking a pipe—twice—while bullets slapped the
ground around him, a demonstration that one of his fellow Lakota called "the
bravest deed possible."[71]

A warrior did not even have to kill to gain status in war. Counting coup,
which involved performing specific acts of bravery, such as touching the enemy, alive or dead, rather than shooting him from a distance, was among the
more respected acts of bravery and honor. Lakota warriors exhibited their
coups by displays of ornamentation, like U.S. soldiers wearing medals. In battle, the first warrior to touch an enemy—with his hand, a bow, lance, whip,
rattle, or other item—won the right to wear a golden eagle feather upright on
the back of his head.[72] The second to count coup wore an eagle feather tilted to
the right. The third wore the feather horizontally, and the fourth wore a vul-
ture feather vertically.

Coups could be won in other ways, too. Killing an enemy in hand-to-hand
combat was coup-worthy, winning the warrior the right to paint a red hand on
his clothing and on his horse. "Saving a friend in battle entitled a man to paint
a cross on his clothing, and if the benefactor rode his friend to safety on the
back of his horse, he might wear a double cross," anthropologist Royal Hassrick reported in his 1964 book, *The Sioux: Life and Customs of a Warrior Society*, perhaps the best description of traditional Lakota culture during its peak
years, from 1830 to 1870.[73]

"Coups might be indicated by painting vertical stripes on leggings; red
stripes indicated that the wearer had been wounded," wrote Hassrick. "Coup
feathers dyed red also signified wounds; notched feathers showed the owner's
horse to have been wounded. Scouts successful in sighting an enemy were
awarded coups. A black feather ripped down the center with the tip remaining
was their badge."[74]

Warriors won coup points for stealing horses, an act of bravery that also
brought material wealth. A warrior showed how many horses he had taken by
painting hoofprints on a coup feather or on his leggings or even on his horse,

with the color of the print matching the color of the stolen horse. If a man captured ten horses, he was entitled to wear a miniature rope and moccasin on his belt. If less than ten, just the rope.[75]

With coups came bragging rights, which the Lakota warrior was quick to claim, taking every opportunity to boast about his own exploits and to mock the less successful or less aggressive. Boasting was a sign of success. "Humility for the Sioux was an indication of stupidity, evidence of a deficiency of personal conviction," Hassrick observed.[76]

Whatever Plenty Horses' intention in shooting Casey, the act fell short of the Lakota standard for bravery. In the world of his own culture, Plenty Horses had lost his way, and in his attempt to win a place for himself there, he had blundered. Nevertheless, the defense might be able to win acquittal with Plenty Horses' claim that he had shot Casey to protect the camp.

CHAPTER 11

On Trial

THE FIRST DAY OF THE trial, the witnesses walked from their lodging at the brick, three-story Merchants Hotel to the courthouse in the Masonic Building, an imposing structure built of stone probably from the local quarry and topped with a clock tower that may have been the tallest structure in town. A heavy, ponderous edifice that filled almost half a city block, the building faced wagon-rutted dirt streets but was fronted with clean wooden sidewalks.[1]

The presiding judges were Civil War veteran Oliver Shiras, on loan from the Iowa federal district court, and South Dakotan Alonzo J. Edgerton, who also had presided at Plenty Horses' grand jury hearing. Edgerton was a civic-minded politico who recently had turned down an opportunity to run for the Senate.[2] The two judges looked out over a packed courtroom. Bevies of brightly dressed women were given priority seating. Men stood at the edges of the room or sat on windowsills. In the front of the courtroom sat Plenty Horses, a red silk kerchief around his neck. Behind him sat the Lakota witnesses, most of them in three-piece suits and boots or shoes. Jack Red Cloud, his long hair parted on the right, wore a gold watch chain on his vest and dangling metal earrings similar to a pair worn by Plenty Horses. Living Bear wore striped slacks and beaded moccasins with his dark jacket and vest. Least dapper of all was Plenty Horses in worn shirt and slacks and tasseled moccasins.

Beside Plenty Horses were Nock and Powers, who were working without pay but in the hope that the Indian Rights Association eventually would cover their costs, including a trip to Pine Ridge by Powers to study the crime scene and ferret out witnesses. Both attorneys wore their hair cropped short, pomaded to their scalps and parted high on their heads with mustaches that would have done a walrus proud. Like prosecutor William Sterling, they wore conservative suits, including frock coats that reached almost to the knee.

Sterling's round face, with prominent nose and sloping chin, looked distinctly twentieth century because he lacked a mustache and combed his hair

The Merchants Hotel in Sioux Falls, South Dakota, provided rooms for participants in the Plenty Horses trial. *(Courtesy of the Siouxland Heritage Museums, Sioux Falls, South Dakota)*

back, parting it low at the side. His assistant in the prosecution, an army captain named J. G. Ballance, made up for Sterling's more futuristic style. With receding hairline and full beard, he looked as if he had just stepped off a box of Smith Brothers cough drops.

The first day of the trial was devoted primarily to jury selection, which was not completed until 4 p.m. Nock and Powers sought to place eastern men on the jury, while Sterling aimed for men born in the West, who were less likely to indulge any sympathies for Indians. The selected jury was made up mostly of farmers who the *New York World* reporter concluded were intelligent men representative of their area and likely to give Plenty Horses a fair trial.[3]

Witness testimony began on the second day, an unusually beautiful one for that time of year, townspeople said.[4] Some Lakota said the weather was the work of the Messiah, although they did not specify whether it was a good or a bad omen for Plenty Horses—they would not discuss the subject with even their most trusted interpreters.

Much of the opening testimony was designed to inform the jury about details of the Casey shooting and related events. The first witness whom Sterling called, for example, was Dr. B. L. Ten Eyck, an assistant army surgeon from Leavenworth, Kansas, who ascertained that Casey was killed by a bullet that "entered the back of his head and came out under the right eye." One witness after another, from White Moon to Pete Richard, from Broken Arm to Philip Wells, laid out the details of Casey's death or of the various battles that had followed Wounded Knee.

When Sterling called for White Moon, the Casey scout walked to the stand with rigid military bearing. He wore his blue uniform with red and white trouser stripes and a white chevron on either arm indicating his corporal's rank. His long braids were tied with strips of mink skin, and he took his oath solemnly. His testimony was translated by William Rowland, the gaunt, white-mustached interpreter from Fort Keogh. Sterling led the scout, who bowed his head at the mention of Casey's name, through the details of the shooting. Every so often, White Moon shot Plenty Horses a withering look. When Sterling asked him, "Do you know who shot Lieutenant Casey?" White Moon almost shouted, "Plenty Horses!" Plenty Horses gazed at White Moon without a flicker of emotion.[5]

Sterling, attempting to define Casey's death as murder, might have built his prosecution on the fact that White Moon, a uniformed army scout, was not killed, as he might reasonably have been had Plenty Horses been engaged in an act of war against enemy troops. But nothing in the existing record suggests that Sterling pursued that line of inquiry. Instead, he asked White Moon what he did after the killing.

"I started back to camp," the scout replied. "I could do nothing else."

"What did you take with you?" Sterling asked.

"I took Lieutenant Casey's horse and led him home, led him to the camp."

"Did you remain there by the side of Lieutenant Casey any length of time after he was killed?"

"I went right away," White Moon said.[6]

During cross-examination Nock asked White Moon about the specific purpose of Lieutenant Casey's mission. Was the officer trying to set up peace talks with a chief or chiefs of the hostile camp?[7] No, White Moon said, Casey wanted only to see the camp, an admission that Nock would use later to suggest that Casey was a spy, not a peacemaker.

White Moon was followed on the witness stand by the other scout who had ridden with Casey the day of the shooting. Rock Road, according to newspaper accounts, sounded almost cheerful as he ran through the events that led to the shooting, though he responded to Sterling's questions with more or less the same story White Moon had told. Then Nock approached the witness for the cross-examination. As with White Moon, Nock asked about Casey's mission. "What did Casey say he was going to the Indian camp for?"

"To get a view of it."

"Were you armed?" Nock asked.

"Yes. We had rifles and revolvers."

"Would you go into that camp alone?"

"No. I was afraid."

"Did Casey say anything about holding a counsel when he left?"

"No, sir, he just wanted to see the Indian camp."

Rock Road had offered scant tidbits to the defense, but some elements were beginning to surface that Nock and Powers might use in their argument that the Indians and the army were at war. Reported the *New York World:* "That the defense will attempt to show that Casey was a spy from Gen. Brooke's company and the Government was at war with the Sioux Nation was made apparent by the line of questioning indulged in by Mr. Nock for the defense when selecting the jury. Today he went further in the same direction, although not quite to the point, probably because he did not desire to show his hand at this early stage."[8]

Nock was playing a crafty game, because he knew the judges would resist any suggestion that the Lakota were an independent nation capable of declaring war. "The great legal battle will be on admitting testimony to show that war was acknowledged on both sides and that the soldiers were there for the purpose of engaging the Indians in battle should the occasion arise for it," explained the *New York World.* "Such a question has not been raised in late years. It will settle the status of the Indians, for, if decided adversely to the defendant here, it will undoubtedly be carried to the Supreme Court."[9]

Rock Road was followed by Bear Lying Down, also called Bear That Lays Down, who was Plenty Horses' uncle, but he added nothing that had not been said before. At the end of his testimony, about 3 p.m., the court adjourned until the following Monday, giving everyone Sunday off. This announcement was "a great relief to the Indians who do not fancy sitting in the hot room," reported the *New York World.* "The defendant stood up, languidly smiled and walked out like a chieftain: too proud to look at any one [*sic*] near."[10]

* * *

BY THE THIRD DAY OF the trial, crowds of would-be spectators had besieged the courthouse since early morning in hope of getting seats. Half the people who jammed sidewalks and doorways were women "radiant in their Spring bonnets and attractive costumes, forming a picturesque group, with the brown-skinned Sioux for a background," according to *New York World* reporter J. J. McDonough. The crowd gawked at the Lakota, who ignored them with a great show of dignity. "These Sioux are wonders of stoical indifference," McDonough wrote. "They have no care for their surroundings, and while preferring to be back on the reservation, they give no sign of discontent at their long stay here."[11]

Plenty Horses seemed now to rise from his lethargy. The courtroom buzzed when he entered, the whispered conversations growing louder until the judges came in and marched to their seats. Plenty Horses, pale and thin, scanned the room, his gaze coming to rest on the jury, studying them closely, minutely, as if trying to read their minds. He had presumed that the trial was a mere formality that the whites wanted to go through before hanging him. But his first two days in court had shown him that his lawyers were putting up a good fight, and he had begun to think that his chances of acquittal were good. He could understand all that the lawyers said, though he was not sure why they were saying it. He was even able to take an objective view of the whole affair, enjoying the lawyerly discourse. "The Indians all like good speakers, and of course we feel pleased to have these men speak," he told a newspaper reporter. He demonstrated what can only be called extreme objectivity when he even praised the quality of Sterling's opening remarks.[12]

During cross-examination of Bear Lying Down, Nock eased into his argument about war on the reservations, asking Bear to describe the condition of the Indian camp. Instantly, William Sterling objected.[13] Nock rose to his feet and said: "I want to show by this man what the condition of the average Sioux in these camps was at the time: that they were in a state of foment bordering on fenzy, quite enough to unsettle any man's mind. This we will present in order to make plain the fact that the defendant was not responsible for the crime alleged against him, which I will now state is to form part of our defense."

Sterling responded by asking that all testimony of that nature be stricken from the record. The judges overruled the objection, permitting Bear Lying Down to say that the camp was fortified because the people in it thought of themselves as combatants. So many Indians had been killed at Wounded Knee,

The Masonic Building, which housed a drugstore and real estate office on the first floor and served as the site of the Plenty Horses trial. *(Courtesy of the Siouxland Heritage Museums, Sioux Falls, South Dakota)*

he said, that all had fled to the White Clay Creek encampment. "We had a battle at White Clay Creek one day and thought there might be another fight," he said. "All were armed in some way with guns, revolvers and knives."

After Bear Lying Down came Pete Richards, Red Cloud's half-white son-in-law, who described the Casey shooting in lurid details that held the crowd in rapt attention but again added nothing of note to the case against Plenty Horses. Broken Arm then recalled stripping Casey's body of its pistols, displaying the dry matter-of-factness with which denizens of the plains dealt with gunfire and sudden death: "Casey had a pistol shoved down along side of his leg, down in the boot. He had two belts on. One of them had a pistol, the other was a cartridge belt. He was lying on his face. He had one leg drawn up and one leg stretched. I took him by the arm and pulled him over on his back so I could take his belt off. His hat was off a little ways from him. I went and picked the hat up and laid it close to his head. Then I jumped on my horse and started off. One pistol I gave to Red Cloud's son and told him to give it to the owner. The other I gave to Little Wound."[14]

The prosecution's final witness was a translator from Fort Keogh who described the area in which Casey was shot.

David Edward Powers then rose to make introductory remarks to the jury, putting the defense's spin on the trial.

> You have heard from the different witnesses who have been called on the part of the Government the story of how the life of Lieutenant Casey came to such a sudden and sad end, and we assure that there is nothing can be said complimentary to Lieutenant Casey that will not meet the unqualified endorsement of the counsel for this unfortunate savage. This calamity is certainly a deplorable one, and we wish it were in our power to return Lieutenant Casey to a life of usefulness on this earth. It probably will not be denied in this case the fatal shot which ended the life of Lieutenant Casey was fired by this poor fellow, but we maintain and shall insist, not only on the jury, but the Court, that the shot was fired under circumstances which, so far as the civil authorities of this Government are concerned, they have nothing at all to do with.
>
> The Messiah craze talked of was the result of abuse by Government agents. Not only the Messiah craze excited those people, but we shall show you that they conceived that the treaty relations existing between the Sioux Nation and the United States Government had been violated. They believed that they had been wronged. The next thing that occurred was the killing of Sitting Bull, and the manner in which that wiley chief came to his end was communicated from tribe to tribe.
>
> Then followed the terrible battle of Wounded Knee. It is true that Plenty Horses was not at that battle and did not participate in it, but the Indians' version of that battle was communicated to the hostile camp of which he was a member. He caught the impression and he believed that at Wounded Knee the United States troops seduced the Indians into giving up their arms and, after they had made a surrender of their arms, they slaughtered them in cold blood. This was the version substantially of the battle of Wounded Knee that reached this hostile camp.
>
> The question of an Indian's rights in case of war will be fully and thoroughly discussed, and I believe you will agree with me that the case in hand was the result of war and one of its unfortunate incidents.

Nock and Powers then called their first witness to the stand, Philip Wells, the Pine Ridge government scout and interpreter who had nearly left his nose at Wounded Knee. Powers established Wells's familiarity with the Lakota and his participation in the Wounded Knee battle, then asked simply, "Who was the battle fought between?"

Sterling stood up. "I object to the introduction of any testimony for the purpose of showing that a state of war existed between the Sioux Indians and the Government of the United States, and before any testimony of that kind is admitted I desire to be heard," he said. "While they may desire to introduce evidence of this nature in order to lessen the degree of his crime, yet I submit that is not admissible evidence in this case. The Government did not concede that there was a war at the time Casey was killed, and no Department held that such was the case."[15]

This objection spurred a prolonged debate, in which Powers countered:

> By the treaty of 1869 the United States Government recognized the Sioux tribes as a nation. As a nation they have certain attributes of nationality, and the right to declare and prosecute a war which is secured by implication to the Sioux Nation by treaty since King Philip's war in 1675.[16] The right of the Indian tribes of this country to appeal to arms has never been questioned, and the United States Supreme Court, in several cases, has distinctly held that the Indian tribes of this country and dependent nations possess certain political powers and functions, and among these powers and functions is the right to declare war. In this case the act of defendant in killing Casey was the act of a belligerent and in the prosecution of a war, and inasmuch as his act in killing Casey has been endorsed by the Sioux Nation, the civil authorities of this Government have no jurisdiction to try him for murder.[17]

Captain J. G. Ballance, who was assisting Sterling in the case, responded, pointing out that all treaties with the Lakota referred to them as a tribe, not a nation.

> These treaties have sometimes been made with one tribe of the Sioux Indians and at other times with more, each time recognizing the particular tribe or tribes with whom they were treating as Sioux Indians. It will be observed on examination that the treaty of 1868 has no signature of any chief or head man

[*sic*] belonging to or pretending to belong to the Sioux Nation, but each signer purports to belong to a particular tribe. These different tribes are called Sioux merely because they speak the same tongue and have common characteristics and interests. Those interests may differ, and under the old system different tribes of the Sioux Indians might be at war with each other, or one tribe might be at war with the whites or an Indian tribe with whom another tribe of Sioux Indians might be at peace.

The Sioux Indians, by an agreement embodied in the law of 1877,[18] especially agree that they will be subject to the laws of the United States, and Congress in 1885 enacted a law providing that offenses committed on an Indian reservation situated within a State should be subject to the exclusive jurisdiction of the United States Courts. This law did recognize the Indians as nations, but it was a legislative declaration that the Congress believed that justice for offenses on an Indian reservation could be better meted out by the United States Courts.[19]

Anyone who had been following the trial would have known that much of Plenty Horses' fate hinged on how Judge Shiras and Judge Edgerton responded to these different points of view about Lakota independence as a nation and their right to conduct a war as well as the court's authority to try Plenty Horses. Most trial aficionados believed the judges would decide in Plenty Horses' favor. But the judges were not about to reach a conclusion on that issue with haste. After hearing the arguments, they adjourned until 9:30 the following morning.

WHEN THE TRIAL RECONVENED ON April 28, the courtroom was crowded with women, who seemed daily more interested in the trial. They were on hand for an important victory for the defense: The judges ruled that the court did have jurisdiction over the case but agreed to allow testimony about war that might offer mitigating circumstances for Plenty Horses. Judge Shiras explained that he and Judge Edgerton were not going so far as to say that the Lakota were an independent nation, but did recognize that the Indians could be a belligerent in a war. Sterling nevertheless would struggle all day to block testimony about the killing of any Indians, and Nock and Powers would fight back just as hard to show that the killing and other events surrounding Wounded Knee had preyed on and distorted their client's mind. "No better battle was ever made for the life of a man than these men have made," reported the ever-present *New York World*, "and that, too, in the face of insurmountable difficulties."[20]

Nock and Powers opened the day by recalling Philip Wells to the witness stand. He described the Drexel Mission fight, the positioning of troops, and the ghost dance. The dance, he said, put the Indians into trances in which they believed that they visited the afterworld. They believed, too, that the whites soon would be wiped out in favor of the Indians and that their ghost shirts would protect them from bullets. "This testimony was introduced by the defense to show that the Indians, including Plenty Horses, were in a peculiar state of mind and hardly accountable for any of their acts," McDonough told his readers.[21]

Next the attorneys put Living Bear before the jury. He talked about the Indians' retreat to the camp on White Clay Creek and how they danced there and built fortifications for the onslaught they expected from the U.S. Army. "We dug rifle pits, dragging pine logs in front of them. They were dug and made so that we could get in there and get sheltered from the fire, and we could shoot from there," he said. "We were surrounded by different camps of soldiers, and we expected they would come after us."[22]

Living Bear said that at the time of the shooting, the Lakota had been in a state of war with the whites for two weeks. He offered a pathetic view of Brulé life during that period, with the military chasing down frightened Lakota in the wake of the Sitting Bull shooting. The slaughter at Wounded Knee had both angered and frightened the Brulé, sending them in flight to the Badlands and to the camp along White Clay Creek, where they united in their willingness to fight the army more from fear than from desire for a war that would have resulted in the destruction not only of warriors but also of women and children. In addition, the Indians were hungry, going for two weeks without promised government rations.

Sterling cross-examined Living Bear severely in an attempt to make him admit that the Indians were about to surrender at the time that Casey was killed, but Living Bear was unshakable in his denial—no, they were entrenched and expecting a fight.

He Dog was next, and he supported Living Bear's description of the fortifications and the Indian belief that they would be attacked soon. Bear Lying

Down followed He Dog and repeated that the Lakota anticipated an attack at any moment, but he also testified that they were about to go to Pine Ridge when Casey was killed. Thus he managed to score points for both sides of the trial.

The defense then reached the anticipated climax of the day and even of the trial, calling Plenty Horses to the witness stand. He stood, pulled his blue blanket up around his shoulders, and strode to the front of the courtroom to be sworn in with Philip Wells, his interpreter.

Sterling immediately stood to object. "This man has had an education and can get along without an interpreter," he said.

"But, Your Honor, I know that he cannot speak English good enough to testify intelligently, and I say that an interpreter is absolutely necessary," Nock responded.

Judge Edgerton asked Plenty Horses several questions, which Plenty Horses answered. The judge ruled that no interpreter would be used unless the defendant failed to understand what was wanted of him.

Nock did not give in. "I have been with the man almost daily, and we have always had an interpreter to conduct our conversations," he said. "In fact, I never tried to talk any length of time with him, after the first futile attempt, without the aid of Philip Wells. The defendant understands some English, but he is unable to describe what it will be necessary to describe on the stand, and in trying to do so he might prejudice his case beyond repair. We ask for an interpreter, because it is absolutely essential for the proper presentation of his evidence, and if that be refused, you will force us to close our case without a word from the defendant in his behalf."

"It is not necessary to make a threat," Judge Shiras replied, angered.

"We are not threatening, but presenting the case in its true light," Nock said.

The judges did not budge.

"Then we refuse to permit Plenty Horses to testify," Nock said, "and we also close our case."

The courtroom hung suspended in utter silence. J. J. McDonough described the scene, at the same time showing how even reporters were being won over to Plenty Horses.

> Over near the witness chair, with his eyes turned to the open window, head erect, arms easily folded, stood the accused, giving no sign that he knew, if indeed he

did know, that the most important ruling of the Court during the trial had just been given against him. All eyes were upon him, yet he gave no heed.

No more striking figure than this proud young Sioux ever appeared under similar circumstances. His life had not been a happy one, but doubtless bright dreams of the future filled his heart until this shadow came over him. Of course, he holds life dearly, and yet he never indicates that he is afraid lest death be decreed, and now, before the very eyes of the twelve men who hold his fate in the balance, he waits with the calm reserve of one who has no sense of fear.

He paused in his reverie and turned his large brown eyes full on the Judge, who had just spoken to him, and then the Deputy Marshal twitched his arm as if to awaken him. Then he knew that there would be no opportunity for him to tell the jury of the wrongs he suffered, of the war which brought about the death of his near relatives, of his entire absence of intent to murder when he shot the officer dead, and so he went back to the jail with the two marshals, followed by his never-absent father.[23]

"I wanted to tell them all that I am not guilty of murder," Plenty Horses later told McDonough. "If they do not care to hear me, I am satisfied. Probably it is better that way."

However, Plenty Horses got his chance to testify to the public if not the jury. In a *New York World* interview he outlined the testimony he might have offered the court.[24] He reiterated that he had come back from the Carlisle school with "no chance to get employment, nothing for me to do whereby I could earn my board and clothes, no opportunity to learn more and remain with the whites." He went on to say, "I was at Pine Ridge with my father last winter when the troops were brought in. Then came the killing of Big Foot's band. I heard the shooting and ran out to help. It was an awful sight. The survivors told such a pitiful tale that we all went into camp not far away, and it was said that there would be war. Everybody seemed to feel that the government had injured him too much to ever give in. There was ghost dancing and much excitement at the time. The day Casey was killed I was out from the camp watching that no troops came to harm my father and relatives. Of course, I was in a very bad frame of mind. Our home was destroyed, our family separated and all hope for good times was gone. There was nothing to live for."

Along came Casey, on horseback in the company of a lone Cheyenne scout, an enemy Indian who had allied with the whites against the Lakota. The

Cheyenne would have added to Plenty Horses' jaundiced view of Casey, who the young Brulé said became very angry when told he could not examine the Indian camp. According to Plenty Horses, Casey said "that he would go away then but would return with soldiers enough to capture our chief. I understood him to say that his object in taking them was to kill them. You can understand my state of mind at hearing that we were to suffer still more because we arose to demand the food and clothing the government owed us. All this passed before my mind, and then I thought that right at my side rode a spy from our enemy who was boldly announcing his determination to come back and do us still further injury." Plenty Horses closed his story as if he personally had had no connection with the way in which Casey died: "He turned to go and a moment later fell dead with a bullet from my gun in his brain."

THE LAST DAY OF THE trial opened with a crowd amassed on the sidewalk in front of the courthouse, eager to attend even though the heat inside was suffocating. To control the crush, court officials issued tickets for admission and brought in Plenty Horses an hour early to avoid the jam. Women, fully a hundred of them, made up more than two-thirds of the audience and even overflowed into the area reserved for the attorneys.

Plenty Horses sat in his usual place behind the rail and during the entire morning, as defense and prosecution delivered closing remarks, made not the slightest movement. When Nock and Powers spoke, he trained his gaze downward and did not look up until the break for lunch. Living Bear sat behind him and, like other Indians in the audience, listened closely to what was said.

Plenty Horses' sad story, his forlorn look, or both had won over the crowd. According to the *New York World*, "It was a cheerful, eager, sympathetic audience." The newspaper reported, probably with more color than accuracy, that women wept during closing remarks when Nock or Powers referred to the "poor savage" and glared at Sterling when he called Plenty Horses "a cold-blooded murderer."[25]

Powers and Nock read from the *New York World* stories about the previous winter's events on the reservations to show that General Nelson Miles had fortified Pine Ridge, putting it into a state of war, and that the Indians had received no rations throughout the hostilities. Nock, most of whose actual words at the trial have been lost, described the fear and confusion that struck the reservations after Sitting Bull's death and after Wounded Knee, where, Nock said, Plenty Horses' cousin was killed. He argued that Plenty Horses and other Lakota had been in a state of high excitement even before these events, crazed by the ghost dance religion. He spoke of the Indians' maltreatment at the hands of the whites for years and years.

Nock's summary, according to the *Argus-Leader,* was very effective and clearly swayed both jury and audience. "He wound about the case such a showing of conditions of hostilities that one might have thought a life-long war had just ceased," effused J. J. McDonough of the *New York World.* "His strong voice filled every part of the court-room. He pleaded for the accused, whom he pictured as a savage who believed he did right in a cause sacred to his race. He was, he truly believed, protecting his people from a spy."[26]

Nock at this point waxed eloquent.

> How did Casey leave his camp? Did he leave it as though peace was lingering on every side? No. Nor as a peace-going citizen, but he starts armed, as he had a right to, and as a warrior should.
>
> It is said that he went over to look at the camp of the hostiles. He did not say that they went over there on a friendly mission to have a talk with the chiefs. When Lieutenant Casey left that camp that morning, it was not for a friendly visit. It was not that he might take the hand of Red Cloud and Two Strike, or any other chief, and say, "Let us have peace." He went out of that camp that morning, if we may believe the testimony of White Moon, for the purpose of inspecting the hostile camp and getting whatever information he could to use against the Indians. He rides along with the defendant, Plenty Horses, and what was said between them God and the accused alone know.
>
> This defendant went out of his camp in the same capacity that Lieutenant Casey left his, not for the purpose of friendship, as they would have you believe, because the evidence shows that over on the hillside was the camp of the United States Army, under General Brooke. They were supplied with all the implements and accoutrements of war, and that every man in the United States camp knew it was war.[27]

Nock next went on to make a plea for a fair trial, the verdict of which would assuage rather than rend the heart of old Living Bear, Plenty Horses' father.

At 2 p.m. Sterling rose to speak for the prosecution, attacking both the idea that the reservation was in a state of war and the notion that Casey was a spy.[28] As with the defense attorneys, most of his comments are lost, covered only in general terms in the contemporary newspapers. He said that the reservation was not at war when Casey was shot and that if there had been a state of war, Plenty Horses had taken no part in it. Moreover, he argued that even if war had been under way, Casey had been killed on neutral ground. He also called specifically upon the jury's Civil War veterans to expose the fallacy of the war argument during deliberations. Finally, he asserted that the condition of Lakota society could have no bearing on Plenty Horses' individual actions. "I ask you to treat this defendant as a white man," he said.

> I do not ask and would be loath to see any other treatment. I call this one of the most inexcusable, one of the most unprovoked, one of the most-cowardly murders in history. Here is a man who shook hands with Lieutenant Casey as a friend, and a minute later, when his back was turned, he deliberately drew his gun and put a bullet through his victim. Could anything be more dastardly, more unprovoked, more cowardly, more inexcusable than that? You must remember that there is testimony that Plenty Horses took no part in the ghost dance, his own statement is that he did not believe in the Messiah.[29] An hour before the murder was committed, Plenty Horses was as cool and deliberate as he was at the time he shot his gallant victim.[30]

Sterling attempted to show that the Indian camp was anything but hostile. He drew a verbal picture of Casey as a brave young soldier riding to his death, then ended his oration with a shot to the jurors' hearts.

> Something has been said about sympathy for the defendant and of sorrow for his old father. My sympathies are with that poor old Indian father; my sympathies are with the family of the defendant; and I appreciate the sorrow of that old man. I do not ask you to forget the sorrow of this poor old father or the grief of his family, but I do ask you not to forget that by this terrible act, by this brutal murder, other hearts have been stricken with sorrow, another broken. I ask you not to forget that while Edward Casey, like the prisoner, had neither wife nor children, he had a mother, and today his mother, who lives by the side of yonder sea, yearns for her son with a mother's love, which never

dies, yearns for her soldier boy who will never return to her. In her heart there
is no thought of revenge, for she is too near her grave, with her head bowed
down with cares and sorrow and her hair whitened with the snows of many
Winters. Before she retires she will take down from its place on the shelf the
well-worn Bible and draw strength from it. She will turn to the page wherein is
written the divine commandment, "Thou shalt not kill," and again to that divine judgment that [a] man who has done this thing shall surely die. So it is
that she awaits the news of the result of this trial with the abiding conviction
that a just God will put into your hearts to mete out even-handed and exact
justice.[31]

This speech was a fabrication. Casey's mother, far from living by yonder
sea, was buried by it, near her soldier son, and had been buried there for nearly
thirty years. The only woman alive who could claim anything akin to a maternal connection to Edward Casey was his father's second wife and widow, with
whom the Casey brothers had had long and acrimonious disputes over inheri-
tance.

But Sterling was not yet finished. In conclusion, he kicked up the emotional
appeal: "I plead not only for the broken-hearted mother; not only for that
young life of Edward Casey which was so sadly and cruelly blotted out, but I
plead for justice; I plead for the sanctity of human life; I plead for the honor
and for the safety of the people of the State and the district of Dakota."[32]

On that note, the case went to the jury. Judge Shiras spent half an hour outlining the case for the jurors, telling them that the Indians had no status as an
independent nation and so could not declare war. Nevertheless, he said that
they could engage in a war against the government, declared or otherwise.
Consequently, he said the jury could come to one of three conclusions about
the Casey shooting. One, that Casey was shot while the United States and the
Lakota were at war, in which case Plenty Horses should be acquitted. Two, if
the United States and the Lakota were not at war, and Plenty Horses shot
Casey with deliberation and malice, the Brulé was guilty of murder. Finally, if
Plenty Horses fired in a state of great mental excitement, without deliberation
and premeditation, even if there were no state of war on the reservation at the
time, he should be found guilty of the lesser crime of manslaughter.

The jurors began deliberations at 3:40 p.m. on April 29, 1891. At 9:15 p.m.
they returned to ask the court about such matters as Plenty Horses' activities

prior to visiting Pine Ridge and what role the ghost dance was permitted to play in their deliberations. Then the jurors went back to casting judgment.

THE CASE FELL INTO THE jury's hands at a time when newspaper accounts might have led Plenty Horses to believe that his own people were disavowing him, perhaps to soften the hard feelings of settlers and soldiers after the ghost dance period. Young Man Afraid of His Horses—Few Tails's close relative—had reported on April 27, 1891, to Captain C. M. Bailey of the Eighth Cavalry that "his people are all right and friendly, perhaps a little more so than ever."[33] Young Man held five councils with Lakota from three reservations and said that "they are satisfied and do not want trouble." They wanted peace and to learn farming, he told Bailey. According to Bailey, " 'Young-man' [sic] is quietly absorbing Brules [sic] in his band, that is, all who so desire, and is obtaining a big influence and following." The Lakota leader promised to do all he could to enlist warriors in the army scouts.

More stinging to Plenty Horses would have been an April 11, 1891, letter that Two Strike himself sent to Richard Henry Pratt, head of the Carlisle school,[34] and that later was quoted in the *Argus-Leader*.[35] Two Strike's words renounced the traditional Lakota ways that had inspired Plenty Horses. "You wrote me about the Indians here making more trouble," Two Strike said in a letter dictated to a lieutenant in the Sixth Cavalry. "There is no intention here of making trouble. If we were going to make trouble why would we enlist our young men as soldiers for the Great Father—as we are now doing? We see that this is a very good chance for our young men to do something for themselves, and make men of themselves and we let them enlist." Wounded Knee, he said, "gave us a lesson. We did not want to fight in the first place, but somebody called for troops. All we think about now is to farm. I received a letter about the same matter from the Lower Brule [sic] Agency, and I told them that we were not going to make any more trouble, and that they must not pay attention to such talk. This talk gives me much trouble, and I do not like it. I do not want to tell my officer friends any lie, for I know they are here for the Great Father." Two Strike signed with an *X*.

And so Plenty Horses' own leader had thrown aside the old way of life. As Plenty Horses sat in the jail at Sioux Falls, awaiting his fate, the world was moving on, and his cause was falling into the past even as it made headlines across the nation, and readers awaited the verdict.

THE JURY RETURNED TO THE courtroom at 9 a.m. on April 30 after a long night of deliberation. "Have you reached a verdict?" asked Shiras.[36]

"We have not, Your Honor," the jury foreman declared.

In an atmosphere of anticlimax, the judges then discharged the inconclusive jury. That afternoon, Sterling called for a retrial. Nock objected to going to Deadwood, where the court would next be in session, because he and Powers were not being paid for their services. Relocating the trial would pose a serious financial burden. Judge Edgerton agreed and concluded that the retrial would be begin on May 25, 1891, in Sioux Falls.

The jurors had failed to reach a verdict because they had fallen afoul of the issue of manslaughter or murder. The first ballot had come out six for murder and six for manslaughter. After clarifying some issues with the court the previous evening, the jurors voted eight for murder and four for manslaughter. At 1 a.m. the vote fell to six against six. The jury went through twenty-three ballots and came up with nothing closer to a verdict than eight to four. "We could have remained out for four days and never come any nearer to an agreement," said one juror.[37] The *New York World* pointed out that although Sterling had called on the jury's Civil War veterans to debunk the war question, all the veterans had voted consistently for manslaughter.[38]

Although the whites of South Dakota seemed less eager to hang an Indian than most observers had expected, a juror named House, distinctly in favor of a murder verdict, remarked casually during the courtroom hubbub, "I have lived over the border too long to look upon the outrages of those savages as permitting of any mitigating circumstances."[39]

Powers quickly responded, "Then you are not without prejudice, although you swore that you had none before becoming a juror."

House, probably uncertain just what penalty such perjury might bring with it, immediately fled the scene.

The jury deliberations were plagued with doubts about the respective punishments for murder and manslaughter. One juror said that several of them voted for murder because they thought the penalty for manslaughter would be only two or three years in jail. Had they known that Plenty Horses could have been locked away for ten years for manslaughter, the jurors might all have voted for that verdict.[40]

Plenty Horses took the jury action in stride with his usual show of stoical indifference. A reporter asked how he felt, but he answered with silence.[41] Not so his father, who had been pacing the hallway outside the courtroom during the tense hours of jury deliberations, wringing his hands and asking the court deputy every few minutes how things were going. When the verdict came down, Living Bear squeezed through the crowd, hands trembling, tears streaming down his face, and seized Nock by the hand, pouring out thanks that "must have compensated the lawyer for the work he had done."[42] Formerly so somber, Living Bear was now shaking hands with anyone who would take his, laughing heartily, and talking about nothing but his son's narrow escape from death. He left that night on a train for Pine Ridge.[43]

A hung Indian, not a hung jury, had been the anticipated result of the trial. But the outcome was not bad for Sioux Falls. Concluded the *Argus-Leader*, with a stunning display of boosterism, "It is likely that the second trial will attract more attention than the first, and, in a cold-blooded sort of way, Sioux Falls is to be congratulated that it is to take place here."[44]

Back in jail that evening, Plenty Horses told the *New York World*'s McDonough: "I thought last night that they would hang me sure. But now I feel that it will not be so. My father is glad once more."[45]

CHAPTER 12

Justice Deferred

INITIALLY, ANY GAMBLER WOULD HAVE bet that the Plenty Horses case would end at the gallows, but somehow Sterling had lost—an inauspicious result for a newly married lawyer with money problems. Then, in early May, he found himself committed to a leading role in another trial involving whites, Indians, and alleged murder. The Culbertson brothers and two South Dakota ranchers, James Juelfs and Alva Marvin, had been arraigned before a grand jury in Sturgis, South Dakota, and charged with killing Few Tails. The U.S. Department of Justice assigned Sterling to help the state attorney try the case. This time, Sterling would be prosecuting whites for killing an Indian, the mirror image of the Plenty Horses trial.

The Few Tails case had gone before the grand jury on May 13, 1891, with the prosecution represented by the state attorney and the assistant U.S. attorney. Few Tails's widow, Clown, and their daughter were among the witnesses. Clown spoke of her dangerous days and nights on the frozen prairie, an experience which, the *Sioux Falls Argus-Leader* reported, had crippled her for life. The paper characterized the slain Few Tails as "one of the most reliable and progressive Indians of [Pine Ridge] agency" and recalled the Culbertsons' "well known reputation as horse thieves and border ruffians." Few Tails's killing was "one of the most cold-blooded and unjustifiable murders ever committed on the frontier," according to the *Argus-Leader*.[1]

Given that the Culbertsons were none too popular locally and that Clown's emotional testimony could not fail to stir juror empathy, Sterling stood a chance of winning in Sturgis. After all, the cowboys had been jailed thanks to a persistent cry for bringing them to justice. They had been arrested even over the protest of Meade County officials, who had been pleading lack of funds as an excuse for ignoring the murder. But a win for Sterling in the Few Tails case would be influenced by the outcome in Sioux Falls.

*   *   *

As Plenty Horses' second trial neared, the *New York World* editorialized:

> The killing of Lieut. Casey was brutal and cowardly. His death was a distinct
> loss not only to the service but to the Indians whom he was teaching to be civ-
> ilized soldiers. He was a brave, conscientious, honorable officer, and his slayer
> was a savage with all the mean as well as honest instincts of the savage.
>
> But is it well for the Government to accuse Plenty Horses of murder?
>
> Plenty Horses and other Sioux went on the warpath because the govern-
> ment starved them. The administration has not yet remedied the evil that caused
> the trouble. Will it help matters to hang for murder an Indian who supposed
> that he did only what war gave him a right to do? Can the United States afford
> to drive them into revolt and then hang them for the killing that they do?[2]

Heartened by the first trial and the hopeful outcome, the defense team was
primed for round two. Despite little time to prepare their case, the two attorneys had every weapon in their arsenal fully loaded. They prepared tough,
clear arguments to convince judges and jurors that Pine Ridge was at war at
the time of Casey's shooting. They lined up excellent new witnesses. During
the first trial they had wanted testimony from American Horse—the well-
known progressive whose bravery had kept the attempted arrest of Little from
breaking into a bloody riot on Royer's office doorstep—but he had not been
able to appear. This time, he was on board.

They also beat William Sterling in the critical matter of getting a witness to
testify on behalf of General Nelson Miles. Sterling had gone to Chicago to enlist Miles for the prosecution, wanting him to deny that the reservations were at
war the previous winter. Miles had dismissed that plan. "My boy, it was a war,"
he told Sterling. "You do not suppose that I am going to reduce my campaign
to a dress-parade affair? Oh no. I am sorry, but I cannot do it."[3] The defense,
on the other hand, wanted Miles to testify that war it had been indeed, and *that*
Miles was eager to do.

But Nock and Powers at the outset of the second trial also found themselves
missing two critical witnesses: Philip Wells and Living Bear. Wells's appear-

ance was blocked by vengeful army officers who feared that his participation would help Plenty Horses.[4] Living Bear's absence was a mystery. The strongest defense witness at the first trial, he had failed to return to Sioux Falls from the Rosebud Reservation. Nock and Powers suspected that someone—perhaps soldiers bent on undermining Plenty Horses' defense—kept Living Bear away. The attorneys stated firmly that the case would not close until Bear had testified. The court immediately sent a telegram to Rosebud, asking where Living Bear was. The next morning came the answer: about twenty miles from reservation headquarters. The court sent a deputy marshal to track him down.

Meanwhile, the trial went on without Plenty Horses' father. When court opened at 9:30 a.m. on Monday, May 25, 1891, Plenty Horses sat behind the rail that separated spectators from judges, jury, and attorneys. He was a bright spot in the room, in scarlet shirt and yellow silk scarf, probably gifts from supporters. These colors had religious significance for the Lakota.[5] Yellow was the color of Inyan, God as rock, the primal source of all things and the patron of revenge, destruction, and violence. It was also the color of Wakinyan, the Winged God or Thunderbird, created by Inyan as his companion. A Lakota who had escaped a personal encounter with an enemy was entitled to wear upright in his hair an eagle tail feather dyed yellow. Red, like yellow, was a favorite color of the Lakota gods, but it was special to the Sun God, Wakan Tonka Kin, the greatest of all the gods. Wakan Tonka Kin was pleased by people who wore red and would listen if they spoke to him.

J. J. McDonough thought he could see signs of wear and tear in Plenty Horses but also praised him as if he were assuming heroic stature: "Long imprisonment has wasted the defendant considerably. His face is quite pale, and his frame has very little flesh on it. But with all his suffering there is the same dauntless spirit in the fellow which no power on earth can subdue. His eyes are bright, he holds his head erect, and the same old smile plays over his face when he greets a friend."[6]

The *Argus-Leader* reporter saw something else in Plenty Horses' countenance: hope. "His face at times lost the stolid indifferent expression and to the careful eye betrayed something very akin to nervous anxiety. This morning he asked his attorney, 'Have you not any new evidence';—the first time he has shown any interest whatever in the evidence or in his case. The fact is that during the former trial Plenty Horses had the idea that he was a prisoner of war and that the trial was only a formality to precede execution. The disagreement of the former jury put new hope in his breast, and now for the first time he takes a keen and almost nervous interest in the testimony."[7]

In his opening remarks William Sterling tried to discredit Plenty Horses' claim that he had shot Lieutenant Casey while defending his people in a time of war. Not so, Sterling said. Plenty Horses' people scorned him for being a "book Indian," one who had attended the white school. Plenty Horses killed Casey to win the approval of the Lakota. Casey was a sacrifice to the would-be warrior's ambition.

Sterling's first witness was Rock Road, who wore "a jaunty spring suit with loud checks and looked very much as though civilization agreed with him," McDonough wrote.[8] He described the killing yet again.

In cross-examination Nock seemed determined to show the antipathy between Rock Road and Plenty Horses, perhaps to suggest that Rock Road's description of the murder, and therefore the motive, was questionable. "You do not like the prisoner?" Nock asked.

"No," Rock Road said firmly.

"You hate him, don't you?"

"Yes," the scout said without a moment's hesitation. He said if he had been there when Casey was shot, Plenty Horses would not now be sitting there alive in the courtroom, or anywhere else for that matter. He hated him because he had killed the lieutenant.

Trying to erode the jury's trust in Rock Road's veracity, Nock asked Rock Road whether, at the previous trial, he had testified that he had been afraid to enter Two Strike's camp. He had in fact said so, but now he denied it. "If I said at the other trial I was afraid, I don't remember it, and it was not true."[9] Nock would get back to that point later.

Next, Sterling brought White Moon to the witness stand. The Cheyenne scout and Casey loyalist also described the shooting, emphasizing how Plenty Horses had acted friendly, shaking hands with the officer and talking with him pleasantly before assassinating him.

But during cross-examination White Moon's truthfulness took severe blows. Powers had traveled to Pine Ridge during the period between the two trials and learned that, after the shooting, White Moon had told two people that he could not identify the man who shot Casey. He also had claimed that he had fired twice at the killer on the outskirts of the Brulé camp. "Did you tell

[William] Thompson [an interpreter from Fort Keogh] on returning to camp, that you did not know who shot Casey, as the man who shot him was painted?" Nock asked.

"No."

"Did you tell Thompson, or say in his presence that you fired two shots at the man who killed Casey?"

"I did not."

"Did you say in his presence that you regretted you had missed killing the party who shot Casey, and that the scouts there applauded you?"

"I think not."

"Do you know a man by the name of William Craven?"

"I do not."

William Craven, an interpreter from the Cheyenne River reservation, would come up again later in the trial, much to White Moon's dismay.

Dr. Ten Eyck followed, describing Casey's fatal wounds, as at the first trial, and the court adjourned.

That evening, a hot rumor circulated through town. Captain Frank Baldwin was coming to Sioux Falls from Chicago to testify on General Miles's behalf that the Lakota and the army had not been at war. If the rumor was true, then Baldwin, the two-time Congressional Medal of Honor winner who had investigated the Wounded Knee fight and related shootings, would be a powerful prosecution witness. Only later, when he actually did take the witness stand, would it become clear that this longtime ally of Miles was anything but a boon to William Sterling.

AT 9 A.M. THE NEXT DAY, U.S. Deputy Marshal F. Curtis Fry's sonorous voice rang out to announce the beginning of day two of the trial. The first witness, Broken Arm, had ridden up to Casey with Plenty Horses. He described the shooting much as White Moon had and repeated the story of how he had taken Casey's pistols and left the body turned on its back when he rode back to camp.

Nock and Power's main interest on cross-examination lay in asking who gave Broken Arm his ration tickets for food. They wanted to establish that the Lakota must have been at war if the Indians were receiving ration tickets not from the Bureau of Indian Affairs in the Department of the Interior but from the War Department. They substantially made their point. "Are there two kinds of tickets issued at the agency, one from the interior [*sic*] and one from the war department [*sic*]?" Nock asked.[10]

Sterling objected and was overruled. Broken Arm answered, "I don't know."

"Isn't it a fact that since you came into the agency, you have been drawing rations from the war department?"

"I don't know that." Referring to the fact that the reservations had been turned over to military control shortly after Royer was discharged as agent, Broken Arm added, "We have a soldier for our father, and we get tickets from him."

"Before you went into the No-water [*sic*] camp who gave you tickets?"

"Before that we had a short, little man [Royer] for a father. He was a new man and he wasn't no soldier."

The spectators got a laugh out of that—Royer's reputation as Young Man Afraid of His Indians still overshadowed him.

Nock switched course, getting now to the question of why Plenty Horses might have had his face painted the day of the shooting. "Do Indians paint their faces when they go on the warpath?"

"Yes."

"Do Indians paint their faces when they go see different nations?"

"Yes." Broken Arm explained that they painted their faces for a variety of reasons, from going to social gatherings to visiting friends, from going to war to preparing to die.

The question of paint came up again in the testimony of the following witness, Bear Lying Down, who was Plenty Horses' uncle by marriage. Nock was trying to establish that the paint indicated a state of war, that the Indians wore it because they thought they might at any moment be attacked and killed, like the members of Sitanka's band. Bear Lying Down admitted that he had worn paint while in Two Strike's camp. "Why were you painted?" Nock asked.

"I expected to die every day," Bear Lying Down said simply.

Sterling called only two more witnesses, Pete Richard and Thomas Flood, the Pine Ridge interpreter, who testified that he had talked with Plenty Horses in English at Pine Ridge and that the young man was fluent in the language. Nock, when his turn with Flood came, established that Plenty Horses usually spoke in Lakota. Clearly, the attorneys were maneuvering for the time when Plenty Horses might be called to the witness stand.

In any event, Flood's testimony ended the prosecution's case, and David Powers gave the opening defense remarks.[11] He described how the government had failed to keep its promises to the Lakota. "We have evidence to show you, thank God, that two years ago men, women and children actually starved because of the failure of this government to keep its treaties and to furnish the proper supplies. . . . [The Lakota] committed no outrages until they heard that the soldiers were coming to exterminate them. When the soldiers came, they took it as a declaration of war. But even the Indians made no move until five or six Indians were shot down by the whites in cold blood, one of them a cousin of the defendant. Then came the news of the death of Sitting Bull, which was either a war measure or a cowardly murder. Then came the battle of Wounded Knee."

When, on top of these dangers, Casey arrived threatening to bring more troops to attack the camp, Plenty Horses sprang into action. "Casey armed himself and went out, as a spy, to learn the strength of the hostile camp," Powers said. "It was while Plenty Horses and Casey were riding together that Casey dropped some remark from which the prisoner inferred that the Indian camp was to be attacked and its members killed." Powers then pointed at Plenty Horses and intoned: "Yes, gentlemen, that incorrigible savage, loving his race with all the fervor of a fanatic, fired the bullet which killed the gallant Casey, and if he went before his God this hour he would go without a twinge of conscience or a fear of damnation. To save his people from such a fate, as a patriotic act, crazed by the wild orgies of the ghost dance, driven mad by the terrible recollections of Wounded Knee, he killed Casey to save his own people." Then the attorney hit his central theme: "Place the responsibility of Casey's blood where it belongs, not upon this deluded chief of the forest, but upon the damnable system of robbery and treaty violations which brought it about."[12]

Nock and Powers' first witness was American Horse. He moved toward the front of the courtroom with "a black scowl on his face, and a red fan in his hand," reported the *Argus-Leader*. "He has been to Washington nine different times. He is one of the brass collars among the Sioux and his face shows him to be a strong character."[13]

Nock went straight to the question of what had motivated Lakota actions in the closing weeks of 1890: "What was the condition of the Sioux before the trouble arose?"

Sterling instantly objected, and Powers explained that he wanted to show the conditions that led the Lakota into a state of war. The court upheld the objection, declaring that "if such a vast field of inquiry were opened, it would open up the whole dealings of the white [*sic*] with the Indians since the time of Columbus. Such an investigation would be simply impossible."[14]

Sterling objected again when Powers started to query American Horse about the ghost dance, which Nock pointedly called "the messiah craze," as if to underscore the cultural insanity that might have visited Plenty Horses. Sterling asked the judges to clarify the limits they had placed on testimony about reservation warfare during the first trial. This question of whether a state of war existed on the reservation was a sticky one for Sterling. He had built his entire case for murder on a single linchpin: that the Lakota were not, and perhaps could not be, at war. If the defense proved anything to the contrary, Sterling's case fell apart.

The judges said that such questions could be asked only to show Plenty Horses' frame of mind, not that of his people. Powers' next questions about the ghost dance and the flight to the Stronghold were all blocked by the court.

The defense veered away from the war question when it called William Thompson, who stated that when White Moon returned from the Casey killing, he said he could not recognize the gunman because his face had been painted. Moreover, Thompson said, White Moon claimed to have fired two shots at the retreating killer. Powers had revealed White Moon as a liar, a revelation with an important effect. "As the Cheyenne are very anxious to secure a conviction of Plenty Horses [White Moon] undoubtedly falsified on the stand," McDonough explained. "The testimony of Thompson was listened to by the jury attentively, and it certainly impressed them."[15]

When Thompson retired, Powers called Captain Frank Baldwin, but he could not be found, and the court adjourned until the following day. Baldwin's arrival in town had already been reported in the press, but his appearance as a witness for the defense rather than the prosecution was something of a surprise. Casey had been a friend to both Baldwin and Miles, and in any event, no one expected that the military would come down on the side of Plenty Horses.

"WAS IT WAR? THAT IS the Vital Question of Today's Testimony," read the headline in the *Sioux Falls Argus-Leader* on the third day of the trial.[16]

Captain Frank Baldwin had been ordered by General Nelson Miles to answer that question, and he did so on the witness stand that day.

Baldwin's appearance followed testimony from R. O. Pugh, the issue clerk at the Pine Ridge agency, who laid another plank in the defense platform. Pugh had served as issue clerk from October 5 to December 15, 1890, and explained that since January 15, 1891, the War Department had issued rations. Before that, he said, the Indians had received no food since the previous November. Those who went to the Stronghold naturally received no rations. They were referred to at the agency as "the hostiles," he said. When they surrendered—among them the people of Two Strike's band, including Plenty Horses and his family—they received food from the War Department. They were, in effect, treated as prisoners of war, Nock and Powers indicated.

During Pugh's testimony, Powers scored a point from which McDonough thought the prosecution could not recover.[17] "Did you ever hear, during your eight years' residence among the Sioux, of the Indians committing any depredations previous to the late trouble?" Powers asked.

Sterling objected, and Powers instantly turned on him. "I am not surprised that the government should be blind to a fact that is cognizant to every man living at Pine Ridge, blind to the suffering of these poor, deluded savages, who are huddled together on as barren a soil as there is in America. Yes, they must be blind, for if the government knew of the actual suffering of these people, the horrors of starvation that has [*sic*] for years stared them in the face, which culminated in the ghost craze, and then again into the war of last winter, and finally in brave Casey's death, it would rise in its might and sweep away the systematic robbery that has been going on for years."

The court overruled the objection.

Under cross-examination, Sterling asked if Plenty Horses had ever joined in the ghost dances. "I do not know," Pugh answered. "The Indians who left the agency and went into the Badlands killed cattle belonging to whites and Indians. They had no rations from the government after they left. The rations issued by the military were issued to Indians not entitled to draw at our agency. We took care of those who were under our charge." This testimony indicated that the government was dividing the Lakota, implicitly or explicitly, into prisoners of war and nonprisoners. Sterling's case was splitting at the seams.

*   *   *

IRONICALLY, EDWARD CASEY'S FATHER IN the mid-1850s had used military imprisonment of an Indian warrior to deny civil officials the authority to hang him for killing a white man. Silas Casey, then a lieutenant colonel commanding the army's Puget Sound District, was up against a difficult personality, the governor of Washington Territory, Isaac T. Stevens. A West Point graduate, Stevens believed that as commander of the state militia he also was in charge of regular army troops stationed in the territory. He wanted to use the army to exterminate local Indians and to try as criminals any who were captured. Casey and his superiors of course did not agree that regular army troops should fall under Stevens' authority and also believed that captured Indians should be treated as prisoners of war, not criminals.

The situation blew up over a Nisqually warrior chief named Leschi. When Leschi was accused in the murder of a man named A. Benton Moses, Stevens wanted him arrested. Casey let him run free. Stevens succeeded in bribing Leschi's brother into betraying his sibling, and Leschi was captured, tried, and sentenced to death in a civil court in December 1857. Casey tried to save him, contending that Leschi was a prisoner of war. Casey held Leschi at Fort Steilacoom, but when all attempts to get Leschi freed had run out, including a second trial, Casey turned over the Indian to the local sheriff. Leschi was hung on January 22, 1858.

Thirty-some years had passed by the time the same issues came up in the murder of Edward Casey, but still the Leschi outcome stood as an ominous portent for Plenty Horses.

CAPTAIN BALDWIN WAS CALLED NEXT to testify. He had visited the Wounded Knee battlefield, and Powers asked him what he saw there. Sterling objected. "There is nothing to show that the Indians who fought at Wounded Knee had anything to do with, or were known by, this defendant. They belonged to different tribes."

The court overruled the objection, and Baldwin described Wounded Knee: "I saw a great many dead Indians. I saw guns, ammunition, cooking utensils, *et cetera,* scattered everywhere. I saw over one hundred dead bodies of Indians, men, women and children. I saw a body which was said to be that of Big Foot. His body was at the west end of the string of bodies."[18]

"How were the bodies dressed?"

"They were dressed as warriors. All had on the 'war shirt.' "

"Did you see the dead bodies of any soldiers?"

"I did not."

"Did you keep a record of the dead and wounded?"

"Yes. There were one hundred and forty-nine Indians killed and thirty-eight wounded. There were forty-nine soldiers killed."

"Was it a battle, Captain, the result of a war?"

"It was without doubt. The Army was equipped as they should have been at such a time, sentinels were stationed, and Pine Ridge fortified."

Sterling broken in: "I object."

And the objection was sustained.

But Baldwin was permitted to discuss the deployment of thousands of troops and the military fortifications, pickets, and sentinels at Pine Ridge.

Then Powers asked, "Where was Plenty Horses first taken when arrested?"

Sterling objected, and the court asked Powers, "What do you propose to prove?"

"That the defendant was arrested as a prisoner of war, and that he was held as such," Powers replied. "I will show that Plenty Horses was held by General Miles as a prisoner of war, and that General Miles absolutely refused to deliver over the prisoner until certain conditions were complied with."

"What do you mean?" Judge Edgerton asked testily. "The defendant was arrested on a warrant from this court, and I am not aware that this court has been put under conditions by General Miles."

"I have seen all the correspondence between the War Department and the attorney general, in which the War Department absolutely refused to deliver over the defendant to the civil authorities until certain whites who had committed outrages were arrested and dealt with," Powers said, referring to the Culbertson brothers and others implicated in the Few Tails shooting.

"The counsel has more light on the question than I had," Edgerton said. "What I meant to correct was that this court had made no conditions with General Miles. General Miles is in no position to exact any conditions from this court."

"But . . . ," Powers began.

Edgerton cut in. "The court is absolutely through with this matter."

Baldwin went on to describe the concentration of forces at Pine Ridge to show that a state of war existed there. Powers asked Baldwin if Casey had been spying on the Indians, as Plenty Horses had contended. Baldwin said that Casey was supposed to report on the movements of the enemy. "We do not call such a thing spying," he corrected. "We call it reconnoitering."

Next came William McGaa, an interpreter, who described the Drexel Mission fight, in which Plenty Horses had participated. He was followed by He Dog, who also described the mission fight and then the ghost dance. Again, Powers drove home a point about war at Pine Ridge: "Do you remember the day Casey was killed?"

"Yes," He Dog said.

"On the day before the killing were there any wounded Indians in your camp?"

"Yes. They came in night and day, by twos and threes. Among them were many women and children—some of the children were very small. This created much excitement and much feeling."

The defense recalled Broken Arm, who outlined the fortifications set up by the Indians, suggesting that their camp was built as a defense against the U.S. military.

The following witness was E. P. White, the stenographer who had taken down the testimony of the first trial. He produced notes on Rock Road's statement that he was "afraid to go into the [hostile] camp." This reading proved that Rock Road's denial of his statement in the current trial was false.

Then William Craven, the Cheyenne River reservation interpreter, testified that White Moon had told him, as he had told Thompson, that he did not know who shot Casey because the killer wore paint. Craven also said that White Moon claimed to have fired twice at the killer. Two witnesses had now debunked White Moon's testimony. A spectator in the crowd, White Moon became deeply troubled by these revelations.

Two more witnesses appeared to corroborate that all the Brulé were hostile and that Plenty Horses was a member of the Two Strike band. On that note, the court adjourned until the next morning. At the close of the day, J. J. McDonough thought that Nock and Powers had the case sewn up: "To all appearances, they have matters in their own hands. All this may be attributed to the determination of the prosecuting attorney to prove that war was not in progress when Casey was shot, with the result of really weakening his case."

By then editorial writers were interested in the case. During the week of the trial, the *Omaha Bee* opined: "Plenty Horses, by the help of the Indian Rights association [*sic*] is making a game fight for his liberty at Sioux Falls. In slaying Lieut. Casey he committed a cold-blooded murder. He should be given a fair trial according to the forms of law, and no technicality should shield him from the penalty of his crime."[19]

ON THE FOURTH MORNING OF the trial, the defense team turned in several documents that bolstered the argument that the Lakota were at war when Casey was shot. They had General Miles's report indicating that Casey was killed while reconnoitering the hostile camp. They had Miles's order forbidding the delivery of Plenty Horses to civilian authorities until something was done about Few Tails's alleged killers, which indicated that Miles had control of Plenty Horses as a war prisoner. They had an order from Miles recognizing Plenty Horses as a war prisoner and directing him to be fed by the War Department as such. And they had the report of the lieutenant who arrested Plenty Horses, which showed that the officer did so without any authority from any civilian source, suggesting that the arrest was a military action. The judges adjourned at midday and said they would determine the standing of these documents that afternoon.

White Moon, Casey's scout, left the courtroom severely depressed. He had been badly homesick for several days, but his sadness had redoubled after the previous day's testimony revealed his lies on the witness stand. From the court, he went to a local store and bought a knife with a two-and-a-half-inch blade, then returned to the Merchants Hotel and went to the room occupied by He Dog and another Lakota witness, Woman Dress, who were at lunch.[20] There, White Moon took out his new knife, poised it over his shoulder, and plunged it down to the hilt behind his clavicle, hoping to reach his heart. He collapsed onto a bed, blood pouring from the wound and his mouth, but he was still conscious when He Dog and Woman Dress showed up. They called for a local doctor, who found that the knife had penetrated a lung. White Moon passed out for about an hour, but he proved his mettle: By 4 p.m. he was up and around again, though still feeling low, and was planning to go home the next day.

Meanwhile, the trial went on. That afternoon, the court was so packed with women that hardly a man could be seen behind the bar railing. "It was ladies' day, sure enough," wrote J. J. McDonough.[21]

At 1:30 or 2 p.m. Sterling announced that he would offer no rebuttal to the defense, and Nock rose confidently to say, "We are ready to argue our case."

"Wait a moment, gentlemen," Judge Shiras cut in. "If you have both concluded the presentation of testimony, I have something to say to the jury." This development was irregular enough to set off alarm bells for the defense, and when Shiras next declared, "There is no need of going further with this case," without question he took away the breath of every man and woman in the courtroom.

Quickly explaining, Shiras instructed the jury to bring in a verdict of not guilty. He told them that it was the court's legal responsibility to instruct them to do this in cases in which only a verdict of not guilty could be sustained. "From the entire evidence," he said, "it clearly appears that on the day when Lieutenant Casey met his death there existed in and about the Pine Ridge Agency a condition of actual warfare between the Army of the United States there assembled under the command of Major General Nelson Miles and the Indian troops occupying the camp on No Water and in its vicinity. It is entirely clear that on the part of the Untied States this condition of actual existing warfare was recognized and the troops of the United States and the Indians had fought several engagements with more or less severity, and that both forces were then actually arrayed against each other."[22]

He went on to say that Casey unquestionably was a combatant.

> While the manner in which Plenty Horses killed Lieutenant Casey was such as would meet the severest condemnation, nevertheless we cannot deny the fact that Lieutenant Casey was engaged in an act of legitimate warfare against the Indians, and was in such condition that he might be legitimately killed as an act of war by a member of the hostile camp against which he was then operating.
>
> It is clearly apparent that if on the same day a portion of the hostile Indians had intended to reconnoiter the fortifications and position of the United States troops, and while they were engaged in such expedition one or more of them had been shot and killed by a soldier belonging to the United States forces, that

such an act would not be deemed to be an act of murder on the part of the white soldier, and justice requires the application of the same rule to the Indian as we would apply to the white soldier under reversed circumstances. It is apparent that the actions and the conduct of the troops of the United States at and about Pine Ridge Agency at the time that Lieutenant Casey was killed cannot be justified in all respects excepting upon the admission of the fact they were engaged in actual hostilities and warfare.

Shiras explained that Casey died in the line of duty and that, consequently, "the judgment of the Court is that this jury would be compelled to hold, first that there was a condition of actual warfare existing at that time, and that Lieutenant Casey was actively engaged in operations as a member of the armed forces of the United States carrying on hostilities against the Indians." He pointed out that, had Casey killed an Indian while reconnoitering the camp, the officer would not have been charged with murder. "Under these circumstances, it is the judgment of the Court that a verdict of guilty could not be sustained and therefore the jury are [*sic*] instructed to return a verdict of not guilty."

The courtroom erupted in cheers, and although Marshal Fry rapped on the clerk's desk for order, the tumult continued. Powers shook Plenty Horses' hand, and Plenty Horses actually broke down, tears streaming, according to the *New York World*. "I'm free," he said. "Good, good, good."[23] The *Sioux Falls Argus-Leader* reported an altogether different reaction, saying Plenty Horses "was the coolest person in the room. His face did not for a moment light up with joy. On his face there was no trace of delight, as before there had been none of anxiety or fear."[24]

When Judge Edgerton announced the discharge of the prisoner and adjourned the court, the crowd rushed to Plenty Horses, reaching out for him. He shook hands with dozens of women, bowing slightly to each and smiling. His attorneys eventually got him out of the courtroom. Outside, he met a dozen or more Indians, among them American Horse, who grasped Plenty Horses' hand and expressed the ambivalence that haunted the trial. "I am glad you are free," he said. "You killed Casey. That was bad. He was a brave man and a good one. He did much for the Indian, but the whites cruelly starved us into such a condition that the young men were crazy and you did not know what you did."[25]

Later, Plenty Horses found time for another interview with the *New York World*'s J. J. McDonough. "I am a free man, and my liberty is as precious to me as anyone living, but I would rather have died than to be called by the court a murderer," Plenty Horses said. "Had it not been for the good fight made by my attorneys I doubt if I should ever had a chance to return to my people. They are entitled to the credit of saving my life, and if ever an Indian had occasion to feel grateful to white men I have towards them. I shall go back to the reservation tomorrow to meet my father and mother. They are broken hearted."[26]

McDonough also interviewed the jurors that evening and learned that all of them agreed with Judge Shiras's decision. The reporter suspected that, had the case been handed over to them for a verdict, they would have freed Plenty Horses. An editorial in the *Argus-Leader* came to a contrary conclusion. After canvassing the jury, the paper's editorial staff concluded that the verdict would have been manslaughter.

Captain Baldwin, who had been a friend of Casey, capped the day by telling a reporter: "Casey was on hostile ground, and he died like a soldier. If he could be alive today and appear as a witness, he would not desire the punishment of this poor savage." But it goes without saying that Baldwin's feelings were mixed. While talking with Nock and Powers after the trial, he broke down in tears.

Plenty Horses, meanwhile, took a room at the Merchants Hotel and went for a drive around town with some friends. "I am awful glad," he told the *Argus-Leader* reporter. "I will go back to the agency and be a good Indian. I will ride my pony and be once more happy."[27]

He did not forget the men to whom he owed his life. He had no money, but he had hospitality, and so he invited Powers and Nock to visit him at home, promising that he would provide them his father's ponies for a tour of the reservation and would fete them with dog soup, a Lakota delicacy.

The next morning, Plenty Horses and his friends visited the local photo parlor, Butterfield & Ralston, to have their pictures taken. Leroy T. Butterfield also had taken photographs after the first trial, shot after shot: Plenty Horses alone; Plenty Horses with his Lakota friends; Plenty Horses with the defense attorneys, prosecuting attorneys, and Cheyenne witnesses, White Moon standing in back gazing with grave dignity into the camera. The photographs illustrated the split that had complicated Plenty Horses' life and contributed to the death of Lieutenant Casey: Plenty Horses is wearing the shirt and slacks of a white man,

After the trial, key participants gathered in a local photo studio for portraits. Left to right, front row: Tom Flood, Living Bear, Plenty Horses, Bear Lying Down. Second row: William S. Sterling, J. G. Ballance (bearded), Pete Richard, Broken Arm, Jack Red Cloud, He Dog, Philip Wells. Back row: William Rowland (white mustache), White Moon, Deputy U.S. Marshal F. C. Fry, Deputy U.S. Marshal Chris Mattheison, Rock Road, William Thompson, George P. Nock, David Edward Powers. (*Courtesy of the Sioux and Heritage Museums, Sioux Falls, South Dakota*)

but he is wrapped in his ever-present blue blanket and sports a pair of moccasins. Butterfield subsequently sold copies of the photographs as souvenirs.

Although too poor to afford a train ticket home, Plenty Horses accepted no
white charity. But he did take payment from three or four young women who
wanted his autographs as "valuable mementos." In this practice he was following in the tradition of Sitting Bull, who had sold autographs while being taken
to Fort Randall shortly after his surrender, charging men three to five dollars.
Unlike Plenty Horses, however, Sitting Bull did not charge women, although
he sometimes traded autographs for a kiss.

Soon, Plenty Horses and the other Lakota boarded a train for the reservation. Among his friends was Broken Arm, who had been there at the beginning, when Casey was shot, and now at the end, when Plenty Horses was free.

FOR U.S. ATTORNEY WILLIAM STERLING, when one case closed, another
opened. In Sturgis, South Dakota, the Culbertsons were about to face their
trial, and getting a conviction in their case would be even more difficult now
that Plenty Horses had been acquitted.

The Culbertson trial began on June 22 in Sioux Falls, with Sterling assisting state's attorney Alex McCall, whose commitment to prosecuting the case
was weak—he did not even want to try the men.

Unfortunately, no known trial transcripts survive, and newspapers did not
cover the Few Tails case as thoroughly as they had Plenty Horses'. In any
event, the trial was perfunctory, to the point, anticlimactic, and heartless in ignoring the grief and anguish, physical and otherwise, of the victims. The editor of the *Sturgis Weekly Record* summed up what was almost certainly the
prevailing attitude about the Culbertson trial in regard to the Plenty Horses
case: "Now, what sort of a newspaper must it be that would advocate or countenance the conviction of any white man for shooting an Indian in the same
time that this other condoned crime was committed. No! The RECORD editor
has lived 'out west' too long. You can't make fish of one and flesh of another.
It don't 'size up right' with these crude ideas of justice that seem to sprout from
the ground."[28]

Four men were being tried, as charges against James Juelfs, a wealthy
rancher, had been dropped. The trial opened with Clown's testimony. The

Bismarck Daily Tribune reported that she identified Andrew Culbertson as one of the gunmen but could not identify the others. The *Daily Tribune* also expressed the widely held belief "that it will be impossible to convict since the acquittal of Plenty Horses at Sioux Falls."[29]

The defense attorneys called Clown back to the witness stand on Saturday, June 27, in an unsuccessful attempt to break down her testimony. The sergeant who had visited the Few Tails camp the night before the shooting also was called, and he testified that the six Indians traveling by wagon were the only Indians in the area.[30]

On June 30, the defense attorneys—one Judge Polk, along with T. E. Harvey and Colonel W. H. Parker—opened their case. As in the Plenty Horses trial, the defense team did not deny that their clients had launched the attack but rather insisted that the fight was a matter of self-protection.

Sterling should have been heartened when three of the defendants took the stand one after another and told similar stories so ludicrous that no one could possibly believe them. The gist of the stories was that the ranchers had found a band of 120 to 150 Lakota attempting to rustle about thirty of the Culbertsons' horses. The cowboys hastily armed themselves with guns furnished by the state (presumably guns issued as part of a plan to arm citizens during the ghost dance scare), and went in pursuit. When they were within a hundred yards of the Indians, the ranchers demanded the horses and were answered with gunfire. "A lively skirmish followed, Indians, horses and whites scattering in every direction," reported the *Argus-Leader* with what sounds like a hint of sarcasm. The same article also mentioned that during the trial on July 1, "facts were disclosed . . . that two of the Culbertsons were indicted in Bon Homme county in 1882 for horse stealing but acquitted through a technicality."[31]

In marked contrast, Sterling brought to the witness stand the sergeant from the Quinn ranch army outpost who had investigated the ambush site. He testified that the cowboys had come to his camp to report that they had been attacked by the Indians. Two army privates had gone with the cowboys and helped them shoot at One Feather and his family. The sergeant outlined how he arrived at the scene later, studied the tracks at the site of the ambush, and concluded that the cowboys had attacked the Indians while hidden.

Despite the strong evidence for the prosecution and the sheer stupidity of the cowboys' testimony, the *Argus-Leader* ominously reminded readers: "It is a popular belief that it will be impossible to get a jury in this part of South

Dakota to convict these men owing to the general bad feeling that exists over the acquittal of Plenty Horses. The prosecution, however, claims to have a chain of evidence that will prove conclusively that the men are guilty of the charge in the indictment."[32]

The attorneys made their closing remarks. Parker spoke for the defense in what the local newspaper reporter called "a masterly effort in every particular."[33] The jury adjourned for two hours and took three ballots. In the first two, only one juror opposed a verdict of not guilty. On the third round, that juror gave up, and the four alleged gunmen were sent home.

The editor of the *Sturgis Weekly Record* did not let the trial close without comment: "Thus ends one of the greatest farces that Meade county [*sic*] has ever experienced. Probably not one man in a thousand has thought for a moment that these men should even have been arrested—much less placed on trial. But the outside pressure has been such that nothing would do but to haul them up, keep them in jail for months, and finally bring them before a court of justice—for what? Simply killing an Indian, that, with others, was engaged in horse stealing."[34]

DESPITE THE OUTCOME OF THE Culbertson trial, the acquittal of Plenty Horses was in many senses a victory for Indians: One of their own had gone peacefully under arrest, had weathered the trial system, and had come out still standing. Perhaps the Indians might find fairness and justice in the hands of the whites after all. Perhaps the trial and the acquittal were signs that the United States wanted to expiate its sins, or at least avoid committing new ones. Or perhaps, after Wounded Knee, the government just did not want to kill another Indian.

Or perhaps another, darker issue helped to drive the verdict. The day after Plenty Horses' acquittal, the *Argus-Leader* weighed in with its opinion, fully agreeing with Judge Shiras' decision while adding: "The defendant is a coward, and his act was treacherous and cruel. Plenty Horses in his heart is not a patriot but an assassin. The ARGUS-LEADER has no sympathy with those who try to put a halo about him and who affect to believe him a hero. But from a legal standpoint he was not guilty of murder, and the court's instruction to the jury was good law." Still, the editorial writer could not resist making a crucial point: "If the Sioux trouble was not a war, the Indians killed at Wounded Knee were simply murdered by our soldiers."[35]

How close to the heart of the court's decision did Wounded Knee lie? Doubtless the U.S. Army and the War Department did not want to resurrect the ghost of Wounded Knee. The battle, the fight, the slaughter—whatever it was called—was widely perceived, particularly in the more populated East, as a national disgrace. That disgrace would have been compounded had Plenty Horses been found guilty of murder and perhaps even if he had been judged guilty of manslaughter. The court virtually *had* to find him innocent or open up a Pandora's box of questions about Wounded Knee that no one wanted answered or even asked. The Plenty Horses verdict made certain that Wounded Knee would never rise again, that the issue could be buried out on the remote South Dakota plains with the bodies of the battlefield dead. Miles himself, determined that Forsyth at least should be punished, tried for twenty-five more years to launch another investigation into the Wounded Knee catastrophe, but never succeeded.

One other mystery remained at the close of the trial. Living Bear was still missing, and Marshal F. Curtis Fry learned that the deputy he had sent to bring in Plenty Horses' father had turned up in Sioux City, where he apparently had paused for a spontaneous holiday all his own. No one was certain whether he had even gone to the reservation to get the crucial witness. According to the conventional wisdom of the time, many at Pine Ridge—presumably military or agency personnel—were bitterly against Plenty Horses and had tried to keep his father from testifying.[36] The *Argus-Leader* editorialized a bit in its report on the incident, opining that the deputy would "have to tell a pretty straight story, or he will be decapitated so quickly that he won't know what struck him. The deputy is said to have been heretofore a courageous and conscientious officer, and there is therefore the greater surprise at the turn affairs have taken."[37] But no matter—the case was closed.

Epilogue

WITH THE PLENTY HORSES CASE finished, the government and the public seemed ready to forget Wounded Knee, and the trial gave them reason to do so. The verdict excused any atrocities perpetrated in December 1890 and January 1891 on Pine Ridge and other Lakota reservations, from the shooting of Sitting Bull to the slaughter at Wounded Knee. The shoot-out holds an infamous place in our history, but it is still recounted not as a massacre of unarmed Indians, including women and children, but as the last battle of the Indian wars. Several soldiers received Congressional Medals of Honor for their role in the one-sided fight.

Today, a movement is afoot to rescind those medals, but that is only a small gesture. The people who perpetrated the massacre are beyond punishment, and the truth of what happened at Wounded Knee is beyond reach. All we have left are whispers and speculation. As time passes, the question of Wounded Knee grows faint, and we forget.

But the Lakota remember, and they preserve that memory as a touchstone with their past. In recent years the Lakota have sponsored an annual trek that follows the path of Sitanka and his people as they moved to their meeting with fate and history. Riding horseback, the Lakota make the journey even in the coldest winters, when windchill indexes can fall past seventy degrees below zero.

Called the "Big Foot Ride," after Sitanka, the yearly odyssey first occurred in 1987 after Birgil Kills Straight, a descendant of a Wounded Knee survivor, had a recurring dream urging him to initiate the ride as a way to heal the wounds of the 1890 massacre.[1] Eighteen other riders joined him that first year. The commemoration has continued since, honoring the dead and offering lessons in leadership to today's young by reviving the memory of Sitanka. The ride extends for 350 miles and takes thirteen days, starting at Standing Rock Reservation on the anniversary of Sitting Bull's death and ending at Wounded Knee on December 28, the day before the anniversary of the massacre.

After gathering in a circle for a prayer at the site of the Wounded Knee massacre, the riders—who may exceed two hundred—move uphill to where army guns once stood and where the dead are now buried. Leaders lay out tobacco, sage, and food and offer a prayer for the women and children, elders and warriors, buried there. Reliving the tragedy each winter, they recall the suffering of their ancestors and find courage for the challenges that still await them today at Pine Ridge.

The broken dream of the ghost dance lingers today at Pine Ridge in the form of deadly government neglect.[2] At more than 2 million acres, Pine Ridge reservation is the second-largest Indian reservation in the United States, roughly the size of Connecticut. It is home to about forty thousand people, 35 percent of them under the age of sixteen. Median annual income is $2,600, with 85 to 95 percent unemployment. Infant mortality is 300 percent higher than the U.S. national average. Cervical cancer is 500 percent higher than the national average, and tuberculosis and diabetes 800 percent higher. Average life expectancy is forty-five years, the shortest for any community in the Western Hemisphere outside of Haiti.

At least 60 percent of Pine Ridge homes need to be burned to the ground because of infestations by the potentially fatal black mold *Stachybotrys*. More than 33 percent of reservation homes lack basic water and sewage systems, and 39 percent have no electricity. Pine Ridge reservation schools are in the bottom 10 percent of school funding provided through the U.S. Department of Education and the Bureau of Indian Affairs. The school dropout rate is 70 percent. The teenage suicide rate is one and a half times that of the U.S. national average for teens.

Alcoholism affects eight out of ten reservation families, and death from alcohol-related problems on the reservation is three times more likely than in the rest of the United States, even though the Oglala Lakota Nation has banned the sale and possession of alcohol on the reservation since the early 1970s.

THE YEARS FOLLOWING THE PLENTY Horses trial have often been harsh for the Lakota. For the actual participants in the trial, fate delivered a more mixed result. The Carlisle school found the Plenty Horses verdict a sort of vindication. But the school did not survive long anyway. Richard Henry Pratt continued to run Carlisle until 1903, when President Theodore Roosevelt, miffed with Pratt after a dispute about the Civil Service Commission, forced the old officer to retire, with the rank of brevet general. The commissioner of Indian Affairs asked Pratt to remain at Carlisle as director, which he did. However, Pratt later publicly criticized the Indian Bureau and was immediately fired. When he died in 1924, the school was a thing of the past, its buildings returned to active military service during World War I.

Plenty Horses disappeared into obscurity, resurfacing only once, at a public appearance at the South Dakota exhibit at the Chicago World's Fair in 1893. William Sterling was there, too, to deliver an address. David Powers told a reporter right after the trial that he did not think Plenty Horses would survive another two years—"It is my opinion that he has consumption"—but Plenty Horses outlived them all: Powers, Nock, Edgerton, Shiras, Sterling.[3] He went back to the Rosebud reservation, married, and raised children. Relatives of his fought in World War I. He lived quietly, disappearing from the historic record until his death in 1933, when Franklin Delano Roosevelt was starting his first term as president, and Adolf Hitler was rising to power in Germany.

Powers, in the Plenty Horses trial and in others, proved himself a capable lawyer, valued enough locally that, in 1892, he was appointed city attorney for Sioux Falls.

Pete Culberston—leader of the bushwhackers who killed Few Tails—reinvented himself, touring the country with his own Indian Pete's Wild West show from 1910 to 1920.

He wasn't the only participant in Wounded Knee and its aftermath whose life became someone else's entertainment. Sitting Bull was dead less than a month before North Dakota senator Lyman Casey (not a relative of Lieutenant Casey) urged the Indian Bureau to move swiftly to acquire as many of the chief's personal effects as possible, including his cabin, which ended up on display at the Chicago World's Fair.

When Cody's Wild West show opened at the World's Fair, the gray horse on which Sitting Bull was to have ridden to prison on December 15, 1890, led the procession, mounted by a man carrying the American flag.

Short Bull and Kicking Bear, the leading ghost dance apostles among the Lakota, left the reservation to join Cody's Wild West show.

Bull Head and the other policemen killed while arresting Sitting Bull were buried with honors. McLaughlin, who went on to become a top official in the Indian Bureau, spent years winning small compensatory pensions from the government for the police widows.

Elaine Goodale married Dr. Charles Eastman. They separated in 1921 after thirty years of marriage. He had a heart attack on January 7, 1939—the forty-eighth anniversary of Casey's death—and died the next day, at the age of eighty. He was buried in Detroit. Elaine survived not only the last Indian war but also both world wars, dying in 1953, at age ninety, after decades of service for the Lakota. She was buried in New England.

Wovoka led a quiet life as a ranch hand and medicine man until his death in 1932. His people, the Paiute, called him "Our Father" until the day he died.

On March 20, 1894, Miles recommended that Lieutenant Edward Casey receive posthumously the Medal of Honor for his role in capturing the horses of Lame Deer's village in the raid of 1877. The medal was never awarded.

Just before he retired in 1903, Nelson Miles was promoted to commanding general of the U.S. Army, the last officer to achieve that exalted rank. He died in 1925 of a heart attack while rising from his chair at a circus as the band commenced playing "The Star-Spangled Banner."

NOTES

PROLOGUE

1 Sources for the spirit ride were local newspaper stories and an April 2003 interview with Birgil Kills Straight.

2 For details on these various developments, see Page Smith, *The Rise of Industrial America*, (New York: McGraw-Hill, 1984).

3 Myriad sources are available on the religious movement called the ghost dance and will be cited more specifically below. However, good general sources include Robert Utley's *The Lance and the Shield: The Life and Times of Sitting Bull* (New York: Henry Holt, 1993); the classic James Mooney work *The Ghost Dance Religion and Wounded Knee* (1896; reprint, New York: Dover, 1973); and W. Fletcher Johnson's *Life of Sitting Bull and History of the Indian War of 1890–'91* (published by Edgewood), an interesting little curiosity that was on sale by March 1891—it was a nineteenth-century quick-and-dirty book that sought to capitalize on sensational current events. Some of its facts are wrong, but it reveals prevailing attitudes about events on the Lakota reservations. Out of print, it can be found with relative ease at various used-book outlets. I purchased two copies from eBay.

4 Sources on Wounded Knee abound. Highly readable books on the subject, used in putting together this chapter, include William Coleman's *Voices of Wounded Knee* (Lincoln: University of Nebraska Press, 2000); Robert Utley's *The Last Days of the Sioux Nation* New Haven, CT: Yale University Press, 1963); Tom Streissguth's *Wounded Knee 1890: The End of the Plains Indian Wars* (New York: Facts on File, 1998); Charles Eastman's *From the Deep Woods to Civilization* (1916; reprinted, Lincoln: University of Nebraska Press); Elaine Goodale Eastman's memoir, *Sister to the Sioux* (Lincoln: University of Nebraska Press, 1978).

5 Quoted in Julia McGillycuddy, *Blood on the Moon: Valentine McGillycuddy and the Sioux* (1940; reprint, Lincoln: University of Nebraska Press, 1990), p. 272.

6 Key sources on the shooting include the *New York World* and *Sioux Falls Argus-Leader* newspapers for April and May 1891. The shooting will be covered and cited later in this book in detail.

CHAPTER 1. AN OFFICER'S LIFE

1 During the battle of Seven Pines, in Virginia, Silas Casey's troops faltered, and he was subsequently vilified in the press for poor leadership. However, he was quickly exonerated, with the difficulties on the field blamed on the greenness of his troops and an overextended line of attack.

2 Material on Thomas Lincoln Casey is found in many sources. Perhaps the best repository of information on him, and certainly on others in his family, is the archive of Historic New England, formerly the Society for the Preservation of New England Antiquities, Boston, Massachusetts, which holds Casey family papers dating to the eighteenth century.

3 As a baby, Edward seems to have gotten off on a good foot. His family was loving, supportive, and highly approving. Thomas Lincoln even took time off from his studies at West Point to write his parents, "It gives me great pleasure to hear that you are all well & that the young chap is progressing fully." (Historic New England, box 102 of Casey family material,

letter dated April 11, 1851.) Edward's mother, Abby—a native Rhode Islander and the daughter of a U.S. congressional representative—was unabashedly proud of the family baby. While living in Athens, Georgia, in 1855—military spouses sometimes took a break from frontier life—she wrote to Silas that four-year-old Eddie went to Sunday school with his older siblings and that "he was the best scholar there, and Mrs. Knight gave him a stick of Candy." (Historic New England, box 29, folder 29.9.) He was just barely five when she wrote Silas on January 9, 1856, that she was teaching Eddie his letters and that he "seems quite ambitious to learn." The following October she wrote: "Eddie is quite improving in his studies—he goes regularly to school—and comes home every day to puzzle me with the spelling of a *very hard word of three letters*. I asked him what I should say to you—he 'says give Pa my love, and tell him I ache to see him' he was delighted with the pictures and arrows, he is growing tall—but—very thin." (Historic New England, box 29, folder 29.10, letter dated October 3, 1856.)

[4] The account of the Lame Deer incident described here is from George Bird Grinnell, *The Fighting Cheyenne* (Norman: University of Oklahoma Press, 1955; reprint of 1915 edition published by Charles Scribner's Sons), pp. 387–97. Other accounts differ slightly, including on matters such as the identity of individual members of Lame Deer's band, but Grinnell drew his information from participants in the battle and seems more reliable.

[5] While at West Point he ran into some domestic problems that probably made him long for the calm of a good Indian fight. In 1882 his father died, and Edward was stuck serving as executor of the estate after Thomas Lincoln refused to do it. Edward and brother Silas attempted to sort out who was to inherit what. Negotiations were complicated by two factors discussed obliquely in family correspondence—the dark underside of the Casey family. (Historic New England, box 121, folder N.)

Edward's mother, Abby, had died in the early 1860s, and his father a few years later had married a woman named Florida, who now wanted more cash than the senior Silas had left her. She threatened to go to the newspapers to tell the world how her war-hero husband had not left her enough money to live on. She was hoping that the publicity would net a bigger government pension. Thomas Lincoln entered the fray, telling her he would see what he could do about the pension. And then the mess got messier—the sons found out their father apparently had been on "intimate" terms with another woman, as they put it delicately in their correspondence. This nameless woman refused to give up bonds Silas had given her. Edward spent a large part of 1882 working out these problems.

[6] Presumably Casey was pleased with this assignment. He had written two years earlier to Thomas Lincoln that he liked the area: "My company goes to [Fort Lewis] with four other companies under the Major. The post is very near Durango Col. where I was encamped during the winter of '79 & '80. It is the post above all others I would select & those I have heard from [there] are well pleased." (Historic New England, box 70, folder Q, p. 30, a letter dated November 1882.)

[7] Maurice Frink and Casey E. Barthelmess, *Photographer on an Army Mule* (Norman: University of Oklahoma Press, 1965), pp. 63–70.

[8] "My proposed route would be upon a right line drawn from the mouth of the La Plata River to the upper end of the Canyon, making such divergences as would enable me to visit one or two of the Moqui and Pueblo villages and also such detours as the nature of the country would of course render imperative." (Ibid., p. 56.)

[9] Barthelmess was a great fan of Lieutenant Casey and would name one of his sons after him. One of Barthelmess' grandsons runs the Range Rider Museum in Miles City, Montana, a treasure trove of photographs and other material about Casey and Fort Keogh. Another Barthelmess grandson lives in California and controls the photo collection that his musician-grandfather put together. His name is Casey.

[10] Casey sought to preserve his expedition in a report he filed on his return to Fort Lewis, including maps, thirty-five photographs shot by Christian Barthelmess, the earnestly collected barometric records, and Casey's field notes. Sent eventually to the National Archives, the report and all the rest are missing now, lost decades ago. All that is left is a fourteen-page letter that the post commander, Colonel Peter Swaine, ordered Casey to write in detail—*in detail*, Swaine emphasized—explaining how the lieutenant had managed to lose two men, four pack mules, and a wagon in the course of the trip. See Frink and Barthelmess, *Photographer on an Army Mule*.

[11] She was either a widow or a divorcée—surviving records do not indicate which.

[12] Casey's debts are discussed in a letter from Lieutenant W. H. Kell to Thomas Lincoln Casey, January 22, 1891, archive of Historic New England, box 83. Letters from Mrs. N. W. Mason to Thomas Lincoln Casey after Edward's death, and a letter from brother Silas Casey—all in the archive at Historic New England—discuss Edward's relationship with Nettie Atchison and his depression over his situation, which his nephew Silas (Thomas' son) suggested in a January 8, 1891, letter to his mother, might have made Edward reckless enough to ride into the White Clay Creek camp virtually alone. "He seems to have exposed himself unnecessarily and—it is my firm conviction—purposely. There has been a great gap in his life, something which he has never told us fully but which has been evident to me. In other words life has not been worth living to him since a certain 'affair.' " Historic New England, box 97, folder 189.

[13] This description of life at Fort Keogh in the 1880s is drawn largely from Josef James Warhank, "Fort Keogh: Cutting Edge of a Culture," master's thesis, Department of History, California State University, Long Beach, 1983. This document is available online. Just run a search for "Fort Keogh."

[14] The list of Casey's personal effects is taken from the complete list, compiled after his death, in Historic New England, box 83, January 1–15, 1891. Two houses of the sort in which Casey lived still survive. One is falling into ruin. The other is restored and open to the public at the Range Riders Museum in Miles City, Montana.

[15] Details on Fort Keogh are from Warhank's 1983 master's thesis. Details about Casey's travels come from West Point sources and from Frink and Barthelmess, *Photographer on an Army Mule*.

[16] Letter from Lieutenant W. H. Kell to Thomas Lincoln Casey, January 22, 1891, archive of Historic New England, box 83.

[17] National Archives, record group 393, box 12.

[18] Robert Lee, "Warriors in the Ranks: American Indian Units in the Regular Army, 1891–1897," *South Dakota History* 121 (1991): 262–302.

[19] Thomas W. Dunlay, *Wolves for the Blue Soldiers* (Lincoln: University of Nebraska Press, 1982), p. 191.

[20] Text on the origins of Casey's involvement with Cheyenne troops comes from Frink and Barthelmess, *Photographer on an Army Mule*, p. 104, as well as other parts of that excellent

source. Box 121 of the Casey family papers at Historic New England includes letters from Lieutenant Casey to his brother Thomas, written in late spring, in which he outlines his activities in
creating the Cheyenne unit.

Officers selected to command Indian scouts, the secretary of War would declare in 1866,
must be of high character, believe in the potential for civilizing the Indians, and be patient and
faithful men "imbued with the missionary spirit." Casey was quite likely such a man. His West
Point obituary reported: "His classmates will tell you his popularity in army circles began with
his cadet days, and that his manliness, gentleness and generosity were proverbial. His sense of
humor was keen, and he was fond of jest, but never to hurt a friend." It continued with praise
tainted to modern ears with a measure of Victorian prejudice: "His selection for [commanding
scouts] was most appropriate, for his good will toward the Indians had been manifested in many
ways, and he possessed, in a peculiar degree, the faculty of controlling them. Those under his
command loved him and were rapidly moulded into the best of light cavalry, and, in what is
more remarkable, into civilized men." His death was reportedly lamented among the Cheyenne
as if he were one of their own.

In addition to the correct character, Casey had experience with Indians. He had led a mixed
group of civilian and Cheyenne scouts while serving with Miles in the late 1870s, and he had
been the first officer to drill Crow scouts at Fort Keogh. However, the Crow had proved
undisciplined—in the sense that they once opened fire on and killed a Lakota delegation approaching Fort Keogh for peace talks—which was why Swaine decided to turn to the northern
Cheyenne. In the Crow's defense, it must be said that scouts brought into service in earlier
years were neither trained by the military nor subject to military discipline. That changed at
Fort Keogh. Casey signed up his Cheyenne scouts as regulars in the army and trained them in
fighting and drill.

[21] Richard Upton, ed., *The Indian Soldier at Fort Custer, Montana, 1890–1895* (El Segundo, CA:
Upton and Sons, 1983), pp. 37–38.

[22] Dunlay, *Wolves for the Blue Soldiers*, is an excellent source of information on Indian scouts
and the military, and much of what follows on that general subject in this book is drawn from
Dunlay.

[23] Frink and Barthelmess, *Photographer on an Army Mule*, pp. 99–100.

[24] See Dunlay, *Wolves for the Blue Soldiers*, for several discussions of this subject.

[25] Ibid., pp. 10–13.

[26] National Archives, record group 393, part 5, entry 28, vol. 2, Fort Keogh, Montana.

[27] This letter, dated May 28, 1890, is from box 121 of the Casey family papers at the archive of
Historic New England.

[28] Historic New England. See note 2 for this chapter.

[29] Frederic Remington, *The Collected Writings of Frederic Remington*, Peggy Samuels and
Harold Samuels, ed. (n.p.: Castle, 1986), p. 64.

[30] This letter, dated May 28, 1890, is from box 121 of the Casey family papers at the archive of
Historic New England.

[31] This letter is from ibid.

32 This letter, dated July 18, 1890, is from ibid.

33 This letter, dated June 8, 1890, is from ibid.

34 Remington also gave a nod to the skills the Indians brought to the military: "An Indian is the best possible light irregular cavalryman, and his methods cannot be improved by introducing ours, and he can learn little indeed from a white trooper." See Remington, *Collected Writings,* pp. 65–66.

35 Robert Wooster, *Nelson A. Miles and the Twilight of the Frontier Army* (Lincoln: University of Nebraska Press, 1993), p. 186.

36 Letter dated December 12, 1891, from box 121, Archive of Historic New England.

37 See note 12 for this chapter *re* the letter from Kell. Kell put the date as December 14 and pointed out that reports citing other dates were wrong. These wrong dates crop up in print even today.

38 Letter to Mrs. N. W. Mason from Mrs. Nettie Atchison, dated January 15, 1891, in which Mrs. Atchison quotes a letter from Lieutenant Casey dated December 21, 1890. From box 83 of the Casey family papers at the archive of Historic New England.

CHAPTER 2. CONFLICT ON THE PLAINS

1 Royal B. Hassrick, *The Sioux: Life and Customs of a Warrior Society* (Norman: University of Oklahoma Press, 1964), p. 350.

2 Stanley Vestal, *Warpath: The True Story of the Fighting Sioux Told in a Biography of Chief White Bull* (Lincoln: University of Nebraska Press, 1984; reprint of 1934 edition published by Houghton Mifflin), p. 268.

3 Robert W. Larson, *Red Cloud: Warrior-Statesman of the Lakota Sioux* (Norman: University of Oklahoma Press, 1997), p. 6.

4 Ibid., pp. 6–7.

5 You can find any number of sources on Lakota history. This thumbnail sketch of that history is put together from Larson, *Red Cloud*; Herbert S. Schell, *History of South Dakota*, 3rd ed., revised (Lincoln: University of Nebraska Press, 1975), and George Hyde, *Spotted Tail's Folk: A History of the Brulé Sioux* (Norman: University of Oklahoma Press, 1961).

6 Larson, *Red Cloud*, p. 10.

7 Ibid., p. 3.

8 Ibid., p. 13.

9 By the late eighteenth century the Lakota were on their way to becoming the mounted, formidable warriors who would resist white encroachment on the northern plains in the 1800s. Nevertheless, when they finally reached the Missouri River, they met a people who, unlike the Omaha and Iowa, would not be moved: the Arikara (Larson, *Red Cloud*, pp. 15–18). In addition to hunting, the Arikara grew crops of corn, squash, sunflowers, pumpkins, and beans and traded their crops for Kiowa horses. Their villages of earth lodges were protected by earthen fortifications. Unable to shove the Arikara aside, the Lakota nevertheless found them useful, sometimes trading with them for corn or other agricultural goods that the Sioux thought it unmanly to grow.

Then came strange, new allies for the Lakota: smallpox and other European diseases against which the Indians had little or no immunity (ibid., pp. 17–18). Tribes like the Arikara, living in villages, were severely punished for their frequent European contacts, which caused illness to burn through them like wildfire across dry prairie. Three smallpox epidemics struck between 1772 and 1780, wiping out 80 percent of the Arikara. The Lakota, far wandering and widely dispersed, were less susceptible to contagions. While more sedentary tribes were virtually wiped out, the Lakota suffered relatively slight losses. In the first half of the nineteenth century, when disease cut some plains-tribe numbers by half, the Lakota increased, from about 8,500 in 1805 to 25,000 in the 1850s (ibid., p. 18).

[10] How the Brulé got their name: In about 1763 the people were camped on a lakeshore in eastern South Dakota, when a grass fire swept through, and the band sought refuge in the lake, but not before they were scarred on their legs. They were dubbed Sichangu or Burnt Thighs, by other Lakota, but the French called them Brulé. From Hyde, *Spotted Tail's Folk*, p. 5.

[11] Larson, *Red Cloud*, pp. 11–12.

[12] Bernard DeVoto, *The Journals of Lewis and Clark* (Boston: Houghton Mifflin, 1953), pp. 33–43.

[13] Schell, *History of South Dakota*, pp. 33–34.

[14] Stephen E. Ambrose, *Undaunted Courage: Meriwether Lewis, Thomas Jefferson, and the Opening of the American West* (New York: Simon & Schuster, 1996), p. 170.

[15] Tom Streissguth, *Wounded Knee 1890: The End of the Plains Indian Wars* (New York: Facts on File, 1998), pp. viii–x.

[16] Hyde, *Spotted Tail's Folk*, pp. 8, 9, 12.

[17] Schell, *History of South Dakota*, p. 50.

[18] Hyde, *Spotted Tail's Folk*, pp. 24–25.

[19] John R. Milton, *South Dakota: A History* (New York: Norton, 1977), p. 54.

[20] Schell, *History of South Dakota*, pp. 50–51.

[21] Ibid.

[22] Hyde, *Spotted Tail's Folk*, p. 41.

[23] And the liquor was truly bad, often concocted by traders themselves. The recipe went something like this: To a barrel of Missouri River water add two gallons of alcohol, three plugs tobacco, five bars of soap, a half pound of red pepper, a touch of sagebrush, and two ounces of strychnine. Boil until the liquid turns brown, strain, and bottle. According to one observer: "Strychnine, it is said, was added for its stimulating properties, while the tobacco was a necessity because of the nausea it produced in the Indians of the time, for no whiskey was of value unless the one who drank it eventually became deathly sick. Of the white man it is said that when he drank the mixture he became so inebriated that he could not close his eyes . . . one bottle was worth a buffalo robe, but increased in value of robes per bottle as the individual became drunker and desired more of this 'fire water.'" (Stanley Young and Edward Goldman, *The Wolves of North America* [New York: Dover, 1964], p. 330.)

[24] Lillian Schlissel, *Women's Diaries of the Westward Journey* (New York: Schocken Books, 1982), p. 24.

[25] Hyde, *Spotted Tail's Folk*, p. 42. The Indians and the pioneers remained on uneasy terms, however, even in the best of encounters. Amelia Stewart Knight, who rolled by wagon past Fort Laramie in 1853, wrote in her journal for June 7: "This afternoon we passed a large village of Sioux Indians. Numbers of them came around our wagons. Some of the women had moccasins and beads, which they wanted to trade for bread. I gave the women and children all the cakes I had baked. Husband [*sic*] traded a big Indian a lot of hard crackers for a pair of moccasins." (Schlissel, *Women's Diaries*, p. 207.) Knight went on to describe the outcome of the trade: "After we had started on he came up with us again making a great fuss, and wanted them back (they had eaten part of the crackers). He did not seem to be satisfied, or else he wished to cause us some trouble, and perhaps get into a fight. However, we handed the moccasins to him in a hurry and drove away from them as soon as possible."

Contact with the Lakota resulted, too, in strange juxtapositions. Lavinia Porter, who at nineteen traveled along the Platte trail in 1859, wrote in her journal, "I would state here that the Sioux Indians were the finest looking warriors we had seen." But she also reported her particular delight at the sight of an almost naked Lakota man wearing a discarded hoop skirt. (Ibid., p. 130.)

[26] The figure was provided by Lieutenant Daniel Woodbury, who had helped build Fort Kearny, in a report dated June 2, 1849, and quoted on the Web site www2.sandi.net/kearneyh/history/swk/fk.html. The fort was a crude affair of mud buildings with trees planted on the perimeter. A reporter for the *New York Herald*, who visited the post in 1857 and 1858, wrote: "Intermixed between these immature trees on the side of the square are sixteen blockhouse guns, two field pieces, two mountain howitzers and one prairie piece. These constitute the artillery defences [*sic*] of the post against the Indians." Built on a slight elevation a few miles from the Platte, the fort had no fortifications. This quote is from the same Web site. See also Hyde, *Spotted Tail's Folk*, p. 51.

[27] Streissguth, *Wounded Knee*, p. xii.

[28] Hyde, *Spotted Tail's Folk*, pp. 56–62.

[29] Ibid., p. 70.

[30] Ibid., p. 14.

[31] Ibid., p. 33.

[32] Ibid., p. 35.

[33] Ibid., p. 40.

[34] Ibid., pp. 67–69.

[35] Ibid., p. 76.

[36] Ibid., pp. 77–78.

[37] As a witty and intelligent man, always quick with a quip, he would have this amiable effect on white associates throughout his life. Once, when he visited the White House, he remarked that the whites had many fine possessions. One of the dignitaries present, interested in pushing the Lakota into farming, remarked that if Spotted Tail would farm, he too could own many fine

things. Spotted Tail countered that if the whites would give him a tepee like the White House, he might give farming a try. On another occasion, his reservation agent, Lieutenant Jesse Lee, jested with Spotted Tail that you could tell an honest man by the growth of hair on his palms. Spotted Tail glanced at his own palms while Lee said, "I used to be ambitious to be honest. I worked at it pretty hard, but I never did get more than a few sprouts of hair on my palms." Spotted Tail laughed out loud and seized Lee by the hand, then looked again at his own palm and said, "My friend, I used to have hair on my palms, but shaking hands with so many dishonest white men has worn the hair all off." (Ibid., p. 279.)

[38] Ibid., p. 78.

[39] Ibid., p. 7.

[40] Ibid., p. 116. Hyde's *Spotted Tail's Folk* informs much of this text on the Brulé. He wrote that the Waglukhe treated the hunting Lakota "like country bumpkins who came to visit the sophisticated Sioux at the fort. These wild bulls from the Powder River were full of airs and big talk about fighting whites, but what did they know about the whites and their strength? They imagined that a fight among fifty warriors, in which two men were killed, was a big fight. The Loafers at the fort had heard details of the mighty three-day struggle at Gettysburg, and they knew what the white men meant when they spoke of battle."

[41] Larson, *Red Cloud*, p. 34. Leadership of a band was generally hereditary, although the choice of leader also was based on an individual's war record and social honors. "The headman of the least of bands achieved his position through an extraordinarily complicated system of family status and individual merit. Of supreme importance to his success was his family background. To be a son of renowned parents fostered political aspirations." (Hassrick, *The Sioux*, pp. 13–14.) A particularly successful headman also might attract members from other bands as his reputation grew. Successful leaders were those who embodied the four Lakota virtues: bravery, fortitude, generosity, and wisdom. See note 6, chapter 3 for details on the virtues.

[42] Ibid., pp. 40–41.

[43] War parties were usually organized by individuals. A warrior would announce his plan and ask others to join him. If he was respected, a large party might agree to go. The warriors would travel as a group, with some assigned to keep eager cohorts from attacking enemies too soon. When seeking enemies, warriors usually brought along their fastest horse but rode a second horse, keeping the swift horse fresh for action. They also adorned themselves and their horses with feathers, paint, and other finery so that, if they should be killed, they would arrive in the afterlife looking their best. (Robert M. Utley, *The Lance and the Shield: The Life and Times of Sitting Bull* [New York: Henry Holt, 1993], p. 14.)

Much of Lakota warfare was driven by the Indians' need as a hunting people to lay claim to a territory large enough to support the quantity of wildlife necessary for their survival. Plains Indians established distinct hunting territories that they defended from other tribes. Between established tribal territories lay unclaimed areas that constituted a sort of no-man's-land. Because few Indians hunted in these areas regularly, bison, the primary prey species, would seek refuge there from lance and arrow. Tribal hunters were safer on their own hunting grounds, where they could be fairly certain of encountering only friends. Nevertheless, the massing of bison in the no-man's-lands attracted hunters, who had to be on guard there constantly, as fighting could break out the moment warriors from different tribes spotted each other. In following bison migrations, Indians also might invade another tribe's hunting grounds (Larson,

Red Cloud, pp. 24–25). An invasion could become permanent or could be merely a temporary arrangement compelled by the need for meat. Either way, following buffalo trails into the hunting grounds of other tribes could lead to war.

44 Larson, *Red Cloud*, pp. 99–101. Fort Phil Kearny should not be confused with Fort Kearny in central Nebraska.

45 Ibid., p. 100.

46 Ibid., p. 102.

47 Michael Fellman, *Citizen Sherman: A Life of William Tecumseh Sherman* (Lawrence: University of Kansas Press, 1995), p. 410.

48 Ibid., p. 271.

49 Ibid., p. 264.

50 Hyde, *Spotted Tail's Folk*, pp. 131–32.

51 Larson, *Red Cloud*, p. 106.

52 Ibid., p. 115.

53 Fellman, *Citizen Sherman*, p. 265.

54 Ibid., p. 267.

55 Larson, *Red Cloud*, pp. 117–18.

56 Ibid., p. 117.

57 Hyde, *Spotted Tail's Folk*, pp. 155–56.

58 Larson, *Red Cloud*, pp. 116–21.

59 Ibid., p. 116.

60 Ibid., pp. 120–22.

61 Ibid., pp. 122–23.

62 Ibid., p. 120.

63 Ibid., p. 116.

CHAPTER 3. FREEDOM'S FINAL DAYS

1 George Hyde, *Spotted Tail's Folk: A History of the Brulé Sioux* (Norman: University of Oklahoma Press, 1961), p. 143. Many Waglukhe were married to whites, and the army paid these whites to pressure the Indians into moving.

2 Ibid., pp. 146–47.

3 Ibid., p. 241.

4 Robert W. Larson, *Red Cloud: Warrior-Statesman of the Lakota Sioux* (Norman: University of Oklahoma Press, 1997), pp. 229–31.

5 For detailed discussion of the breakdown of Lakota culture under the reservation system, see Robert M. Utley, *The Last Days of the Sioux Nation* (New Haven, CT: Yale University Press,

1963); George Hyde, *A Sioux Chronicle* (Norman: University of Oklahoma Press, 1956); Hyde, *Spotted Tail's Folk*; and Larson, *Red Cloud*.

[6] Successful leaders were those who embodied the four Lakota virtues: bravery, fortitude, generosity, and wisdom. The discussion here of the Lakota virtues is from Royal B. Hassrick, *The Sioux: Life and Customs of a Warrior Society* (Norman: University of Oklahoma Press, 1964), pp. 32–38. Bravery was, Hassrick wrote, "foremost for both men and women. To be considered full of courage, to have a strong heart, was an honor of extreme importance and worth great effort." That effort included fearlessness in the face of death. One precept of the Lakota was that "it is better to die on the battlefield than to live to be old."

Training for bravery started in childhood. "The toddler who struck the prowling dog was cheered by older brothers and sisters, who urged the youngster to beat still harder," Hassrick wrote. "This encouragement was believed to aid the child in gaining a conviction of his own courage."

The virtue of fortitude entailed what Ernest Hemingway called grace under pressure: The successful Lakota would show reserve during times of emotional stress and would endure physical pain without complaint. The sun dance, which included a painful and prolonged blood sacrifice, was a ritualized expression of fortitude.

Demonstrations of generosity required property, which only a brave warrior could acquire, such as horses captured from enemy tribes. The Lakota were ambivalent about owning things. They believed that failure to acquire property was pitiable, but that holding on to property for its own sake was a disgrace. The most important aspect of owning things was giving them away. One Lakota whom Hassrick interviewed told him, "A man must take pity on orphans, the crippled, and the old. If you have more than one of anything, you should give it away to help these persons." Chiefs gained status by how much they gave away, leading to an interesting social dynamic among the Lakota: The incapable, the inept, and the merely poor were critical to the society because giving them things allowed leaders and aspiring leaders to build prestige. Among the Lakota, keeping up with the Joneses was a matter not of keeping but of giving. When a boy killed his first animal, his parents would give away something, a horse perhaps, in his honor. Similar rituals occurred when a girl reached puberty. "Families saved up in order to make a good showing, for the more gifts that were given, the deeper was the respect displayed for the person honored," Hassrick reported. "Actually, people vied with one another over who could give the most and the finest presents." The chief and holy man Sitting Bull would give away entire buffalo to people less skilled or lucky in hunting. In later life, when he traveled to towns and cities, he would give away to street beggars the money he earned in Buffalo Bill's Wild West show. He did not understand how whites with great material wealth could ignore the poor among them.

The final virtue, wisdom, was not something that could be measured and observed like bravery or generosity. But the Lakota recognized wisdom when a man had it. Wisdom included the ability to inspire others, to settle arguments, to offer sound advice, and to get along well with others.

Women also aspired to perfection in four virtues, but theirs differed by half from those of men. Like men, women were expected to show bravery and generosity. A woman "might display bravery in killing an enemy, in warding off an attacker, or in protecting her family against any harm," Hassrick wrote. "Bravery among women was equally meritorious and deserving of recognition as it was among men." But the four virtues of women replaced fortitude and wisdom with truthfulness and childbearing. (Although one could argue that bearing children is a form of fortitude.)

[7] The reservation infighting led to tragedy in the case of Spotted Tail. On August 5, 1881, Spotted Tail was riding home on horseback from the agency with three other chiefs, one of whom was Two Strike (Hyde, *Spotted Tail's Folk,* p. 332). Near his house, Spotted Tail saw ahead of him a wagon, with a woman holding the reins, and kneeling beside it, as if tying his moccasins, a headman named Crow Dog. Spotted Tail and Crow Dog had been feuding for two or three years. A respected warrior who had escorted Crazy Horse to Fort Robinson when Horse surrendered, Crow Dog saw himself as a rival for Spotted Tail's chieftainship, a rivalry based in part over animosities generated while Crow Dog was head of the reservation police. When the chiefs rode up, Spotted Tail in the lead, Crow Dog snatched up a rifle he had placed strategically on the ground beside him and blasted Spotted Tail in the chest. Spotted Tail fell to the ground, dragged himself to his feet, and advanced on Crow Dog while trying to draw a revolver. But Crow Dog's bullet had done its work. Spotted Tail, one of the last of the great Lakota chiefs, fell backward and died in his tracks.

Crow Dog was punished in the traditional Lakota way, paying a blood fee of six hundred dollars, several ponies, and a number of blankets to Spotted Tail's family. Nevertheless, white authorities arrested him and took him to Deadwood for trial. Convicted of murder and sentenced to hang, he was released when the U.S. Supreme Court ruled that Dakota courts had no authority over crimes committed by Indians against Indians on a reservation. Ironically, Crow Dog did not rise to high power in the vacuum left by Spotted Tail's death, but Two Strike did, becoming chief of a large portion of the Brulé.

[8] Ibid., pp. 303–6.

[9] Ibid., pp. 152–55.

[10] Ibid., pp. 193–94.

[11] Elaine Goodale Eastman, a New England teacher who lived at Pine Ridge in the 1880s and 1890s, described the process in her autobiographical book *Sister to the Sioux,* published in 1978 by University of Nebraska Press. The quotes here are from pp. 61–62.

> The next morning finds us gathered in a big, bare structure, cold as a barn, with a round-bellied wood stove in the middle doing its little utmost. Up and down the white-washed walls are ranged in orderly piles the dark blue blankets, the gay calico quilts, the bolts of flannel, linsey, gingham, sheeting, the shirts and suits, hats and shoes each year doled out to these wards of the nation. Men of every shade of complexion, in buffalo coats, enormous mufflers, and felt boots, are sitting or standing in easy attitudes about the red-hot stove. A high counter shuts off a narrow space at one end of the long room. The issue clerk bends over the counter with a big book open before him and begins to call off the names in order. His assistants take their places before their respective piles. The doors are guarded by tall Indian police.
>
> The head chief, Iron Nation, is first named by the clerk and his name is repeated in Dakota by the interpreter, who stands beside him. The captain of police unbolts the door and sends out a ringing call. The old man comes forward with what dignity he can muster and touches the pencil which signs the receipt. Each article due him is then named in turn and the person who has it in charge must repeat the call in a loud sing-song.
>
> "ONE AND A HALF BLANKETS! One and a half blankets!" echoes from the far end of the room. "ONE FLANNEL SHIRT—MEN'S! One flannel shirt—men's! ONE BOY—DUCK! One boy—duck! FOURTEEN SHEETING! Fourteen sheeting!

TWENTY-FIVE BUTTONS! Twenty-five buttons!"—and so on and so on. Boys run to and fro with each article as named, and by the time the end of the list is reached, a huge bundle is made up on the counter. The blanket, upon which everything else is deposited, is gathered by the four corners and lifted or dragged out, after which exit Iron Nation and enter the next on the roll.

Eastman added: "How much do the Indians receive on average? . . . The men get a shoddy blanket apiece, the women a cheap quilt. Each man is issued a full suit of clothes, hat, and boots; each woman six or eight yards of linsey for a dress, some flannel, gingham, unbleached cotton, a shawl, and a few sundries. Yet so poor is the quality that the total cost to the government is only about ten dollars, according to the agent's estimate."

[12] Elaine Goodale Eastman left an account of a beef distribution at Pine Ridge in *Sister to the Sioux*, pp. 59–60:

As each excited animal was released from the corral, a crier with stentorian voice named the heads of families to whom the meat was assigned. A mob of a hundred or more Indians, each mounted on his best pony, and armed with a repeating rifle, surrounded the exit. Wild, long-horned Texas cattle galloped madly over the open prairie, each one closely followed by several yelling horsemen. Shots rang out, and screams of exultation were mingled with howls of contemptuous laughter when someone's aim was bad. Dead and dying beasts lay all about. Carcasses were butchered while yet warm by the women and old men. Soon blue curls of smoke began to steal upward from frugal small fires and hungry families to gather about the teasing fragrance of boiling meat. Liver and other tidbits were eaten raw while mothers prepared portions for the pot. The greater part was sliced in thin strips to be dried in the open air—their only means of preservation until the next Issue Day.

[13] The Lakota even made war while hunting. In 1873 they ran into Pawnee hunters who had just shot widely scattered bison. About one hundred Lakota attacked as a unit, and the Pawnee, caught spread out over the plains skinning buffalo, retreated to a ravine where their women and children were arriving with ponies laden with meat. The Pawnee warriors then turned and attacked the Lakota, fighting them off for about an hour when, seemingly out of nowhere, between eight hundred and one thousand Lakota came charging across the plains. As the Lakota would do at Wounded Knee when the military opened fire on them, the Pawnee retreated into the ravine. The Lakota stormed down the ravine from both ends and attacked relentlessly, killing about one hundred Pawnee, including thirty-nine women and ten children. They chased the Pawnee out onto the plains along the Republican River and probably would have killed many more had not a bugle call warned that the U.S. Cavalry was coming to the rescue. The Lakota retreated, taking with them eleven Pawnee women and children and about one hundred ponies. (Hyde, *Spotted Tail's Folk*, pp. 207–8.)

[14] Ibid., pp. 263–70.

[15] Getting the Brulé to change locations was no easy feat for either the reservation agents or the chiefs. Initially, the government ruled that no new supplies were to be shipped to the White River area, so the Brulé had to move or go hungry. Over the objections of Spotted Tail and other chiefs, the Brulé chose hunger. As a result, Spotted Tail went to Washington, D.C., to discuss the deadlock with President Rutherford B. Hayes, who explained that food for the Brulé was already waiting at the new Ponca reservation and could not be moved to the White River.

He promised that if the Lakota moved to the new site for the winter, in spring 1878 they could choose a new site for their reservation. And so in October 1877 Spotted Tail started leading his people back to the Missouri. Among those who traveled with him were Crazy Horse's parents, who carried with them the famous warrior's bones—he had been killed in an attempt by the army to jail him. His parents buried the bones somewhere in the Wounded Knee area. See ibid., pp. 286–97, for details of the account described here.

[16] Ibid., pp. 287–88.

[17] Ibid., p. 289.

[18] Ibid., pp. 290–91.

[19] Ibid., p. 291.

[20] Ibid., p. 294.

[21] See ibid., pp. 286–98, for details on the following story.

[22] Ibid., p. 296.

[23] Utley, *The Last Days of the Sioux Nation*, p. 42.

[24] John R. Milton, *South Dakota: A History* (New York: Norton, 1977), pp. 67–68.

[25] Hamlin Garland quoted in Herbert S. Schell, *History of South Dakota*, 3rd ed., revised (Lincoln: University of Nebraska Press, 1975), p. 168.

[26] Thomas J. Schlereth, *Victorian America: Transformations in Everyday Life, 1876–1915* (New York: HarperCollins, 1991), p. 115.

[27] The following paragraph draws on ibid., pp. 23–25, and the Web site of the Museum for the Preservation of Elevating History.

[28] Some people lamented the decline of the horse. The new forms of transportation were so bloodless, so mechanical, so heartless; they did not interact with the rider the way a horse did. But they also were not as demanding and as unreliable as horses, which had to be rested and fed and which fell sick, sometimes on a grand scale. In 1872 a mosquito-borne disease killed almost 25 percent of America's more than 16 million horses. In some cities men resorted to pulling wagons themselves. Home deliveries for items such as fuel failed. Garbage collectors were forced to neglect their pickups. Firemen could not race to blazing buildings. The business losses brought on by the dwindling number of horses contributed to the financial collapse of the following year, the Panic of 1873. Electric streetcars were more than a convenience. See Schlereth, *Victorian America*, pp. 23–25.

[29] Ibid., p. 219.

[30] Ibid., pp. 219–20.

[31] Mark Twain, *Mark Twain: Plymouth Rock and the Pilgrims*, ed. Charles Nieder (New York: Harper & Row, 1984), pp. 61–62.

[32] Schlereth, *Victorian America*, pp. 89–90.

[33] As newcomers to the area in which they staked claims, individual pioneers often wanted help picking out their farmland, so they hired professional land locators, who might charge up to twenty-five dollars for their services (ibid., p. 175). To mark the claim once it was made, the

settler would dig a three-foot-deep hole to symbolize a well, or set up four fence posts to mark out the corners of a house, or erect a "straddlebug," which was a tripod of boards with the would-be landowner's name on it. Official claims were made at federal land-claim offices.

[34] Schell, *History of South Dakota*, p. 170.

[35] Ibid., pp. 171–74.

[36] Ibid., p. 174.

[37] Most of the prairie newcomers were poor and could not survive on farming alone in the early years of soil preparation. They had to supplement their income with other work. If a farmer owned a team of horses or oxen, he or she might hire out to plow the fields of more destitute, teamless cultivators. Settlers might work in town or on the railroads. "In many cases, a settler's first earnings came from collecting the buffalo bones which littered the prairie and also were found in the low places along the James River," Schell reports (ibid., pp. 177–78). "Often the first outward-bound freight from a new town would have aboard a load of bones and horns; many tons of them were shipped out of Dakota Territory and found a ready market in Chicago and elsewhere for processing into fertilizer."

[38] The flavor of the frontier mining town comes out in Mark Twain's description of his first day in the silver-mining capital, Carson City, Nevada, in 1861.

> We were introduced to several citizens, at the stage-office and on the way up to the Governor's from the hotel—among others, to a Mr. Harris, who was on horseback; he began to say something, but interrupted himself with the remark:
> "I'll have to get you to excuse me for a minute; yonder is the witness that swore I helped to rob the California coach—a piece of impertinent intermeddling, sir, for I am not even acquainted with the man."
> Then he rode over and began to rebuke the stranger with a six-shooter, and the stranger began to explain with another. When the pistols were emptied, the stranger re-sumed his work (mending a whip-lash), and Mr. Harris rode by with a polite nod, homeward bound, with a bullet through one of his lungs, and several in his hips; and from them issued little rivulets of blood that coursed down the horse's sides and made the animal look quite picturesque. I never saw Harris shoot a man after that but it re-called to mind that first day in Carson. (Mark Twain, *The Unabridged Mark Twain*, vol. 2, ed. Lawrence Teacher [Philadelphia: Running Press, 1979], pp. 632–33, from *Roughing It*.)

[39] Milton, *South Dakota*, p. 66.

[40] Schell, *History of South Dakota*, p. 243. Theodore Roosevelt, who tried ranching in Dakota Territory in the 1880s, in part to assuage his grief over the death of his mother and his wife on the same day, described the winter of 1886–87.

> The snow fall was unprecedented, both for its depth and for the way it lasted; and it was this, and not the cold, that caused the loss. About the middle of November the storms began. Day after day the snow came down, thawing and then freezing and piling itself higher and higher. By January the drifts had filled the ravines and coulées almost level. The snow lay in great masses on the plateaus and river bottoms; and this lasted until the end of February. The preceding summer we had been visited by a prolonged drought, so that the short, scanty grass was already well cropped down; the snow covered what

pasturage there was to the depth of several feet, and the cattle could not get at it at all, and could hardly move round. . . . The starving cattle died by scores of thousands before their helpless owners' eyes. The bulls, the cows who were suckling calves or who were heavy with calf, the weak cattle that had just been driven up on the trail, and the late calves suffered most. (Theodore Roosevelt, *Theodore Roosevelt's America,* ed. Farida A. Wiley [New York: Devin-Adair, 1955], pp. 47–49.)

CHAPTER 4. THE COMING OF THE GHOSTS

[1] Robert M. Utley, *The Last Days of the Sioux Nation* (New Haven, CT: Yale University Press, 1963), p. 42.

[2] The text on the Lakota's discovery of the Black Hills is based on Robert W. Larson, *Red Cloud: Warrior-Statesman of the Lakota Sioux* (Norman: University of Oklahoma Press, 1997), p. 20.

[3] John R. Milton, *South Dakota: A History* (New York: Norton, 1977), p. 24.

[4] Larson, *Red Cloud,* p. 160. See also George Hyde, *Spotted Tail's Folk: History of the Brulé Sioux* (Norman: University of Oklahoma Press, 1961), p. 225.

[5] Stephen E. Ambrose, *Crazy Horse and Custer: The Parallel Lives of Two American Warriors* (New York: Anchor Books, 1996), pp. 372–73.

[6] Milton, *South Dakota,* pp. 24–25. The soldiers and scientists on the trip all agreed that the hills were imposing and beautiful, cooler than the sun-blasted prairies the men had crossed and alight with flowers. A *New York Herald Tribune* reporter who accompanied the expedition wrote that "no one, from the commanding general on down to the humblest private or the most profane teamster," could ignore the profusion of flowers. "Men who had never picked a flower since their childhood days bent and paid the long-neglected homage. Cavalrymen and teamsters decorated their horses and mules; infantrymen plumed their hats; officers gathered nosegays; pocket-books and note-books were brought into requisition to press and preserve the free gift of this valley." (Ernest Grafe and Paul Horsted, *Exploring with Custer: The 1874 Black Hills Expedition* [Custer, SD: Golden Valley Press, 2002], p. 36.) There is an image only the Old West could have created: the grim, gaunt Custer picking flowers in a valley the nation was about to steal from the Lakota, then leading a column of one thousand men decked out in blossoms.

Thoughts turned to those who were not there. "Some said they would give a hundred dollars just to have their wives see the floral richness for even one hour," reported the Aberdeen, South Dakota, *Pioneer.* A reporter for the *Inter-Ocean* recalled the evening of July 24, 1874. "One who has never seen colors mixed as nature mixes them, in her own rare conservatories like these, can realize the artistic effect that is produced; but let the reader imagine if he can such a valley as I have described . . . darkened by the heavy shade to the tinge of twilight, and illuminated—yes, fairly illuminated—by the gold, and the scarlet, and the blue of its flowers. But the picture is not finished. The regimental band is playing on a shelf of one of the walls, and the 'Mocking Bird,' 'Garryowen,' 'Artist Life,' 'The Blue Danube,' and snatches of 'Trovatore,' and other strains of music for the first time heard in paradise." (Grafe and Horsted, *Exploring with Custer,* p. 37.)

[7] Quoted in Grafe and Horsted, *Exploring with Custer,* p. 79.

[8] Quoted in Milton, *South Dakota,* pp. 25–26.

[9] Larson, *Red Cloud*, pp. 190–91.

[10] Quoted in Robert M. Utley, *The Lance and the Shield: The Life and Times of Sitting Bull* (New York: Henry Holt, 1993), pp. 232–33.

[11] Quoted in Hyde, *Spotted Tail's Folk*, p. 255.

[12] Herbert S. Schell, *History of South Dakota*, 3rd ed., revised (Lincoln: University of Nebraska Press, 1975), p. 140.

[13] Quoted in H. L. Williams, *The Picturesque West . . . Our Western Empire Beyond the Mississippi* (New York: Hurst, 1891), p. 248.

[14] Schell, *History of South Dakota*, p. 147.

[15] Ibid., p. 144.

[16] For accounts of these land-allotment schemes, see Larson, *Red Cloud*, and Utley, *The Last Days of the Sioux Nation* and *The Lance and the Shield*.

[17] Under this process, by 1934 the amount of land owned by Indian people nationwide fell from 138 million acres to 55 million. See Larson, *Red Cloud*, p. 252.

[18] Ibid.

[19] Of course, none of this would happen until three-fourths of adult Lakota men had signed on to the plan. To gather these signatures, the government sent to the reservation another commission of three men, this one headed by Captain Richard Pratt, the founder of the federal Indian school in Carlisle, Pennsylvania—a place to which the Lakota had seen their children sent off, like it or not, some of them never to return. The Lakota bore no affection for the man who was assigned the task of persuading them to give up more than half their land.

The commission launched its mission at the Standing Rock Reservation in what is now south-central North Dakota. There James McLaughlin, who over the years would earn a reputation as one of the best agents—firm but honest in his dealings with Indians—concluded that the terms the commission offered were unfair. Nevertheless, as a good team player, he helped the commissioners state their case, although he also let the Lakota know that he did not like the deal. Pratt told the Lakota that the United States had determined that no "threat, menace or force was to be used to induce them to assent; that it was a matter which was to be left to their own free will." Then he promptly threatened them with the menacing suggestion that refusal to sign the agreement would render "further action which may be taken in regard to the reservation problematical and uncertain." In other words, rations might be cut, goods might not be delivered, the land might be taken anyway—who knew? All was "problematical and uncertain."

[20] Ibid., p. 254.

[21] The Lakota also had time to enjoy their trip, learning to smoke cigarettes, then a fad. Sitting Bull joined other smokers in the lobby of the Belvedere Hotel, but he savored a cigar given to him by a Texas senator. Gall, one of the fiercest of warriors in the old days, went to dinner with Captain Edward Godfrey at one of Washington's finest restaurants. The dinner was another of those ironies of the Old West. Godfrey and Gall had fought against one another at the battle of the Little Bighorn. Godfrey had been under Major Marcus Reno's command, which had nearly gone the way of Custer's unit. See Utley, *The Lance and the Shield*, p. 275.

[22] Utley, *The Last Days of the Sioux Nation*, p. 50.

[23] Utley, *The Lance and the Shield*, p. 278.

[24] About his discussion with Grass, McLaughlin recalled, "I told him that if the act was not concurred in, a worse thing might happen: that legislation might be enacted which would open the reservation without requiring the consent of the Indians; and I labored with him until he agreed that he would speak for its ratification and work for it." In James McLaughlin, *My Friend the Indian* (Lincoln: University of Nebraska Press, 1989; reprint of 1910 edition, published by Houghton Mifflin), pp. 284–85.

[25] Frederic Remington, *The Collected Writings of Frederic Remington*, ed. Peggy Samuels and Harold Samuels (n.p.: Castle 1986), p. 62.

[26] This quote pops up in just about every history of the Lakota. You can find it, for example, in Utley, *The Last Days of the Sioux Nation*, p. 59; Utley, *The Lance and the Shield*, p. 280; and Larson, *Red Cloud*, p. 263.

[27] Larson, *Red Cloud*, p. 264, and James Mooney, *The Ghost Dance Religion and Wounded Knee* (New York: Dover, 1973; reprint of 1896 edition of *The Ghost Dance Religion and the Sioux Outbreak of 1890* published by the Government Printing Office, Washington, DC), pp. 26–28.

[28] Quoted in Mooney, *Ghost Dance Religion*, p. 827.

[29] Ibid., pp. 827–28.

[30] Quoted in ibid., p. 827.

[31] For details on Wovoka and the origins of the ghost dance, see Alice Beck Kehoe, *The Ghost Dance: Ethnohistory and Revitalization* (Fort Worth, TX: Holt, Rinehart and Winston, 1983). Also see Mooney, *Ghost Dance Religion*.

[32] Kehoe, *The Ghost Dance*, p. 56.

[33] Mooney, *Ghost Dance Religion*, p. 791.

[34] John Sugden, *Tecumseh, a Life* (New York: Henry Holt, 1997), pp. 117–20.

[35] Quoted in ibid., pp. 118–19.

[36] Quoted in ibid., p. 119.

[37] Ibid., pp. 119–20.

[38] Elaine Goodale Eastman, a New Englander who had come to the Great Sioux Reservation in 1886 to teach school, told in her autobiography, *Sister to the Sioux*, pp. 96–7, how she first encountered the spreading word of the ghost dance. Restless at the close of her third year out west and wishing to get to know the "wilder" Lakota better, she talked a family into letting her join them for several weeks on a summer deer hunt into the Nebraska Sandhills. "After my first full day on horseback I was stiff and very sleepy and, in fact, fell asleep before supper was ready," Goodale recalled. "I ate and slept again. Later in the night there arose a cry: 'Someone comes!' "

That someone proved to be a lone rider, Chasing Crane, who arrived with a strange tale: Christ had returned to Earth. Goodale continued:

> "God," he declares, "has appeared to the Crows across the Stony Mountains. They say he arrived out of nowhere, announcing himself as the Savior who once before came

upon earth and was killed by the white people. He told the Indians he could no longer bear to hear parents crying for their children, dying everywhere of hunger and strange diseases brought by white men. He promised to let down the sky upon all the whites and to bring back the buffalo for our use. The Messiah was beautiful to look upon, with waving hair. He bore paint as a sign of power."

All listened spellbound as to a revelation from heaven to these words out of the night and the vast empty spaces. Presently the men prepared a vapor bath (which had for them a religious as well as a hygienic meaning), and I fell asleep once more to the soothing, monotonous beat of ritual songs—never dreaming of the strange and cruel events destined to grow out of Chasing Crane's fantastic story.

[39] Wrote E. W. Forester, the agent at South Dakota's Yankton agency, to T. J. Morgan, commissioner of Indian affairs, on November 25, 1890: "Most of our Indians treat these revelations with derision and ridicule; yet there is, I observe, in the heart of the *old* Indian a sort of hope, and perhaps belief, that it is true. These old fellows, who are half fed and half starved, dream with delight of the old days when the buffalo bounded on these plains, and to them such a doctrine is as savory as was the advent of Christ to the old Jews who longed for the old days of Solomon and all this glory to be repeated." National Archives microfilm 983, roll 2, p. 2,040.

[40] Utley, *The Last Days of the Sioux Nation*, p. 85.

[41] Ibid., p. 62; the following text on Short Bull also comes from this source.

[42] Kehoe, *The Ghost Dance*, p. 14.

[43] For background on L. Frank Baum and racism, see Katharine M. Rogers, *L. Frank Baum: Creator of Oz* (New York: St. Martin's Press, 2002). The quote here is from www.bluecorn comics.com/baum.htm.

[44] McLaughlin, *My Friend the Indian*, p. 185, with minor changes to punctuation.

[45] Ibid., p. 15.

[46] Weldon is a mysterious figure from the ghost dance period, arriving seemingly out of nowhere and then vanishing from the historical record. Newspapers reported her activities but were often so inaccurate that they did not even get her name right, although with apparent relish they called her Sitting Bull's white squaw. Weldon blamed the Standing Rock agent James McLaughlin for these stories, believing that he planted them to discredit her; see Stanley Vestal, *New Sources of Indian History, 1850–1891: The Ghost Dance, the Prairie Sioux: A Miscellany* (Norman: University of Oklahoma Press, 1934), pp. 92–98. The text here is based on material in Utley, *The Lance and the Shield*, pp. 282–86, as well as Vestal, *New Sources of Indian History*, pp. 97–115, in which several of her letters appear, providing some tangible sense of her personality. Robert Utley, in a personal communication, told me he calls her the "crazy lady." Her letters do indeed suggest that she was emotionally intense, but then she was dealing with intensely emotional issues.

[47] See the preceding note for sources on Weldon's thoughts and concerns.

[48] William S. Coleman, *Voices of Wounded Knee* (Lincoln: University of Nebraska Press, 2000), p. 73.

[49] Quoted in Vestal, *New Sources of Indian History*, p. 101.

⁵⁰ She was not alone in fearing for his life. Sitting Bull—who believed he could understand the language of birds—had told her that meadowlarks were warning him that his own people would kill him.

⁵¹ Vestal, *New Sources of Indian History*, p. 104.

⁵² Utley, *The Lance and the Shield*, p. 292.

⁵³ Mooney, *Ghost Dance Religion*, p. 892. Not all local journalists agreed with the scare tactics of their brethren. However, their more-reasoned concerns were based on self-interest, not fairness to the Indians. Bad press—which included stories about hostile Indians, drought, and other forms of bad weather—was likely to discourage new settlers and investors. And as every editor worth his newsprint well knew, one of the primary purposes of the many small-town prairie newspapers was to promote local interests and attract eastern investors and settlers. The *Chadron Democrat* on November 27, 1890, lodged a protest to the sensationalized stories of other papers. "On Monday some of our citizens circulated for signature a protest to the Omaha Bee [*sic*] and World Herald [*sic*], asking them to discontinue the publication of sensational reports of the Indian troubles which have filled the columns of the Omaha papers for the past few weeks. Although the protest will probably not do any good, it is no doubt a move in the right direction, as the wholesale publication of outlandish and improbable falsehoods as have appeared in the state papers cannot but prove detrimental to this part of the country, and will be the means of retarding settlement for years to come. Let it be stopped at once." Quoted in Don Huls, *The Winter of 1890 (What Happened at Wounded Knee)* (Chadron, NE: Don Huls, 1988), p. 15.

A week later, the *Chadron Democrat* revisited the issue, declaring, "The Indian excitement is accounting for one thing at least, that of having produced a crop of fine, large sensational mongers and liars of the first water, chief among which stand C.H.C., special correspondent of the Omaha Bee [*sic*], and W.F.K., of the State Journal [*sic*]. From the very beginning of the present trouble they have shown a marked proclivity to enlarge upon every trivial incident and distort the truth far beyond the bounds of reason, besides having at times manufactured stories of blood and rapine in order to pander to the depraved tastes of the lovers of the marvelous and create a sale for the papers which they represent." Quoted in Huls, *The Winter of 1890*, pp. 21–22.

⁵⁴ Charles Eastman, *From the Deep Woods to Civilization* (Lincoln: University of Nebraska Press, 1977; reprint of 1936 edition published by Little, Brown), pp. 93–98.

⁵⁵ Quoted in Utley, *The Last Days of the Sioux Nation*, p. 111.

⁵⁶ Ibid., p. 114.

CHAPTER 5. DEATH COMES FOR SITTING BULL

¹ Robert M. Utley, *The Last Days of the Sioux Nation* (New Haven, CT: Yale University Press, 1963), p. 118.

² Ibid., pp. 120–42, 191–92, 232–35, 251.

³ Quoted in ibid., p. 141.

⁴ Crow Dog had achieved a form of fame about a decade earlier when he killed Spotted Tail. See note 7 for chapter 3, p. 215.

⁵ Utley, *The Last Days of the Sioux Nation*, drew upon several firsthand sources and military records to put together his more detailed description of the Stronghold peace missions. See

pp. 140–42 of his book for his sources. One of his key sources was Thomas S. Bland, *A Brief History of the Late Military Invasion of the Home of the Sioux* (Washington, DC: National Indian Defense Association, 1891). Bland interviewed many of the Lakota who were involved in these affairs.

[6] Utley, *The Last Days of the Sioux Nation*, p. 145.

[7] Quoted in Flora Warren Seymour, *Indian Agents of the Old Frontier* (New York: Appleton-Century, 1941), p. 300.

[8] Quoted in ibid., p. 305. McLaughlin could be quite the autocrat. In his autobiography, *My Friend the Indian* (Lincoln: University of Nebraska Press, 1989; reprint of 1910 edition published by Houghton Mifflin), he described how he, like some other agents, would perform marriages among the Indians even though he lacked the authority for doing so. He felt that any ceremony would help to give the Lakota "a sense of the importance of government." He performed so many faux marriages that "a facetious army officer at Fort Yates, in speaking with some eastern tourists of the religious denominations on the reservation, said that there were Catholics, Episcopalians, Presbyterians, and McLaughlinites" (p. 67).

[9] Letter from William J. Cleveland at Standing Rock to Herbert Welsh, January 12, 1891, at the Philadelphia Historical Society, Indian Rights Association correspondence, series 1, reel 6.

[10] For details see Robert M. Utley, *The Lance and the Shield: The Life and Times of Sitting Bull* (New York: Henry Holt), and John M. Carroll, *The Arrest and Killing of Sitting Bull* (Mattituck, NY: Amereon House, 1986). Both draw on eyewitness accounts of the arrest and the events leading up to it.

[11] An army lieutenant stopped another Indian from cutting up a portrait of Sitting Bull that Catherine Weldon had painted. He later bought it from Sitting Bull's wives for two dollars.

[12] Quoted in Utley, *The Last Days of the Sioux Nation*, p. 167.

[13] Philadelphia Historical Society, Indian Rights Association correspondence, series 1, reel 6.

[14] The quote is from www.bluecorncomics.com/baum.htm.

CHAPTER 6. GUNFIRE AT WOUNDED KNEE

[1] For accounts of the pursuit of Sitanka and the fight at Wounded Knee, see William Coleman's *Voices of Wounded Knee* (Lincoln: University of Nebraska Press, 2000); Robert Utley's *The Last Days of the Sioux Nation* (New Haven, CT: Yale University Press, 1963); Tom Streissguth's *Wounded Knee 1890: The End of the Plains Indian Wars* (New York: Facts on File, 1998); Charles Eastman's *From the Deep Woods to Civilization* (Lincoln: University of Nebraska Press, 1977; reprint of 1936 edition published by Little, Brown); Elaine Goodale Eastman's memoir, *Sister to the Sioux* (Lincoln: University of Nebraska Press, 1978); and Forrest W. Seymour's detailed *Sitanka, The Full Story of Wounded Knee* (West Hanover, MA: Christopher Publishing House, 1981).

[2] One story says that the creek was named in memory of a man who was wounded in the knee with an arrow on the bank of the stream. The literal translation is "shot in the knee." Streissguth, *Wounded Knee*, p. 78.

[3] The number of dead and wounded on each side is still hard to determine. Various sources say 34 dead troops, or 39; 350 dead Lakota, or 153, as well as other numbers. See Coleman, *Voices*

of Wounded Knee, pp. 354–56, for a useful discussion of numbers, as well as Utley, *The Last Days of the Sioux Nation*, p. 228; Streissguth, *Wounded Knee*, p. 95; and especially James Mooney, *The Ghost Dance Religion and Wounded Knee* (New York: Dover, 1973; reprint of 1896 edition of *The Ghost Dance Religion and the Sioux Outbreak of 1890* published by the Government Printing Office, Washington, D.C.), pp. 871–72.

[4] Elaine Goodale Eastman, *Sister to the Sioux*, p. 162.

[5] Ibid.

[6] Charles Eastman, *From the Deep Woods to Civilization*, pp. 108–9.

[7] Utley, *The Last Days of the Sioux Nation*, p. 251.

[8] Robert Wooster, *Nelson A. Miles and the Twilight of the Frontier Army* (Lincoln: University of Nebraska Press, 1993), p. 186.

[9] Charles Eastman, *From the Deep Woods to Civilization*, p. 111.

[10] Ibid., p. 114.

[11] John G. Neihardt, *Black Elk Speaks: Being the Life Story of a Holy Man of the Oglala Sioux* (Lincoln: University of Nebraska Press, 1970), 276.

[12] Archive of the Indian Rights Association (IRA), at the Philadelphia Historical Society, series I, reel 6, IRA correspondence.

[13] Quoted in Don Huls, *The Winter of 1890 (What Happened at Wounded Knee)* (Chadron, NE: Don Huls, 1988), p. 34.

[14] Political enemies in the East began telling newspaper reporters in November that Miles was using the reservation troubles to boost himself as a potential presidential candidate in 1892 (Wooster, *Nelson A. Miles*, pp. 181–82, 250–51). The *Washington Evening Star* published comments from an unnamed "prominent army officer" stationed in Washington, who said: "Miles is predicting a general Indian war and virtually asks that the command of the entire army be turned over to him. He wants to create a scare and pose as the savior of the country. I have no doubt in the world that he is honest in his candidacy. He has shrewdly enlisted the favor of nearly every newspaper man in California, and has by his agreeable manners and the expenditure of his means managed to make himself very popular in a certain way in the west. He is one [of] the most ambitious men in the army and he is pulling the wires shrewdly."

Miles in 1888 had supported unsuccessfully his father-in-law, John Sherman, the brother of Civil War general William Tecumseh Sherman, for the Republican presidential nomination and would support him again in 1892. In 1902 Miles himself would jump to the Democratic Party to seek its nomination for a run against Theodore Roosevelt. It is not likely, nor entirely unlikely, that he had presidential aspirations in 1891. Regardless, he was angered by the nameless "prominent officer" and wanted the matter investigated.

CHAPTER 7. CASEY'S LAST RIDE

[1] Frederic Remington, *The Collected Writings of Frederic Remington*, ed. Peggy Samuels and Harold Samuels (n.p.: Castle, 1986), p. 74.

[2] Ibid., p. 73.

[3] Ibid., p. 74.

[4] Ibid.

[5] Ibid., p. 76.

[6] Letter from Lieutenant Robert Getty to assistant adjutant general, April 13, 1891, National Archives, microfilm 983, roll 1, p. 838.

[7] Robert M. Utley, *The Last Days of the Sioux Nation* (New Haven, CT: Yale University Press, 1963), pp. 256–57.

[8] Letter from Lieutenant Robert Getty to assistant adjutant general, April 13, 1891, National Archives, microfilm 983, roll 1, p. 838; see also Utley, *The Last Days of the Sioux Nation*, p. 257.

[9] Dee Brown, *Bury My Heart at Wounded Knee: An Indian History of the American West* (New York: Holt, Rinehart & Winston, 1970), pp. 411–12.

[10] Coincidentally, both Casey and Gatewood were lieutenants under General Nelson Miles's command. Also, there was the matter of the nose: The Apache had dubbed Gatewood "Big Nose Captain," and the Cheyennes called Casey "Big Red Nose."

[11] Casey might have commiserated with an officer, quoted anonymously in the *Washington Star*, who said that after Wounded Knee he felt "like throwing aside the uniform that honors me with its covering and donning in its place the blanket of the savage. Then I could fight and be sure that my cause had a just foundation." Cited in William S. Coleman, *Voices of Wounded Knee* (Lincoln: University of Nebraska Press, 2000), p. 379. Casey also would have agreed with a comment made by an officer who commanded Crow Indian troops: "For seventy-five years our little army, always the friend and benefactor of the Indian in time of peace, has been called upon from time to time to do battle with him in cruel and bloody wars. The justice of the case was well known to lie often with the so-called 'hostile' tribe, and many a gallant officer and man have, in the very act of destroying its camps and shooting down its warriors in the bloody fight, deplored the iniquity of the cause they represented." From *Harper's Weekly* 36:156–60. Reprinted in Richard Upton, ed., *The Indian Soldier at Fort Custer, Montana, 1890–1895* (El Segundo, CA: Upton and Sons, 1983), pp. 156–60.

[12] Thomas W. Dunlay, *Wolves for the Blue Soldiers* (Lincoln: University of Nebraska Press, 1982), p. 181.

[13] For general information on Casey's meeting with Plenty Horses, see Utley, *The Last Days of the Sioux Nation*, pp. 256–68; Robert M. Utley, *The Lance and the Shield: The Life and Times of Sitting Bull* (New York: Henry Holt, 1993); and Maurice Frink and Casey E. Barthelmess, *Photographer on an Army Mule* (Norman: University of Oklahoma Press, 1965). The National Archives files, especially record groups 75 and 393, include important materials on the ghost dance and the military response to it. The Casey-family collection at the archive of Historic New England and various contemporary newspaper accounts, particularly those published in May 1890 in the *Sioux Falls Argus-Leader*, provide details of Casey's encounter with Plenty Horses.

[14] National Archives, record group 393, part 5, entry 28, vol. 2, Fort Keogh, Montana, p. 26 for Rock Road and p. 44 for White Moon.

[15] Letter from Lieutenant Robert Getty to assistant adjutant general, April 13, 1891, National Archives, microfilm 983, roll 1, p. 838; and the *New York World*, April 26, 1891.

[16] *New York World*, April 26, 1891.

[17] Ibid.

[18] For an excellent account of the Red Cloud wars and Red Cloud's life on the reservation, see Robert W. Larson, *Red Cloud: Warrior-Statesman of the Lakota Sioux* (Norman: University of Oklahoma Press, 1997).

[19] Quoted in Utley, *The Last Days of the Sioux Nation*, pp. 232–33.

[20] Red Cloud's reaction can be found in National Archives, microfilm 983, roll 2, pp. 1, 172–76.

[21] Ibid., pp. 1, 175.

[22] Ibid.

[23] Ibid.

[24] Ibid., pp. 1, 172–73.

[25] Ibid., pp. 1, 176.

[26] Casey's body did not lie abandoned for long. On the day of the shooting, the military retrieved the frozen corpse, which was found naked but without such traditional Lakota mutilations as scalping, removal of ears, and slashes to the thighs—wounds the Lakota believed the dead would continue to suffer the afterworld.

The military turned over Casey's body to a doctor and undertaker in Oelrichs, South Dakota, for embalming and dressing. The physician injected the body with enough zinc chloride to preserve it for a month. The face was disfigured, presumably from the exit wound, so that Casey was unrecognizable except when viewed in right profile. On the evening of January 8, the coffined body was placed on the 9 p.m. train and shipped east, escorted by a corporal. Cost of embalming and undertaking totaled fifty-five dollars. (Casey archive at Historic New England, box 83, folder B3, p. 77, letter dated January 9, 1891, written to Thomas Lincoln Casey by a captain with an illegible signature.)

The body arrived in New York City, three hours late, on January 11. The burial was at the family farm in Warwick, Rhode Island. Thomas Casey hired two carriages for the burial at a cost of four dollars. (Historic New England, box 83.)

The Silas Casey Post of the Grand Army of the Republic, named for Casey's father, sent a wreath. Casey's older brother Silas put a small bouquet of violets on the coffin before it was lowered into the ground. The family then retreated to the Casey house for dinner. (Historic New England, box 106, Thomas Lincoln Casey's diary entry for January 11, 1891. Frink and Barthelmess, *Photographer on an Army Mule*, pp. 101–2, as well as genealogical information from various Web sites and particularly, for most of the details about the burial, records at Historic New England.)

Nettie Atchison urged the family to bury Casey at West Point, which she wrote "was the wish of his heart." She added, "He had a dread of being buried at the farm." She continued to protest his burial after it was completed, but his brother Thomas decided to leave the dead lie. Historic New England, box 83, January 15 to 31, 1891.

[27] Historic New England, box 121, Thomas Lincoln Casey's day diary for January 8, 1891.

[28] Historic New England, box 121, folder M, news clip in Thomas Lincoln Casey's scrapbook.

[29] Historic New England, box 83, January 1 to 15, 1891.

[30] Casey had written to Nettie around Christmastime, telling her: "Do not worry about me. A man's time comes only when the Almighty is ready for it. But pray that I may do what my duty requires and that my Scouts may deserve credit." Nettie's letters can be found in box 83, January 15 to 31, 1891, at Historic New England.

[31] Ibid.

[32] Historic New England, box 121, folder E, p. 104, Thomas Lincoln Casey's scrapbook.

[33] A shoot-out between Chippewa Indians and troops in Minnesota in 1898 left six soldiers dead, but it resulted from military support for a marshal arresting an Indian and was not an event in the Indian wars.

CHAPTER 8. AMBUSH OR SELF-DEFENSE?

[1] *Black Hills Weekly Journal*, January 16, 1891.

[2] *Sturgis Weekly Record*, January 23, 1891.

[3] *Sioux Falls Argus-Leader*, May 16, 1891.

[4] Marshall's report can be found on National Archives, microfilm P2187, roll 45, item 10937. A similar report from Marshall can be found in microfilm 983, pp. 1, 188–1, 197; although the two reports are nearly identical, some wording differs between them.

[5] National Archives microfilm P2187, roll 4, item 10937, p. 1,065.

[6] *Sioux Falls Argus-Leader*, July 2, 1891, 8. The comment about the warning appeared in the *Sturgis Weekly Record* for January 23, 1891.

[7] National Archives, microfilm 983, p. 1,188.

[8] I found two reports by Marshall, one in National Archives, microfilm P2187 (D-G), roll 45, item 10937 and the other in National Archives, microfilm 983, beginning on p. 1,188. In the latter, dated January 22, Marshall states that he visited the wagon on the morning of the twelfth, and in the former, dated January 25, on the thirteenth. Given that the shooting occurred on the eleventh, and that Marshall reports in 10937 that he arrived at the Quinn ranch in the evening of the twelfth, I presume that the thirteenth is correct. I suspect that the date he reported in the document on microfilm 983 was a typo.

[9] National Archives, microfilm 983, p. 1,191.

[10] National Archives, microfilm P2187, roll 45, item 10937, p. 1,065.

[11] Ibid.

[12] Ibid.

[13] Miles had left his Chicago headquarters in early December in favor of a command post in Rapid City, South Dakota, where he could keep a closer eye on military operations. A month later he moved to Pine Ridge itself.

[14] Robert Wooster, *Nelson A. Miles & the Twilight of the Frontier Army* (Lincoln: University of Nebraska Press, 1993), p. 188.

[15] The *Pioneer*, Deadwood, South Dakota, probably April 1891. Undated clipping found in National Archives, microfilm P2187, roll 45, item 11944.

[16] The following biographical sketch of Nelson Miles is based on material in Wooster, *Nelson A. Miles*.

[17] Ibid., p. 35.

[18] Like Casey, Miles could trace his family history in the New World back to the 1630s. One of his father's ancestors, the Reverend John Myles (as with so many immigrants in all eras, the family would adopt a new spelling in the New World), served as a captain in the colonial militia during King Philip's War (see note 16 for chapter 11 for more on that war). Miles's great-grandfather and three of his great-uncles fought the British during the Revolutionary War.

[19] Quoted in Wooster, *Nelson A. Miles*, p. 3.

[20] Quoted in ibid., p. 125.

[21] Ibid., p. 192.

[22] Robert Lee, *Fort Meade & the Black Hills* (Lincoln: University of Nebraska Press, 1991), p. 127.

[23] Ibid., p. 126.

[24] Robert Utley, "The Ordeal of Plenty Horses," *American Heritage* 26, no. 1 (1974): pp. 19–20.

[25] Indian Rights Association, *Ninth Annual Report* (1891), p. 43, quoted in Robert M. Utley, *The Last Days of the Sioux Nation* (New Haven, CT: Yale University Press, 1963), p. 265. The name indicated that his reputation as a warrior was so fearsome that merely the sight of his horses frightened his enemies.

[26] Many sources outline the events covered in this chapter. A good thumbnail description appears in Utley, *The Last Days of the Sioux Nation*. The story of the shooting of Few Tails, as related here, is pieced together from testimonies by Clown, One Feather, Red Owl, and U.S. soldiers as they appear in National Archives microfilm, P2187, roll 45, 10937. Other citations appear below. The quote here is from Clown's testimony.

[27] See note 1 for this chapter.

[28] *Sioux Falls Argus-Leader*, May 13, 1891.

[29] *Sturgis Weekly Record*, January 23, 1891.

[30] Clown's testimony in National Archives, microfilm, P2187, roll 45, item 10937.

[31] The *Sioux Falls Argus-Leader* for May 16, 1891, reported that the Culbertsons plotted the attack the night of January 10 but does not cite a source for this information.

[32] Clown's testimony to military officials is in National Archives, microfilm P2187, roll 45, item 10937.

[33] Ibid.

[34] National Archives, microfilm P2187, roll 45, item 10937.

[35] *Black Hills Weekly Journal* (Rapid City, South Dakota), January 16, 1891, and the *Sioux Falls Argus-Leader*, May 16, 1891.

[36] One Feather's actions won the admiration of Captain F. E. Pierce, the acting Indian agent at Pine Ridge, who wrote to the assistant adjutant general of the Division of the Missouri in

Chicago: "The determination and genuine courage, as well as the generalship he [One Feather] manifested in keeping at a distance the six men who were pursuing him, and the devotion he showed toward his family, risking his life against great odds, designate him as entitled to a place on the list of heroes. His wife was badly wounded at the first fire. One daughter is only 13 or 14, and the other girl a baby, less than one year of age, yet he protected and saved and took them to a place of safety." National Archives, microfilm P2187, roll 45, item 10937.

[37] National Archives, microfilm P2187, roll 45, item 10937.

[38] *Sioux Falls Argus-Leader*, May 16, 1891.

[39] *Sturgis Weekly Record*, January 23, 1891.

CHAPTER 9. THE LAST BATTLE

[1] The account of Plenty Horses' arrest is based on Cloman's official report, which can be found in National Archives, microfilm 983, pp. 1, 163–68.

[2] The accusation against Young Skunk proved to be a case of mistaken identification, and later he was released. The Indian who did kill Miller was never prosecuted, in large part because of the Plenty Horses trial and its outcome.

[3] The source for quotes about Rushville is W. Fletcher Johnson, *Life of Sitting Bull and History of the Indian War of 1890–'91* (n.p.: Edgewood, 1891). This curious little book, fraught with inaccuracies but also offering interesting contemporary perspectives on the Wounded Knee conflict and related events, was published by March 1891, only three months after Sitting Bull was shot. The author also wrote other books about recent contemporary events, such as the Johnstown, Pennsylvania, flood.

[4] "Towns not on railroad lines, struggling to survive, not uncommonly concluded that their only hope for prosperity was to prevail on a railroad to run a spur to the town, thereby connecting it to the great national network of rails. Railroads often 'auctioned off' a lifesaving spur line to the town that made the highest bid; towns not infrequently bankrupted themselves to win a railroad line that, it was hoped, would make them flourishing cities, only to find their hopes defeated and their future bleaker than ever." Page Smith, *The Rise of Industrial America: A People's History of the Post-Reconstruction Era*, vol. 6, McGraw-Hill (New York: 1984), p. 101.

[5] For details on the grand jury, see Robert Lee, *Fort Meade and the Black Hills* (Lincoln: University of Nebraska Press, 1991), p. 130. This grand jury also investigated the case of Young Skunk, accused of killing the shepherd Henry Miller. With the help of Fast Horse, a Lakota friend of the jury foreman, the jury determined that Young Skunk was the wrong man and that Miller's killer was Leaves His Women, from the Rosebud Reservation east of Pine Ridge. Charges against Young Skunk were dropped. A June 9, 1891, letter from the acting agent at Pine Ridge to the commissioner of Indian affairs mentioned that Leaves His Women was indicted for Miller's murder by that date but that no action had been taken to arrest him and that none would be taken until the acting agent conferred with William Sterling, the U.S. attorney for South Dakota. The letter is item 21359 from microfilm P2187, roll 46, in the National Archives.

[6] Joseph G. Rosa, *They Called Him Wild Bill: The Life and Adventures of James Butler Hickok* (Norman: University of Oklahoma Press, 1974), p. 353.

[7] J. W. Buel, *Heroes of the Plains* (Philadelphia: Standard Publishing, 1886), pp. 186–87; quoted in John R. Milton, *South Dakota: A History* (New York: Norton, 1977), p. 29.

[8] Unreferenced newspaper clipping from microfilm P2187, roll 45, item 10773. Apparently it was sent by former reservation agent Dr. Valentine T. McGillycuddy to Indian Bureau director T. J. Morgan with the former's letter of March 19, 1891.

[9] See items 1183, 1260, and 1264 from record group 73, National Archives, which include Sterling's letter complaining about Miles's unwillingness to turn over Plenty Horses.

[10] Quoted in Robert Utley, "The Ordeal of Plenty Horses," *American Heritage* 26, no. 1 (1974): 82.

[11] Lee, *Fort Meade and the Black Hills*, pp. 130–31.

[12] National Archives, microfilm P2187, roll 44, item 3512.

[13] National Archives, microfilm P2187, roll 45, item 10775.

[14] National Archives, microfilm P2187, roll 45, item 10773.

[15] Lee, *Fort Meade and the Black Hills*, p. 131.

[16] Burns's March 27, 1891, letter to military authorities at Pine Ridge is in National Archives, microfilm P2187, roll 45, item 12561.

[17] Burns's March 28, 1891, letter to Herbert Welsh is in National Archives, microfilm P2187, roll 45. The item number is illegible but may be 12562.

[18] The details on Welsh's life are drawn from William T. Hagan, *The Indian Rights Association: The Herbert Welsh Years, 1882–1904* (Tucson: University of Arizona Press, 1985).

[19] Burns's March 28, 1891, letter to Herbert Welsh is in National Archives, microfilm P2187, roll 45. The item number is illegible but may be 12562.

[20] Sumner's letter to Welsh, dated March 29, 1891, is item 12504 in National Archives, microfilm P2187, roll 45. See chapter 1 for Casey's similar attempt, in the name of fair play and justice, to defend four of his scouts accused of murder.

[21] See Hagan, *The Indian Rights Association*, pp. 5–7, for this and the following information on the trip west.

[22] Ibid., p. 4.

[23] Ibid., p. 5.

[24] Ibid.

[25] Ibid., p. 7.

[26] Ibid., p. 6.

[27] Ibid., p. 4.

[28] Ibid., p. 3. In 1873 Welsh married Fanny Frazer, the daughter of a leading Philadelphia family. The wedding marked the beginning of sixty-six years of a marriage so bad that even Welsh's brother-in-law urged him to get a divorce in an era and a social stratum in which divorce was virtually unthinkable. Fanny did not share his interests or his energy—she was frequently ill or said she was—and so had no involvement in the active side of his frenetic life.

[29] Ibid., pp. 9–10. These points are discussed throughout Hagan's book and appear at various points in the text.

³⁰ Ibid., p. 14.

³¹ Ibid., pp. 16–19, for the story of the meeting.

³² Ibid., pp. 22–32. See also Lee, *Fort Meade and the Black Hills*, and Utley, "The Ordeal of Plenty Horses."

³³ The information on Powers and Nock comes from the *New York World*, April 25, 1891, and from Dana R. Bailey, *History of Minnehaha County, South Dakota* (Sioux Falls, SD: Brown & Sanger, 1899), pp. 498 and 669.

³⁴ The information on Sterling comes from Anonymous, *Biography and Speeches of William B. Sterling with Memorial Addresses and Resolutions* (Chicago and New York: W. B. Conkey, 1897).

³⁵ Ibid., p. 311.

³⁶ David Laskin, *The Children's Blizzard* (New York: HarperCollins, 2004), p. 126.

³⁷ Anonymous, *Biography and Speeches of William B. Sterling*, p. 112.

³⁸ Ibid., p. 30.

³⁹ Ibid., p. 3.

⁴⁰ For an exhaustive source of information on western railroads, see David Haward Bain, *Empire Express: Building the First Transcontinental Railroad* (New York: Penguin Putnam, 1999). For a shorter study, see Robert Edgar Reigel, *The Story of the Western Railroads* (1926; reprint, Lincoln: University of Nebraska Press, 1964). For a thumbnail sketch of rail history in the late 1800s, see Smith, *The Rise of Industrial America*, pp. 89–112. The data cited here are from Smith.

⁴¹ Quoted in Anonymous, *Biography and Speeches of William B. Sterling*, p. 322.

⁴² Ibid., p. 331.

⁴³ Ibid., p. 15.

⁴⁴ Ibid., p. 319.

⁴⁵ Ibid., pp. 15–16.

⁴⁶ Ibid., pp. 48–49. Many of those points sound familiar to modern ears, but none so much as his use of Benjamin Harrison's war record in promoting Harrison for president. He pointed out that the Democratic incumbent, Grover Cleveland, had not even served in the Civil War, but instead had hired someone to go in his place—which was legal during the war, but not something to be proud of in the postwar years. Harrison, on the other hand, had risen to the rank of general in the war, which made him into "a man who knows what it costs to be a soldier; a man whose fidelity and devotion to the interests of the soldier have never been questioned; a man who will see to it that the remnant of the great army of the Republic, which still remains, shall be treated not only justly, but generously." (Ibid., pp. 52–53 and 171 [the latter from an 1892 campaign speech].)

⁴⁷ Sterling became a popular speaker at events throughout South Dakota, addressing various civic groups, such as the state firemen's association and the graduating classes of colleges and universities. He was famed for his eloquence—even Plenty Horses would compliment Sterling's style. At a girls' school in 1891, Sterling revealed relatively modern ideas, pointing out

that in the previous half century, opportunities for the education of women had "grown from the narrowest limits, until today, they are equal almost to those which are afforded men; and I hope, and believe, that before the close of the present century, there will be no single avenue of education, or improvement open to men, to which access will be denied to women." (Ibid., p. 119.)

He would wax poetic when he spoke about Dakota Territory—he was inspired by the booster spirit and would stretch the truth until it snapped and became a lie—and he took issue with anyone who suggested that the territory was anything but ideal even in matters so fundamental as climate. Speaking of a land in which broiling summer temperatures sometimes turned into prolonged droughts and winter brought pummeling arctic winds and blizzards, he said, "In the Winter, when our own people are basking in the open air, in the warm sunshine of a perfect Winter day, the people of the East huddle closely together around blazing hearth, while their teeth chatter and their bones ache with the dampness of Northern blasts." (Ibid., pp. 202–3.) Summers, he said, were kept cool by breezes blowing in from the snowcapped Rocky Mountains.

[48] *Sioux Falls Argus-Leader*, April 29, 1891. Sterling expressed these feelings in court.

[49] Frederic Remington, *The Collected Writings of Frederic Remington*, ed. Peggy Samuels and Harold Samuels (n.p.: Castle, 1986), pp. 70–77. The quote is on p. 77.

CHAPTER 10. A FRACTURED LIFE

[1] Wayne Fanebust, *Where the Sioux River Bends, a Newspaper Chronicle* (Freeman, SD: Pine Hill Press [for the Minnehaha County Historical Society], 1984), p. 302.

[2] Ibid., p. 330.

[3] For details on Pettigrew's plans, see Wayne Fanebust, *Echoes of November: The Life and Times of Senator R.F. Pettigrew of South Dakota* (Freeman, SD: Pine Hill Press), 1997, pp. 225–38.

[4] Fanebust, *Where the Sioux River Bends*, p. 328.

[5] Ibid., pp. 355–56. The population today stands at a little more than 130,000.

[6] Ibid., pp. 328–30.

[7] The city of Sioux Falls itself became one of the quarries' biggest customers in the boom years of the late 1880s, consuming thirty thousand paving stones a day when Phillips Avenue, a major thoroughfare, required eight hundred thousand stones. Once paved, the avenue created a new problem: Drivers of horse-drawn carriages couldn't resist speeding over the new, hard surface. See ibid., p. 278.

[8] Ibid., p. 339.

[9] *Sioux Falls Argus-Leader*, April 11, 1891.

[10] Fanebust, *Where the Sioux River Bends*, pp. 302–3.

[11] *Sioux Falls Argus-Leader*, April 23, 1891.

[12] *Sioux Falls Argus-Leader*, May 25, 1891.

[13] *New York World*, April 25, 1891.

[14] Clipping in Thomas Lincoln Casey's scrapbook, box 121, folder C, p. 1, Casey archive at Historic New England: The source of the clipping is unknown.

[15] Pulitzer had promised readers a newspaper that would "expose all fraud and sham, fight all public evils and abuses, and . . . battle for the people with earnest sincerity." It would also focus on scandals and other sensational material. In 1887 Pulitzer—a native Hungarian who came to the United States in 1864 and worked as a mule skinner and waiter before learning English and striking it rich in the newspaper business—would send the reporter Nelly Bly on a trip around the world to see if she could beat the author Jules Verne's fabled deadline for circumnavigating the globe in eighty days. (She did, completing the feat in seventy-two days, six hours, eleven minutes, and fourteen seconds. The *World* sponsored a contest to see who could most closely guess the time, and more than a million people participated.) In 1890 the new headquarters for the *New York World* opened as the tallest building in the world, standing 305 feet tall. Pulitzer competed ferociously with William Randolph Hearst's *New York Journal* in pursuit of lurid stories, and without question the Casey shooting fell into the right category, which is fortunate, because the *World* left for posterity perhaps the most detailed surviving reports of the courtroom activities. A transcript apparently was made of the trial—letters in the Indian Rights Association archive at the Philadelphia Historical Society indicate that the association paid for one—but apparently the transcript is lost.

[16] *New York World*, April 25, 1891, for this and following quotes in this chapter.

[17] Although Standing Bear describes in some detail living in a tepee, hunting with his father, and the joys of traditional Lakota life, he neglects to mention that his father was perhaps half white and owned a general store on the Brulé reservation. (Luther Standing Bear, *My People the Sioux* [Lincoln: University of Nebraska Press, 1975; reprint of 1928 edition published by Houghton Mifflin], pp. xiv–xv.) How accurately Standing Bear's description of Brulé childhood in the 1870s matches Plenty Horses' experiences is uncertain, but they were born only a year or so apart and both were Brulé, so similarities would be inevitable. Given that Plenty Horses' father, Living Bear, apparently owned a large number of horses, the son might have had the opportunity, in the 1870s, to learn the rudiments of hunting and other traditional skills as Luther Standing Bear did.

[18] Luther Standing Bear, *My Indian Boyhood* (Lincoln: University of Nebraska Press, 1988; reprint of 1931 edition, published by Houghton Mifflin), p. 5.

[19] Standing Bear, *My People the Sioux*, p. 9.

[20] Standing Bear, *My Indian Boyhood*, p. 16.

[21] Ibid., p. 21.

[22] Ibid., pp. 17–20.

[23] Ibid., p. 177.

[24] Ibid., p. 31.

[25] Ibid., p. 37.

[26] Standing Bear, *My People the Sioux*, p. 63.

[27] Standing Bear, *My Indian Boyhood*, pp. 59–60.

[28] Ibid., p. 94.

[29] Ibid., p. 29.

[30] Flora Warren Seymour, *Indian Agents of the Old Frontier* (New York: Appleton-Century, 1941), p. 267. Prevailing ideas about saving the Indians were outlined succinctly in an article from the *Philadelphia Manufacturer* and reprinted in the Carlisle school bimonthly newspaper, the *Red Man* (December 1890–January 1891).

> Nothing in the history of the American people is more discreditable to them than the methods employed in dealing with the Indians. The story of our Indian policy is a record of injustice, falsehood and imbecility. The practice we now pursue of maintaining large bodies of these savages in idleness, feeding them at the public cost, treating them as if they were independent, and permitting them to retain their tribal organizations, is probably the worst for them, and for us, that could be devised by the wit of man. . . . The whole body [of 250,000 Indians in the United States] should be brought East of the Mississippi, the tribes should be broken up and the families of each tribe distributed so that they could never again come together. . . . They should be supplied with machinery, cattle and seeds, and proper instruction in the arts of civilization should be given to them, with the distinct understanding that they must either support themselves by their own labor within two or three years or starve. . . . It will produce good results for us and far better results for the Indian, for it will give him a chance, which he does not now possess, of being transformed from a useless vagabond into a civilized and useful man.

[31] Quoted in Tom Streissguth, *Wounded Knee 1890: The End of the Plains Indian Wars* (New York: Facts on File, 1998), p. xii.

[32] Quoted in Seymour, *Indian Agents*, p. 159.

[33] Quoted in Linda F. Witmer, *The Indian Industrial School: Carlisle, Pennsylvania, 1879–1918* (Carlisle, PA: Cumberland County Historical Society, 2002), p. 7.

[34] Quoted in Seymour, *Indian Agents*, p. 263.

[35] Pratt was so proud of the transformations his policies wrought that he gave away before-and-after photos as newsletter-subscription premiums, showing students as they looked when they arrived at Carlisle with long hair and native garb and how they looked after a period of schooling, shorn of their locks and armored in Euro-American clothing.

[36] *Indian Helper*, March 20, 1891.

[37] Michael L. Cooper, *Indian School: Teaching the White Man's Way* (New York: Clarion Books, 1999), pp. 48–49.

[38] Charles Eastman, *From the Deep Woods to Civilization* (Lincoln: University of Nebraska Press, 1977; reprint of 1936 edition published by Little, Brown), p. 57.

[39] Quoted in the *New York World*, April 25, 1891.

[40] Quoted in the *Red Man*, April–May 1891.

[41] Frederic Remington, *The Collected Writings of Frederic Remington*, ed. Peggy Samuels and Harold Samuels (n.p.: Castle, 1986), p. 63.

[42] Copies of the *Indian Helper* and the *Red Man* can be found at the Cumberland County Historical Society in Carlisle, Pennsylvania. The *Indian Helper* is also available online through the historical society.

[43] National Archives, record group 35, stack area 11E-3, compartment 3, shelf 2.

[44] *Red Man,* February–March 1891.

[45] Ibid.

[46] *New York World,* April 25, 1891.

[47] Ibid.

[48] *New York World,* April 26, 1891.

[49] Ibid.

[50] *New York World,* April 25, 1891.

[51] Ibid.

[52] *New York World,* April 28, 1891.

[53] The views expressed here are gleaned from a reading of the *Argus-Leader* and *New York World* accounts of the trial, including commentary that appears throughout the April and May coverage, as well as accounts provided in other papers, such as the *Omaha Bee, Chadron Democrat,* and *New York Times.*

[54] *New York World,* April 26, 1891.

[55] *Sioux Falls Argus-Leader,* April 28, 1891.

[56] Plenty Horses, according to some sources, had a dubious control of English, although other sources said he spoke it fluently. His quotes in the press indicate a fine control of the language, but likely were edited by the reporter.

[57] Plenty Horses' quote in the previous paragraph, about the military shooting an Indian, is so much like the comment attributed to Miles that you have to wonder if perhaps Plenty Horses read about Miles's view in the *Red Man* or another publication and paraphrased him.

[58] Accounts of the investigation of Wounded Knee abound. For a succinct version, see Streissguth, *Wounded Knee,* or Robert Wooster, *Nelson A. Miles & the Twilight of the Frontier Army* (Lincoln: University of Nebraska Press, 1993).

[59] Miles reserved special and personal enmity for Forsyth, who in 1875 had been openly critical of George Armstrong Custer, of whom Miles was a great fan. Streissguth, *Wounded Knee,* pp. 95–99, offers a nice thumbnail sketch of the proceedings against Forsyth. For more detail, see Wooster, *Nelson A. Miles.*

[60] Robert Wooster, *Nelson A. Miles & the Twilight of the Frontier Army* (Lincoln: University of Nebraska Press, 1993), p. 188.

[61] Quoted in Wooster, *Nelson A. Miles,* p. 190.

[62] Quoted in William S. Coleman, *Voices of Wounded Knee* (Lincoln: University of Nebraska Press, 2000), pp. 329–32.

[63] Quoted in Julia B. McGillycuddy, *Blood on the Moon: Valentine McGillycuddy and the Sioux* (1940; reprint, Lincoln: University of Nebraska Press, 1990).

[64] Robert W. Larson, *Red Cloud: Warrior-Statesman of the Lakota Sioux* (Norman: University of Oklahoma Press, 1997), p. 47–48.

[65] Robert M. Utley, *The Lance and the Shield: The Life and Times of Sitting Bull* (New York: Henry Holt, 1993), p. 14.

[66] Ibid., p. 19.

[67] For excellent details on Crazy Horse, see Stephen E. Ambrose, *Crazy Horse and Custer: The Parallel Lives of Two American Warriors* (New York: Anchor Books, 1996).

[68] Larry McMurtry, *Crazy Horse* (New York: Viking, 1999), p. 44.

[69] Larson, *Red Cloud*, pp. 58–60.

[70] Utley, *The Lance and the Shield*, pp. 3–25. Of course, Lakota warfare was not all gore. They never tortured captives, and they were not without mercy. Even a matchless fighter like Sitting Bull was noted for his merciful qualities. He once not only kept fellow warriors from killing a boy captured from an enemy tribe but even adopted the youngster and made him part of his own family. He was instrumental in forcing a member of his band to release a captured white woman. When Sitting Bull's own father was killed by Crow Indians, Sitting Bull kept his people from slaughtering captive Crow women and children in revenge.

[71] Ibid., pp. 108–9.

[72] Royal B. Hassrick, *The Sioux: Life and Customs of a Warrior Society* (Norman: University of Oklahoma Press, 1964), p. 96.

[73] Ibid., p. 97.

[74] Ibid.

[75] Ibid.

[76] Ibid., p. 33.

CHAPTER 11. ON TRIAL

[1] *New York World*, April 26, 1891.

[2] Edgerton had served as a member of the committee that had written South Dakota's constitution and at the time of the trial was head of the local board of education. Like Shiras, he was a Civil War veteran. During the war, he rose from the rank of private to brigadier general.

[3] *New York World*, April 26, 1891.

[4] Ibid.

[5] Ibid.

[6] Ibid.

[7] Sterling cited a witness as having said that Casey was on a peace mission, but Sterling did not say who that witness was.

[8] *New York World*, April 26, 1891.

[9] Ibid.

[10] Ibid.

[11] Ibid.

[12] Ibid.

[13] Ibid.

[14] Ibid.

[15] Ibid.

[16] Presumably Powers is referring to the 1868 treaty. The 1869 figure appears in the newspaper account from which the quote is taken, but may have been an error on Powers's part, or the reporter's, or the typesetter's. In his response, Ballance refers to the 1868 treaty. King Philip was a chief of the Wampanoag and the son of Massasoit, the chief who had helped the Plymouth, Massachusetts, Pilgrims in their first years. King Philip's Indian name was Metacomet. He was called King Philip by English settlers who wanted to befriend him. In the 1670s he led a war against the New England Puritans that ended in his death.

[17] *New York World*, April 28, 1891.

[18] He is referring to the treaty of 1877 that ended the wars with the Lakota.

[19] *New York World*, April 28, 1891.

[20] Ibid.

[21] Ibid.

[22] Ibid.

[23] Ibid.

[24] *New York World*, April 25, 1891, and *Sioux Falls Argus-Leader*, April 28, 1891.

[25] *New York World*, April 30, 1891.

[26] Ibid.

[27] Ibid.

[28] Ibid., *Sioux Falls Argus-Leader*, April 29, 1891.

[29] The statement to which Sterling refers is unclear, since Plenty Horses never took the stand. Sterling may be drawing on one of Plenty Horses' newspaper interviews or on his grand jury testimony.

[30] *Sioux Falls Argus-Leader*, April 29, 1891.

[31] *New York World*, April 30, 1891.

[32] Ibid.

[33] National Archives, microfilm P2187, roll 46, item number illegible but may be 21358.

[34] Record group 107, entry 80, general correspondence 1891: 1641–2841, box 11.

[35] *Sioux Falls Argus-Leader*, May 1, 1891.

[36] Ibid.

[37] Ibid.

[38] *New York World*, May 1, 1891.

[39] Ibid.

[40] Ibid.

[41] *Sioux Falls Argus-Leader*, April 30, 1891.

[42] Ibid.

[43] *New York World*, May 1, 1891.

[44] *Sioux Falls Argus-Leader*, April 30, 1891.

[45] *New York World*, May 1, 1891.

CHAPTER 12. JUSTICE DEFERRED

[1] *Sioux Falls Argus-Leader*, May 16, 1891.

[2] *New York World*, April 29, 1891.

[3] *New York World*, May 27, 1891.

[4] *New York World*, May 26, 1891.

[5] See James R. Walker, *Lakota Belief and Ritual* (Lincoln: University of Nebraska Press, 1991), pp. 108, 186, 235, and others, as well as Royal B. Hassrick, *The Sioux: Life and Customs of a Warrior Society* (Norman: University of Oklahoma Press, 1964), pp. 20 and 255. No one can say whether Plenty Horses wore these colors with any of this in mind, but surely he knew their symbolism.

[6] *New York World*, May 25, 1891.

[7] *Sioux Falls Argus-Leader*, May 25, 1891.

[8] The following trial coverage is from the *New York World*, May 26, 1891.

[9] *Sioux Falls Argus-Leader*, May 25, 1891.

[10] *New York World*, May 27, 1891, and *Sioux Falls Argus-Leader*, May 26, 1891.

[11] *Sioux Falls Argus-Leader*, May 26, 1891.

[12] Ibid. and *New York World*, May 27, 1891.

[13] *Sioux Falls Argus-Leader*, May 26, 1891.

[14] Ibid.

[15] *New York World*, May 27, 1891.

[16] *Sioux Falls Argus-Leader*, May 27, 1891.

[17] *New York World*, May 28, 1891.

[18] Ibid. and *Sioux Falls Argus-Leader*, May 27, 1891.

[19] Quoted in the *Sioux Falls Argus-Leader*, May 29, 1891.

[20] *New York World*, May 29, 1891, and *Sioux Falls Argus-Leader*, May 28, 1891.

[21] *New York World*, May 29, 1891.

[22] Ibid.

[23] Ibid.

[24] *Sioux Falls Argus-Leader*, May 28, 1891. The contrast between this description and that of the *New York World* suggests that the New York reporter may have been coloring the news or even creating scenes that he thought would appeal to his readers. Pulitzer's newspaper was no stranger to sensationalism, an element that no doubt drew it to the Plenty Horses case in the first place.

[25] *New York World*, May 29, 1891.

[26] *New York World*, May 29, 1891.

[27] *Sioux Falls Argus-Leader*, May 28, 1891.

[28] *Sturgis Weekly Record*, June 19, 1891.

[29] Ibid.

[30] *Bismarck Daily Tribune*, June 28, 1891.

[31] *Sioux Falls Argus-Leader*, July 2, 1891.

[32] *Sioux Falls Argus-Leader*, June 23, 1891.

[33] *Sioux Falls Argus-Leader*, July 3, 1891.

[34] *Sturgis Weekly Record*, July 3, 1891.

[35] *Sioux Falls Argus-Leader*, May 29, 1891.

[36] *Sioux Falls Argus-Leader*, May 28, 1891.

[37] Ibid.

EPILOGUE

[1] Sources for the spirit ride were local newspaper stories and an April 2003 interview with Birgil Kills Straight.

[2] For statistics on Pine Ridge, see www.unpo.org, the Web site of the Unrepresented Nations and People Organisation. See also www.wambliho.com, a Pine Ridge Web site.

[3] *Sioux Falls Argus-Leader*, May 29, 1891.

BIBLIOGRAPHY

Adams, David Wallace. *Education for Extinction: American Indians and the Boarding School Experience*. Lawrence: University Press of Kansas, 1995.

Ambrose, Stephen E. *Crazy Horse and Custer: The Parallel Lives of Two American Warriors*. New York: Anchor Books, 1996.

——. *Undaunted Courage: Meriwether Lewis, Thomas Jefferson, and the Opening of the American West*. New York: Simon & Schuster, 1996.

Anonymous. *Biography and Speeches of William B. Sterling with Memorial Addresses and Resolutions*. Chicago and New York: W. B. Conkey, 1897.

Bailey, Dana R. *History of Minnehaha County, South Dakota*. Sioux Falls: Brown & Saenger, 1899.

Branch, E. Douglas. *The Hunting of the Buffalo*. Lincoln: University of Nebraska Press, 1962.

Brown, Dee. *Bury My Heart at Wounded Knee: An Indian History of the American West*. New York: Holt, Rinehart & Winston, 1970.

Carroll, John M. *The Arrest and Killing of Sitting Bull*. Mattituck, NY: Amereon House, 1986.

Coleman, William S. *Voices of Wounded Knee*. Lincoln: University of Nebraska Press, 2000.

Connell, Evan S. *Son of the Morning Star: Custer and the Little Bighorn*. New York: Harper Perennial, 1984.

Cooper, Michael L. *Indian School: Teaching the White Man's Way*. New York: Clarion Books, 1999.

Dary, David A. *The Buffalo Book: A Saga of an American Symbol*. New York: Avon Books, 1974.

DeBarthe, Joe. *Life and Adventures of Frank Grouard*. Norman: University of Oklahoma Press, 1958.

DeVoto, Bernard. *The Journals of Lewis and Clark*. Boston: Houghton Mifflin, 1953.

Dunlay, Thomas W. *Wolves for the Blue Soldiers*. Lincoln: University of Nebraska Press, 1982.

Eastman, Charles. *From the Deep Woods to Civilization*. Lincoln: University of Nebraska Press, 1977. (Reprint of 1936 edition published by Little, Brown.)

——. *The Soul of the Indian: An Interpretation*. Lincoln: University of Nebraska Press, 1980. (Reprint of 1911 edition published by Houghton Mifflin.)

Eastman, Elaine Goodale. *Sister to the Sioux*. Lincoln: University of Nebraska Press, 1978.

Fanebust, Wayne. *Echoes of November: The Life and Times of Senator R.F. Pettigrew of South Dakota*. Freeman, SD: Pine Hill Press, 1977.

——. *Where the Sioux River Bends, A Newspaper Chronicle*. Freeman, SD: Pine Hill Press (for the Minnehaha County Historical Society), 1984.

Fellman, Michael. *Citizen Sherman: A Life of William Tecumseh Sherman*. Lawrence: University of Kansas Press, 1995.

Frink, Maurice, and Casey E. Barthelmess. *Photographer on an Army Mule*. Norman: University of Oklahoma Press, 1965.

Grafe, Ernest, and Paul Horsted. *Exploring with Custer: The 1874 Black Hills Expedition*. Custer, SD: Golden Valley Press, 2002.

Grinnell, George Bird. *The Fighting Cheyenne*. Norman: University of Oklahoma Press, 1955. (Reprint of 1915 edition published by Charles Scribner's Sons.)

Hagan, William T. *The Indian Rights Association: The Herbert Welsh Years, 1882–1904*. Tucson: University of Arizona Press, 1985.

Hassrick, Royal B. *The Sioux: Life and Customs of a Warrior Society*. Norman: University of Oklahoma Press, 1964.

Huls, Don. *The Winter of 1890 (What Happened at Wounded Knee)*. Chadron, NE: Don Huls, 1988.

Hyde, George. *A Sioux Chronicle*. Norman: University of Oklahoma Press, 1956.

———. *Spotted Tail's Folk: A History of the Brulé Sioux*. Norman: University of Oklahoma Press, 1961.

Johansen, Bruce E., and Donald A. Grinde, Jr. *The Encyclopedia of Native American Biography*. New York: Da Capo Press, 1998.

Johnson, W. Fletcher. *Life of Sitting Bull and the History of the Indian War of 1890–'91*. N.p.: Edgewood, 1891.

Kehoe, Alice Beck. *The Ghost Dance: Ethnohistory and Revitalization*. Fort Worth, TX: Holt, Rinehart and Winston, 1983.

Larson, Robert W. *Red Cloud: Warrior-Statesman of the Lakota Sioux*. Norman: University of Oklahoma Press, 1997.

Laskin, David. *The Children's Blizzard*. New York: HarperCollins, 2004.

Lee, Robert. "Warriors in the Ranks: American Indian Units in the Regular Army, 1891–1897." *South Dakota History* 121 (1991): 262–302.

———. *Fort Meade & the Black Hills*. Lincoln: University of Nebraska Press, 1991.

McGillycuddy, Julia B. *Blood on the Moon: Valentine McGillycuddy and the Sioux*. Lincoln: University of Nebraska Press, 1990. (Reprint of 1940 edition published by the board of trustees of the Leland Standford Junior University.)

McGregor, James H. *The Wounded Knee Massacre from the Viewpoint of the Sioux*. Rapid City, SD: Fenwyn Press Books, 1997. (Originally published in 1940.)

McLaughlin, James. *My Friend the Indian*. Lincoln: University of Nebraska Press, 1989. (Reprint of 1910 edition published by Houghton Mifflin.)

McMurtry, Larry. *Crazy Horse*. New York: Viking, 1999.

Miles, Nelson A. *Personal Recollections and Observations of General Nelson A. Miles*. Lincoln: University of Nebraska Press, 1992. (Reprint of 1896 edition published by Werner.)

Milton, John R. *South Dakota: A History*. New York: Norton, 1977.

Monaghan, Jay. *Custer: The Life of General George Armstrong Custer*. Lincoln: University of Nebraska Press, 1971. (Reprint of 1959 edition published by Little, Brown.)

Mooney, James. *The Ghost Dance Religion and Wounded Knee*. New York: Dover, 1973. (Reprint of 1896 edition of *The Ghost Dance Religion and the Sioux Outbreak of 1890* published by the Government Printing Office, Washington, DC.)

Neihardt, John G. *Black Elk Speaks: Being the Life Story of a Holy Man of the Oglala Sioux*. Lincoln: University of Nebraska Press, 1970.

Remington, Frederic. *The Collected Writings of Frederic Remington*. Edited by Peggy Samuels and Harold Samuels. N.p.: Castle, 1986.

Robertson, S. C. "Our Indian Contingent." *Harper's Weekly* 36 (1892): 156–60.

Rogers, Katharine M. *L. Frank Baum: Creator of Oz*. New York: St. Martin's Press, 2002.

Roosevelt, Theodore. *Theodore Roosevelt's America*. Edited by Farida A. Wiley. New York: Devin-Adair, 1955.

Rosa, Joseph G. *They Called Him Wild Bill: The Life and Adventures of James Butler Hickok*. Norman: University of Oklahoma Press, 1974.

Sajna, Mike. *Crazy Horse: The Life Behind the Legend*. New York: Wiley, 2000.

Schell, Herbert S. *History of South Dakota*. 3rd ed., revised. Lincoln: University of Nebraska Press, 1975.

Schlereth, Thomas J. *Victorian America: Transformations in Everyday Life, 1876–1915*. New York: HarperCollins, 1991.

Schlissel, Lillian. *Women's Diaries of the Westward Journey*. New York: Schocken Books, 1982.

Seton, Ernest Thompson. *Lives of Game Animals*. Boston: Charles T. Branford, 1953.

Seymour, Flora Warren. *Indian Agents of the Old Frontier*. New York: Appleton-Century, 1941.

Seymour, Forrest W. *Sitanka: The Full Story of Wounded Knee*. West Hanover, MA: Christopher Publishing House, 1981.

Smith, Page. *The Rise of Industrial America: A People's History of the Post-Reconstruction Era*, Vol. 6. New York: McGraw-Hill, 1984.

Standing Bear, Luther. *My Indian Boyhood*. Lincoln: University of Nebraska Press, 1988. (Reprint of 1931 edition published by Houghton Mifflin.)

———. *My People the Sioux*. Lincoln: University of Nebraska Press, 1975. (Reprint of 1928 edition published by Houghton Mifflin.)

Streissguth, Tom. *Wounded Knee 1890: The End of the Plains Indian Wars*. New York: Facts on File, 1998.

Sugden, John. *Tecumseh, a Life*. New York: Henry Holt, 1997.

Twain, Mark. *Mark Twain: Plymouth Rock and the Pilgrims*. Edited by Charles Nieder. New York: Harper & Row, 1984.

————. *The Unabridged Mark Twain*. Vol. 2. Edited by Lawrence Teacher. Philadelphia: Running Press, 1979.

Upton, Richard, ed. *The Indian Soldier at Fort Custer, Montana, 1890–1895*. El Segundo, CA: Upton and Sons, 1983.

Utley, Robert M. *The Lance and the Shield: The Life and Times of Sitting Bull*. New York: Henry Holt, 1993.

————. *The Last Days of the Sioux Nation*. New Haven, CT: Yale University Press, 1963.

Vestal, Stanley. *New Sources of Indian History, 1850–1891: The Ghost Dance, the Prairie Sioux: A Miscellany*. Norman: University of Oklahoma Press, 1934.

————. *Sitting Bull: Champion of the Sioux*. Norman: University of Oklahoma Press, 1989. (Reprint of 1932 edition published by Houghton Mifflin.)

————. *Warpath: The True Story of the Fighting Sioux Told in a Biography of Chief White Bull*. Lincoln: University of Nebraska Press, 1984. (Reprint of 1934 edition published by Houghton Mifflin.)

Walker, James R. *Lakota Belief and Ritual*. Lincoln: University of Nebraska Press, 1991.

Warhank, Josef James. "Fort Keogh: Cutting Edge of a Culture." Master's thesis, Department of History, California State University, Long Beach, 1983.

Williams, H. L. *The Picturesque West: Our Western Empire Beyond the Mississippi*. New York: Hurst, 1891.

Wilson, Raymond. *Ohiyesa: Charles Eastman, Santee Sioux*. Urbana: University of Illinois Press, 1999.

Witmer, Linda F. *The Indian Industrial School: Carlisle, Pennsylvania 1879–1918*. Carlisle, PA: Cumberland County Historical Society, 2002.

Wooster, Robert. *Nelson A. Miles & the Twilight of the Frontier Army*. Lincoln: University of Nebraska Press, 1993.

Young, Stanley, and Edward Goldman. *The Wolves of North America*. New York: Dover, 1964.

Index

Note: Page numbers in *italic* indicate photographs.

Aberdeen Saturday Pioneer, 68, 84–85
agents, 42–44
Agreement (1876), 63
agriculture, Lakota and, 32, 38, 42–43
Alkali Creek ambush:
    Clown's, Red Owl's, and One
      Feather's stories, 111–14
    decision to prosecute killers, 110, 118,
      121–23
    investigation, 104, 105–6
    newspaper accounts, 103–6
    trial, 179, 196–98
American Horse, *74*
    Fetterman Massacre, 33
    at Plenty Horses second trial, 185–86,
      193
    and Royer-Little encounter, 73–74, 180
Argus-Leader. See Sioux Falls Argus-
    Leader
Arikara, 209n.9
Atchison, Nellie, 12, 101–2, 117n.16

Baldwin, Frank:
    at Plenty Horses second trial, 183,
      186, 188–90, 194
    Wounded Knee investigation, 152,
      153, 154
Ballance, J. G., 160, 166–67
Barthelmess, Christian, 10
Baum, Lyman (L. Frank), 68, 84–85
Bear Lying Down:
    and Casey, 98, 100

    testimony at Plenty Horses' first trial,
      162, 163–64, 168–69
    testimony at Plenty Horses' second
      trial, 184
Big Foot (Sitanka), 2, 67, 85, 87, 88
Big Foot Ride, 201–2
Bismarck Daily Tribune, 197
Black Buffalo, 23
Black Coyote, 2–3
Black Elk, 92
Black Hills, 51, 53–58, 219n.6
Black Hills Weekly Journal, 102
Bozeman Trail, 38
bravery, Lakota virtue, 155–57, 214n.6
Broken Arm:
    and Casey, 97, 100–101
    testimony at Plenty Horses' first trial,
      148–49, 164
    testimony at Plenty Horses' second
      trial, 183–84, 190, 196
Brooke, John, 77–78, 88, 90
Brulé Lakota:
    agriculture and, 42–43
    Grattan affair, 27–28
    and Lewis and Clark expedition,
      23–24
    name of, 210n.10
    rations, 44
    at Rosebud reservation, 45, 46
    Spotted Tail (*see* Spotted Tail)
    as teamsters, 47
    Two Strike, 77–78, *78*, 90, 95, 175

Brulé Lakota: (*continued*)
  Waglukhe (Loafers), 32, 41, 46, 47
  wagon trains and, 26, 211n.25
  at Whetstone Creek reservation,
    41–45
  in White River area, 25–26, 45
Buel, J. W., 120
buffalo, 22, 25–26, 141–42
Bull Head, 61, 83, 203
Burns, John, 123–25
Butterfield, Leroy T., 194, 196

Carlisle School (Pennsylvania), 142–48,
    202–3
Carruth, F. H., 118–20
Casey, Edward Wanton, 7–20, *8. See
    also* Plenty Horses' first trial;
    Plenty Horses' second trial
  and Cheyenne recruits, 15–20, *19*
  death of, 4, 97–102
  early life, 7
  family, 7
  at Fort Keogh, 12–15, *14*
  funeral and burial, 227n.26
  Grand Canyon expedition, 9–12,
    11
  at Muddy Creek, 9
  at Pine Ridge reservation, 93, *94*,
    95–100
  at the Stronghold, 93–95
  at West Point, *8*, 9, 207–08n.20
Casey, Silas, 7, 188, 206n.5
Casey, Silas, III, 7
Casey, Thomas Lincoln, 7, 101
"Casey's Last Scout" (Remington),
    134
cereals, 49
Chadron Democrat, 92

Chasing Crane, 221n.38
Cheyenne troops, 15, 16–20, 93–95,
    94. See also Rock Road; White
    Moon
cigarettes, 50
Cloman, S. A., 117
Clown, 111–13, 114–15, 179, 196–97
Coca-Cola, 50
Cody, Buffalo Bill, 82–83, 203
Corn Brulé, 46, 47, 57–58
Corn Man, 117
cottonwood trees, 142
coups, 156–57
Craven, William, 183, 190
Crazy Horse, 33, 45, 46, 155
Crook, George, 60–61
Crow Dog, *78*, 79, 215n.7
Crow Foot, 56, 83, *85*
Culbertson brothers (Andrew, Nelson,
    Pete):
  Alkali Creek ambush, 103–6, 112–15
  arrest, 107
  decision to prosecute, 110, 118,
    121–23
  Pete's Wild West Show, 203
  trial, 179, 196–98
cultural extinction, 128–29, 143–48,
    235n.30
Custer, George Armstrong, 54, 56

Dakota Territory, 47–48, 50–52, 58–62
Dawes, Henry, 59
Dawes Act, 59
Deadwood (South Dakota), 120
Dickson, Sarah, 92
Drexel Mission, 90–91, 190
Drum, William, 82–83
Duke, James Buchanan, 50

Eastman, Charles, 146, *147*
  death of, 204
  Royer-Little encounter, 73, 74
  Wounded Knee massacre, 89, 90, 91
Edgerton, Alonzo, 120, 159, 176, 189–90
Edison, Thomas, 48
Edmunds, Newton, 58–59
Eighth Cavalry, 104, 106
electricity, 48
elk, 142

face painting, 184
Fanebust, Wayne, 135, 136–37
Fetterman, William, 33
Fetterman Massacre, 33–34
Few Tails, 103, 104, 111–13. *See also*
  Alkali Creek ambush
Flood, Thomas, 184
Forsyth, James, 88, 90–91, 152–54
fortitude, Lakota virtue, 214n.6
Fort Kearny, 26
Fort Keogh, 12–15, *14*
Fort Laramie, 26–27
Fort Leavenworth, 30–31
*Four Weeks Among Some of the Sioux
  Tribes* (Welsh), 128
Fry, F. Curtis, 183
fur trade, 25–26

Gatewood, Charles, 96, 97
General Allotment Act, 59
generosity, Lakota virtue, 43, 127, 214n.6
Geronimo, 96, 97
Getty, Robert, 95
ghost dance religion:
  origins of, 2, 64
  retreat to the Stronghold, 75, 77–79
  Royer and, 72–75

rumors and fears about, 2, 68, 71, 72,
  223n.53
Short Bull and Kicking Bear, Lakota
  apostles of, 66, 68–70, 71
Sitting Bull and, 68, 70–72
Two Strike's surrender at Pine Ridge
  reservation, 78–80
ghost shirts, 66
gold, 51, 53, 54–55, 58
Goodale, Elaine, 73, 89–90, 204,
  221n.38
Grand Canyon expedition, 9–12, *11*
Grant, Ulysses S., 54, 55, 108
Grass, John, 61, 82
Grattan, John L., 27–28
Gray Eagle, 72
Great Dakota Boom (1878–87), 50
Great Mystery, 65, 66
Great Sioux Reservation, 58–64, 63

Hare, William, 54, 62, 126
Harney, William S., 28, 29–30, 41–42
Harper's Weekly, 134
Harrison, William Henry, 62
Harvey, T. E., 197
Hassrick, Royal, 156, 157, 214n.6
Hayt, Ezra, 14–20
He Dog, 149, 168
Heroes of the Plains (Buel), 120
Hollow Horn Bear, 47
Homestead Act, 51
horses, 48–49, 140–41, 217n.28
Hunkpapa Lakota, 23, 71. *See also*
  Sitting Bull

Indian Peace Commission, 34–35,
  38–39
Indian police forces, 43, 82, 83

Indian Rights Association, 124–25, 126,
    130
Indians in the military, 14–20

Jarvis, Nathan S., 11
Jones, F. B., 11
Juelfs, James, 179
Jutz, John, 77

Kearny, Stephen W., 26
Kent, Jacob Ford, 152, 153
Kicking Bear, 69
    as apostle of ghost dance religion,
        66–67
    in Cody's Wild West Show, 203
    and Sitting Bull, 68–70
    at the Stronghold, 75, 77, 79–80, 88,
        90
Kills Straight, Birgil, 1, 201
Kirkham, Henry, 103
Knight, Amelia Stewart, 211n.25

Lakota. See also Brulé Lakota;
    Miniconjou Lakota; Oglala Lakota
    agriculture and, 32, 38
    Black Hills, loss of, 53–58
    and buffalo, 22, 25–26, 141–42
    at Carlisle School, 142–43, 144–48
    colors, significance of, 181
    counting coup, 156–57
    Crazy Horse, 33, 45, 46, 155
    cultural extinction, 128–29, 143–48,
        235n.30
    face painting, 184
    Fetterman Massacre, 33–34
    four virtues of, 127, 155–57, 212n.41,
        214n.6

fur trade, 25–26
ghost dance religion (see ghost dance
    religion)
Great Sioux Reservation breakup,
    58–64, 63
horses and, 22–23, 140–41
Indian Peace Commission and, 34–35,
    38–39
names of children, 145
names of years, 21
origins, 42
police forces, 43, 83
railroads and, 35, 38
rations and annuities, 61, 62, 64,
    215n.11, 216n.12
Sioux Acts (1888, 1889), 59–62
Sitting Bull (see Sitting Bull)
Standing Bear's description of way of
    life, 140–43
sun dances, 43, 44, 127
traditionalists vs. progressives, 32,
    42–43, 46
Treaty (1825), 25
Treaty (1851), 27
Treaty (1866), 34
Treaty (1868), 39, 41, 53, 58–59, 63
tribes, 23
warfare, 155–57, 212n.43, 237n.70
at White River area, 80
Lakota Wars (1860s and 1870s), 36–37
    (map), 55–56
Lame Deer, 9
land claims, 50–51
Leschi, 188
Lewis and Clark expedition, 24
Little (Oglala ghost dancer), 73
Little Big Horn, Battle of, 56

Little Wound, 66

Living Bear, 123, 124, 149, 159, 168, 177, 181, 199

Love, William T., 132, 133

Marshall, F. C., 104, 105–6

Marvin, Alva, 179

Mattheison, Chris, 123

McCall, Alex, 122

McDonough, J. J.:
   interviews of Plenty Horses, 138–39, 170–71, 177, 194
   trial coverage, 163, 168, 169–70, 172, 181, 186, 190–91, 192

McGaa, William, 190

McGillycuddy, Valentine T., 121–23, 124

McLaughlin, James, 61, 71, 80–84, 81, 203–4, 220n.19

milahanska (long knives), 26

Miles, Nelson, 108, 108–9, 204
   and Alkali Creek ambush, 104, 107
   and Casey, 102
   and Cheyenne scouts, 16
   during Civil War, 107–9
   at Fort Keogh, 8–9, 12
   on government bad faith and mismanagement, 109
   at Muddy Creek, 9
   orders to avoid conflict, 93
   and Plenty Horses, 110–11, 121, 151–52, 180, 191
   as potential presidential candidate, 228n.16
   on rations, 62, 64
   and Sitanka (Big Foot), 87
   Sitting Bull's arrest, 82
   and Stronghold surrender, 76, 77

troop build-up at Pine Ridge reservation, 20
   and Wounded Knee massacre, 90, 92–93, 107, 110, 152–54

Miles City, 12

Miniconjou Lakota, 9, 23, 87–88. *See also* Big Foot (Sitanka)

Mitchell, D. D., 27, 143

Mooney, James, 72

Mouser, H. S., 133

Muddy Creek, 9

Murray, W. H. H., 84

nativist religions, 65–68

Neolin, 65

New York Tribune, 54, 58

New York World, 234n.15
   Plenty Horses first trial, 137, 138–39, 148, 149, 151, 162, 163, 168, 170–71, 172, 176, 177
   Plenty Horses' second trial, 180, 193, 194
   Sitting Bull's death, 84

Ninth Cavalry, 75, 91

Nock, George:
   Plenty Horses first trial, 150, 159
      closing remarks, 171–72
      cross-examination of Bear Lying Down, 163–64
      cross-examination of Rock Road, 162
      cross-examination of White Moon, 161
      on interpreter for Plenty Horses, 169
   Plenty Horses second trial, 182, 184, 185–86

Oglala Lakota, 23, 53. *See also* Red
    Cloud
Omaha Bee, 191
One Feather, 111–14

Pancoast, Henry, 126–27, 129–30
Panic of 1873, 54
Parker, W. H., 197, 198
Pemberton, John, 50
Pettigrew, Richard, 58, 72–73, 135
Pine Ridge Reservation, 20, *45*, 89, 90,
    202
Plenty Horses. *See also* Plenty Horses' first
        trial; Plenty Horses' second trial
    arrest, 110–11, 117
    at Carlisle school, 3, 146, 147–48
    childhood, 3, 139–40
    at Fort Meade, *99*, 117, *122*
    indictment, 120
    interviews of, 138–39, 151, 152,
        170–71, 194
    after second trial, 194, *195*, 196, 203
    shooting of Casey, 4, 97–98, 100
    in Sioux Falls jail, 123
    after Wounded Knee massacre, 3
Plenty Horses' first trial, 5, 148–77
    act-of-war defense, 151–52, 165,
        166–68
    Bear Lying Down's testimony, 162,
        163–64, 168–69
    Broken Arm's testimony, 164
    change of venue, 120
    closing remarks, 171–74
    defense attorneys (*see* Nock, George;
        Powers, David Edward)
    defense introductory remarks, 165
    judges, 120, 159
    jury, 174–75, 176–77

Living Bear's testimony, 168
newspaper coverage of, 137–38
photographs, 195, *196*
Plenty Horses' courtroom demeanor,
        150–51, 163, 169–70
Plenty Horses' testimony, 169
prosecuting attorneys (*see* Ballance, J.
        G.; Sterling, William B.)
public opinion, 150
Rock Road's testimony, 161–62
self-defense motive, 154–55
Ten Eyck's testimony, 160–61
translator, 150
verdict, 176–77
Wells' testimony, 166, 168
White Moon's testimony, 161
Plenty Horses' second trial, 180–96
    act-of-war defense, 180, 185–86,
        188–90, 191, 192–93
    American Horse's testimony, 180,
        185–86
    Baldwin's testimony, 183, 186, 188–90
    Bear Lying Down's testimony, 184
    Broken Arm's testimony, 183–84,
        190
    Craven's testimony, 190
    McGaa's testimony, 190
    opening defense remarks, 185
    Plenty Horses' courtroom demeanor,
        181–82
    Pugh's testimony, 187
    Rock Road's testimony, 182, 190
    Thompson's testimony, 186
    verdict, 192–93, 194, 198–99
    White Moon's testimony, 182–83
Polk, Judge, 197
Pollock, W. J., 46–47
Ponca Creek, 46

Porter, Lavinia, 211n.25

Powers, David Edward, 130–31, 203
    Plenty Horses first trial, 150, 159, 165,
        166, 168
    Plenty Horses second trial, 182–83,
        185–86, 187, 188–90

Pratt, Richard Henry, 143–44, 202–3,
    220n.19

Proctor, Redfield, 101

Pueblo Revolt (1680), 22–23

Pugh, R. O., 187

railroads, 35, 38

ranching, 51–52

rations and annuities, 44, 61, 62, 64,
    215n.11, 216n.12

Red Cloud, 32–33, 74
    and Casey, 98, 100
    Fetterman massacre, 33, 34
    prestige and status of, 155–56
    and sale of Black Hills, 55, 58
    and Treaty of 1868, 38, 39

Red Cloud, Jack, 73–74, 149, 159

Red Owl, 111–14

Reid, Charles, 10

Remington, Frederic:
    on Carlisle School, 146–47
    with Casey, 93, 94, 95
    on Casey's death, 134
    on Indian rations, 61
    on Indian soldiers, 17–18, 20

reservation agents, 42–44

Richard, Pete, 100–101, 164, 184

Robertson, S. C., 15

Rock Road, 97, 161–62, 182

Royer, Daniel, 72–73, 74–75

Rundquist, Adolph, 114

Rushville (Nebraska), 118–20

Sans Arc Lakota, 23

Santee Reservation, 127

settlers:
    Dakota Territory, 31–32, 47–48,
        50–52
    in Kansas, 30
    wagon trains (1840s), 26–27

Seventh Cavalry, 87–88

Shafter, William, 121

Shangreau, Louis, 78, 79

Sheridan, Philip, 33–34, 53

Sherman, William Tecumseh, 33–34, 35,
    38–39, 153

Shiras, Oliver, 120, 159, 167–68, 174,
    192–93

Short Bull, 70
    as apostle of ghost dance religion, 66,
        68
    in Cody's Wild West Show, 203
    at the Stronghold, 75, 77, 78–79,
        79–80, 88, 90

Siha Sapa Lakota, 23

Sioux, 21–22. See also Lakota

The Sioux: Life and Customs of a Warrior
    Society (Hassrick), 156, 157, 214n.6

Sioux Act (1888), 59–60

Sioux Act (1889), 60–61, 63

Sioux Falls (South Dakota), 120,
    135–37

Sioux Falls Argus-Leader:
    Alkali Creek ambush and Culbertson
        brothers' trial, 104, 179, 197–98
    Plenty Horses' first trial, 135, 136, 137,
        150, 172, 175
    Plenty Horses' second trial, 177,
        181–82, 186–87, 193, 194,
        198–99

Sitanka (Big Foot), 2, 67, 85, 87, 88

Sitting Bull, *57*
  in battle, 155, 237n.70
  belief in supernatural powers, 64
  death of, 82–85, 203
  and 1889 commission, 61
  and ghost dance religion, 68, 70–72
  and McLaughlin, *81*, 81–82, 84
  surrender of, 56
Smith, Edward, 55, 105
Smith, Frank, 104, 112
South Dakota statehood, 62
speculators, 50–51
Spotted Tail, *29*
  and agents, 43–44
  and Crazy Horse, 45
  death of, 215n.7
  mail-wagon attack, 28–31
  at Rosebud Creek, 46–47
  and sale of Black Hills, 55, 58
  Treaty of 1866, 34
  Treaty of 1868, 38, 39
Standing Bear, Luther, 140–43
Standing Bull, 53
Standing Elk, 57–58
Standing Rock reservation, 80–81, *81*
Sterling, William B., 131–34
  Culbertson brothers' trial, 122, 179,
    196, 197
  Plenty Horses' first trial, 131, 134,
    159–60
    closing remarks, 173–74
    Living Bear, cross-examination, 168
    Rock Road's testimony, 161–62
    Wells' testimony, 166
    White Moon's testimony, 161
  Plenty Horses second trial, 182, 187
  speaking ability, 232–33n.47
Stevens, Isaac T., 188

Stewart, Thomas, 84
Stronghold, 75, 77–79
Sturgis Weekly Record, 104, 115, 196, 198
Sumner, Edwin "Bull," 125
sun dances, 43, 44, 127
Swain, Peter, 14–15, 18

teamsters, 47
Teller, Henry, 43
Ten Eyck, B. L., 160–61, 183
the Prophet, 65
Thompson, William, 186
Thorpe, Jim, 146
timber-culture claims, 50, 51
Treaty (1825), 25
Treaty (1851), 27
Treaty (1866), 34
Treaty (1868), 39, 41, 53, 58–59, 63
Truteau, Jean Baptiste, 24
Twain, Mark, 49, 218n.38
Two Kettle Lakota, 23
Two Strike, 77–78, *78*, 90, 95, 175

U.S. Army, Indians in, 14–20

Victorian Era, 48–50
virtues, Lakota, 127, 155–57, 212n.41,
  214n.6

Waglukhe (Loafers), 32, 41, 46, 47
Wallace, George, 88
warfare, Lakota, 155–57, 212n.43,
  237n.69
Washington Star, 101
Weldon, Catherine, 70–72
Wells, Philip, 150, 166, 168, 180–81
Welsh, Herbert, 59, 124, 125, 126–30
Welsh, John, 128, 129

Welsh, Mary, 128
Welsh, William, 128
West Point, 7, 8, 9, 208n.20
Whetstone Creek reservation, 41–45
White, Zimri, 58
White Clay Creek, 90, 91
White Moon:
   with Casey, 97, 100, 101
   testimony and Plenty Horses' first
      trial, 161
   testimony at Plenty Horses' second
      trial, 182–83, 190, 191–92
White River area, 25, 45, *80*, 95
Whitside, Samuel, 87–88
Wilson, Jack, 64–65

wisdom, Lakota virtue, 214n.6
Wounded Knee massacre, 2–3, 88–90,
   89
   burial party, 91
   commemoration of, 1, 201–2
   Indian response to, 90–91, 92
   Miles investigation of, 152–54
   white response to, 92
Wovoka, 64–65, 66–67, 204

Yankton Daily Press and Dakotaian,
   54–55
Young Man Afraid of His Horses, 111,
   175
Young Skunk, 110–11, 117, 230n.5